# ARCHY LEE'S STRUGGLE FOR FREEDOM

# Archy Lee's Struggle for Freedom

*The True Story of California Gold,*
*the Nation's Tragic March Toward Civil War,*
*and a Young Black Man's Fight for Liberty*

## Brian McGinty

LYONS
PRESS

*Guilford, Connecticut*

An imprint of The Rowman & Littlefield Publishing Group, Inc.
4501 Forbes Blvd., Ste. 200
Lanham, MD 20706
www.rowman.com

Distributed by NATIONAL BOOK NETWORK

British Library Cataloguing in Publication Information available

**Library of Congress Cataloging-in-Publication Data**

Names: McGinty, Brian, author.
Title: Archy Lee's struggle for freedom : the true story of California gold, the nation's tragic march toward Civil War, and a young black man's fight for liberty / Brian McGinty.
Other titles: True story of California gold, the nation'stragic march toward Civil War, and a young black man's fight for liberty
Description: Guilford, Connecticut : Lyons Press [2020] | Includes bibliographical references and index. | Summary: "Against the backdrop of the run-up to the Civil War, a young African American man in San Francisco in 1858 was freed from the claims of a white man who sought to return him to slavery in Mississippi. Archy Lee was the name of the man who, with the aid of anti-slavery lawyers and determined opponents of human bondage, won his freedom from the claims of Charles Stovall. With the aid of pro-slavery lawyers and equally determined supporters, Stovall had sought to capture him and carry him back to a far-away slave plantation. This is the story of Archy Lee, and the fight against slavery in a non-slave state"— Provided by publisher.
Identifiers: LCCN 2019022083 (print) | LCCN 2019981564 (ebook) | ISBN 9781493045341 (hardcover) | ISBN 9781493045358 (ebook)
Subjects: LCSH: Lee, Archy—Trials, litigation, etc. | Slavery—Law and legislation—California—History—19th century—Cases. | Slavery—United States—Legal status of slaves in free states. | Fugitive slaves—California—Biography.
Classification: LCC KF228.L444 M38 2020 (print) | LCC KF228.L444 (ebook) | DDC 342.79408/7—dc23
LC record available at https://lccn.loc.gov/2019022083
LC ebook record available at https://lccn.loc.gov/2019981564

*To the memory of Edward Dickinson Baker,*
*Lincoln's "dearest personal friend" and*
*Archy Lee's victorious trial lawyer in San Francisco*

# Contents

# INTRODUCTION

A POPULAR HYMN WAS PUBLISHED IN LONDON IN 1750 WITH WORDS BY Charles Wesley, one of the founders of Methodism. Titled "Blow Ye the Trumpet, Blow," it celebrated the freedom from spiritual bondage that faith can bestow on Christians.[1] A little over a century later and more than five thousand miles away, the same hymn was adapted by the congregation of the African Methodist Episcopal Zion Church in San Francisco, California, to celebrate the joy they experienced when a young African American was freed from the claims of a white man who sought to return him to slavery in Mississippi. It was 1858, in the midst of a city created by California's fabulous Gold Rush. The refrain of Wesley's hymn was:

> The year of jubilee is come!
> The year of jubilee is come!
> Return, ye ransomed sinners, home.

In San Francisco, the Zion congregation's refrain was:

> The year of Archy Lee is come!
> The year of Archy Lee is come!
> Return, ye ransomed Stovall, home.[2]

Archy Lee was the name of the young black man who, with the aid of anti-slavery lawyers and determined opponents of human bondage, had just won his freedom from the claims of Charles Stovall, a white man from Mississippi who, with the aid of pro-slavery lawyers and equally determined supporters of the American South's peculiar institution, had sought to capture him and carry him off to a far-distant slave plantation.

California had entered the Union in 1850 as a "free state." Its constitution, approved by Congress and President Millard Fillmore as part of the long and bitterly debated Compromise of 1850, proclaimed that "all men are by nature free and independent" and "neither slavery nor involuntary servitude, unless for the punishment of crimes, shall ever be tolerated" in the state.[3] But the constitution was only a stopgap, for the promise of quick and easy riches from the gold that was discovered in 1848 in the foothills of the Sierra Nevada attracted hundreds of thousands of men and women from all over the nation and the world to the new state. Arriving in a sudden flood of humanity, they brought with them different backgrounds, different skin colors, and dramatically different attitudes regarding freedom and bondage. Many came from free American states north of the Mason-Dixon Line, and an approximately equal number from slave states below it. What were then called "persons of color" came from both the North and the South, some with firm claims to freedom and others as the servants of whites, forming a small but determined community of miners, common laborers, and enterprising businessmen.

Bitter differences of opinion about the future of slavery in America—and the place that African Americans would occupy in American society—were then moving the United States closer and closer to the outbreak of civil war. And so, in seeming disregard of California's constitutional prohibition against slavery, legislators passed laws preventing blacks from testifying in court against whites, disqualifying them from sitting on juries, barring them from voting, and authorizing slave owners from outside the state to capture blacks they claimed were their slaves and, with the aid of the courts, compel their return to southern plantations. And, with equal fervor, anti-slavery legislators, lawyers, and judges were fighting back against the laws, seeking to invalidate them as violations of the Constitution and to summon the popular support necessary to repeal them. A frightening storm was gathering over the United States that would soon erupt into one of the bloodiest conflicts in the history of the world; and, despite the glitter and abundance of its gold, California found itself deeply embroiled in the storm.

Because of the uncertain facts surrounding his arrival in California in late 1857 (did he come as a slave or as a free man voluntarily emigrating to the land of gold?), his residence while in the state (was he regarded as a slave there or as a free man?), and the explosive legal battles that soon erupted about his status as a free man or a slave, Archy Lee came to personify the struggle being waged in the state about slavery and the future of the nation. Would an African American who was labeled a slave in another state remain a slave when in California, despite the state constitutional provision saying there were no slaves? Could a slave owner from the American South come to the Golden State with a black man, live with him there, and then force his return to bondage when he decided to return to his plantation?

Archy Lee spent much of the year 1858 in the center of the turbulent controversy, first trying to elude the reach of his captor, then confined behind bars while pro- and anti-slavery forces contested his status. He was secretly put on a steamship bound for Panama, from there to return to slavery in the American South, but he managed to escape, only to be rearrested by police officers and taken before judges who would decide his fate. News of his struggle was publicized in newspapers all over California, and even nationally, and debated in the broader forums of public opinion. All the while, California's small but determined black community stood by him, crowding into courtrooms when his future was being debated, cheering in the streets when decisions favorable to him were announced, protesting when there were adverse decisions, raising money to pay his lawyers, celebrating the victories his supporters gained over his enemies in their churches, enshrining his name in the adapted words of the Wesley hymn, and, when his chance for freedom came, helping him escape aboard a steamship bound for the British Crown Colony of Victoria, soon to become the Crown Colony of British Columbia and a few years later part of the Confederation of Canada. In the northern land there was no slavery at all (the English Parliament had abolished slavery throughout the British Colonies by an act that took effect in 1834), and there were no laws mimicking the institution, so blacks seeking lives of freedom flocked there. The British-ruled territory north of the United States was the ultimate destination of the Underground Railroad in the eastern United States, and Victoria performed a similar if not exactly identical function along the Pacific coast.

The little-known story of Archy Lee dramatizes the angry struggle over slavery that was building in force and fervor in the United States in the 1850s, not just in a few adamantly pro- and anti-slavery states in the North and the South, but throughout the country—even in the new and gold-rich American West. The struggle was not new—it had racked the United States from its early days in the 1790s. But it had recently been fueled by the US Supreme Court's controversial decision in *Dred Scott v. Sandford*, delivered in 1857 under Chief Justice Roger Taney, which seemed to indicate that slaveholders could take their slave property anywhere in the country, that property rights in slaves were guaranteed by the US Constitution, and that African Americans had no rights that whites were bound to respect. It continued in the struggle over the efforts of pro-slavery settlers beginning in 1854 to extend slavery into the Kansas Territory, and in 1858 over the bitterly contested "Lecompton Constitution" which, if approved by Congress, would have made Kansas the newest slave state in the Union. And it found volatile and eloquent expression in the seven debates between Illinois's Democratic senator Stephen Douglas and his Republican challenger, Abraham Lincoln, conducted between August 21 and October 15, 1858, that raised the debate over slavery's future to a peak and elevated Lincoln to the national presidency a little more than two years later. All of these events—all of these arguments and contests and controversies—were the background against which "The Year of Archy Lee" played out. A black newspaper published in San Francisco, looking back on Archy Lee's 1858 struggle for freedom, remembered it as "the famous Archy case which agitated California to its very centre, and was the first triumph for freedom."[4] A later historian, with a touch of poetry, called Archy Lee's struggle for freedom a *cause célèbre* "which in the end set the heather on fire."[5] Another wrote that it was a large blot on the California Supreme Court's escutcheon.[6] Yet another described it as "California's Dred Scott case."[7]

This book is not solely about the black man named Archy Lee. It is also about the travel routes that the gold-seekers followed to California in the 1850s, some by land over the Great Plains, some by sea around Cape Horn, yet others by sailing from the East Coast of North America to Central America, where they crossed over the land there, first by horse and wagons and ultimately by trains, and then continued on by sea to San Francisco. It is about the efforts of the state's racially motivated lawmakers to suppress the rights of all of its residents except whites, and to subject people of African, Asian, Hispanic, and Native American descent to second-, third-, or even fourth-class citizenship. It is about the brave men and women— including many whites—who fought back against those efforts, seeking to ameliorate or repeal the discriminatory laws and introduce a measure of fairness and justice into California's civil life. It is about the lawyers and judges who participated in Archy Lee's legal struggles in 1858, some supporting his claims for freedom while others ferociously opposed them and, in the process, elevated their own political and professional profiles. It is about men who made names for themselves in the history of California and ultimately the entire United States as they took sides in the struggle that confronted them. And it is about Donati's Comet, the celestial body first observed in Italy that appeared in California's night sky in 1858 and went on to appear over the town of Jonesboro, Illinois, where it fascinated Lincoln during his debates with Stephen Douglas, before earning a place in history as the first comet ever photographed, by many accounts the most beautiful comet ever seen in the nineteenth century, and a celestial object that was an emblem of social and political ties that would soon be felt from California over the rest of the world. It is a story of important persons and important events, all of which helped to tie the nation and the world together in the "Year of Archy Lee."

Of course, 1858 was not the only crucial year in the nation's fateful march toward secession and civil war. Other years also played important parts in the advancing drama: 1850, the year of the controversial compromise that permitted California to become a free state and abolished the Missouri Compromise line that forbade the progress of slavery into northern territories; 1854, the year in which the Kansas-Nebraska Act was passed, opening the northern territories to the possibility of slavery if local voters chose to permit it; 1857, the year in which the Supreme Court handed down its astounding decision in the *Dred Scott* case, assuaging slavery's proponents while at the same time outraging its opponents; 1859, the year in which the abolitionist John Brown led his raid on Harper's Ferry, Virginia, in an effort to spark fighting between the pro- and anti-slavery states;[8] and 1860, the year in which Abraham Lincoln, the first Republican president, won the election that would send him from Springfield, Illinois, to the White House in Washington, DC, thus unleashing the tide of southern secession that soon led to the formation of the Confederate States of America.

Nor was Archy Lee's the only case in which African Americans, some free, some enslaved yet still hoping to become free, sought justice in the courts. African Americans had been trying for many years before 1858 to break the legal bonds that held them in servitude, some successfully, most quite unsuccessfully, and they would continue to do so thereafter. There had been many judicial efforts by slave owners to recover escaped slaves through the means provided by the Fugitive Slave Act of 1850, and a surprisingly large number of slaves themselves had asked lawyers and courts to fight for their freedom in trials under the provisions of state laws.[9] But 1858 was one of the most dramatic years, and the Archy Lee case was one of the most notable of the judicial trials, a case in which the contest reached a peak of bitterness and hope, in part because it was so close to the actual outbreak of the war, in part because Archy Lee's judicial effort was in fact successful—even as Dred Scott's was not. "The Year of Archy Lee" thus deserves a place in the mounting national drama, one that it has not previously had because its history was not told in full.

This book tells a true story. It does not include imagined scenes or dialogue invented to make it more exciting or more dramatic. Quotations set forth in the text are those that my research has discovered in memoirs, in letters, in court transcripts, and in on-the-scene newspaper stories, not any that I have imagined. Of course, truth is an elusive thing, not an absolute inscribed in stone and preserved for all time. Historical truth is particularly elusive. The sequence of events preserved in the past has gaps that must be recognized. Some speculation is necessary to bridge over these gaps, to make the individual facts that historical evidence has left us coherent and understandable. I have tried to inform readers where I have found it necessary to speculate, to assume, or to suppose. Enough of the true facts have survived to tell a true story that, I sincerely believe, will help readers understand the past, the lessons it teaches us, and how those lessons can help us understand the future.

# DRAMATIS PERSONAE

**Archy Lee,** young black man from Mississippi who became the subject of the most controversial legal case tried in California in the 1850s. He was the man celebrated in the joyous hymn sung in San Francisco's African Methodist Episcopal Zion Church to "The Year of Archy Lee."

**Simeon Stovall,** slave owner in Mississippi's Carroll County touted as the master of Archy Lee. His ownership was widely assumed but never convincingly proved.

**Charles A. Stovall,** young son of Simeon Stovall who traveled across the plains to California, part of the way with Archy Lee, but after spending some time in Sacramento attempted to take Archy back with him to Mississippi, setting off the ferocious legal battle that followed.

**George Pen Johnston,** one-time sheriff of Issaquena County, Mississippi, and pro-slavery US commissioner in San Francisco who, after a hotly fought trial brought under the Fugitive Slave Act of 1850, decided that Archy Lee was not a fugitive slave but a free man in California.

**Edwin Bryant Crocker,** an anti-slavery Republican attorney in Sacramento who served for a short time as one of Archy Lee's attorneys. He was a brother of one of the "Big Four" investors who built the Central Pacific Railroad.

**Peter H. Burnett,** Tennessee-born, pro-slavery attorney and politician who was elected as first governor of the State of California in 1849 and served as one of the three justices of the California Supreme Court when the case of *Ex Parte Archy* came before it for decision. He wrote the widely condemned opinion that, in the words of a subsequent Supreme Court justice, "gave the law to the North, and the nigger to the South."

**Stephen J. Field,** Connecticut-born judge who was a member of the California Supreme Court when the case of *Ex Parte Archy* came before it. Due to illness, he took no part in the decision, but he later made a public statement in which he said he did not concur in it. He was named a justice of the US Supreme Court by President Lincoln in 1863 and continued to serve in that post until his resignation in 1897, thus earning distinction as the longest-serving US Supreme Court justice up to that time.

**David S. Terry,** knife-wielding, pro-slavery chief justice of the California Supreme Court who in February 1858 delivered the widely condemned decision in *Ex Parte Archy* (written by then–associate justice Peter Burnett) ordering Archy Lee back to slavery in Mississippi. Terry killed anti-slavery US senator David C. Broderick in an 1859 duel only to be killed himself when, in 1889, he attempted to physically attack US Supreme Court justice Stephen J. Field and was shot to death by Field's bodyguard.

**James H. Hardy,** pro-slavery lawyer for Charles A. Stovall who waged a determined but ultimately unsuccessful battle to return Archy Lee to bondage in Mississippi. In 1859, he became a trial judge in Marin County, north of San Francisco, where he presided over the trial of David S. Terry for killing Senator Broderick in a duel. Terry was acquitted in part because of Hardy's "indecent haste" in conducting the trial, but Hardy was soon impeached and removed from office for his virulent pro-slavery statements and actions, thus becoming the first and only California judge ever removed from office by impeachment.

**Edward Dickinson Baker,** brilliant anti-slavery lawyer, orator, and "dearest personal friend" of Abraham Lincoln, who won Archy Lee's case in the San Francisco courtroom of US commissioner George Pen Johnston in April 1858. He went on to become US senator from Oregon, to personally introduce Lincoln at his inaugural on the steps of the US Capitol in Washington, DC, and to die while leading a regiment of Union troops at the battle of Ball's Bluff on October 21, 1861, thereby becoming the first and only sitting US senator ever to die in military combat. A marble statue of Baker was erected in the US Capitol in 1876 and moved to the Capitol's Hall of Columns in 1979. A state holiday honoring Baker was authorized in Oregon in 2011.

**John Jamison (J. J.) Moore,** founder of San Francisco's all-black African Methodist Episcopal Zion Church, in which the congregation celebrated Archy Lee's freedom by singing the hymn to "The Year of Archy Lee." Moore went north to British Columbia with Archy and other African Americans from California, but later returned, first to California and then to the Atlantic states, where he became a bishop and, in 1884, published *A History of the A.M.E. Zion Church in America.* He was regarded as one of the greatest preachers of his time.

**Mifflin Wistar Gibbs,** one of the leaders of the free African-American community in California who went north with Archy Lee and other members of the black community in 1858. Born a free man in Philadelphia, he had come to San Francisco aboard a steamship from Panama in 1850, where he became a successful store owner and an active member of the African Methodist Episcopal Zion Church. After a successful career in British Columbia, he returned to the United States where, in Arkansas, he became the first black elected as a judge in the United States and later was appointed by President William McKinley as the American consul in Tamatave, Madagascar. His autobiography, *Shadow and Light,* was published in 1902 with an introduction by the pioneering black educator Booker T. Washington.

**James Douglas,** official of the Hudson's Bay Company who became governor of the Crown Colony of Victoria after gold was discovered on the Fraser River. He welcomed blacks who came north from California in 1858, in part because he had some African-American ancestry and in part because the Fraser River gold rush depleted the pool of workers he needed in the northern colony. He was later knighted by Queen Victoria.

**Jeremiah Nagle,** veteran Irish-born shipmaster who regularly carried passengers and freight between San Francisco and the Crown Colony of Victoria in what was soon to become British Columbia. At a crowded meeting in the Zion Church in 1858, he told the congregation about the opportunities that would be available to them in the northern land. His assurances that they would be warmly welcomed there played a large part in their decision to migrate north.

**William M. Gwin,** Tennessee-born attorney and medical doctor who owned many slaves in Mississippi when Archy Lee lived there. He came to California in 1849 with lofty political ambitions and became the first man elected to represent it in the US Senate. A firm supporter of slavery (although he agreed to prohibit the institution in California), he became the chief rival of the free soil, anti-slavery Democrat David C. Broderick.

**David C. Broderick,** New York-born leader of the anti-slavery, or free soil, branch of California's Democratic Party who was elected to the US Senate in 1857 and in March 1858 delivered a stinging rebuke to the pro-slavery President James Buchanan in a speech delivered in the Senate. The very next year, he was killed by the pro-slavery Judge David S. Terry in a sensational duel fought on the outskirts of San Francisco, after which Edward D. Baker gave a long and impassioned eulogy over his body.

**James Buchanan,** Democrat elected president of the United States in 1856 who, in "The Year of Archy Lee," led a bitter campaign for the admission of Kansas to the Union as a slave state under the Lecompton Constitution. He was opposed by California's anti-slavery David C. Broderick, who ascribed Buchanan's pro-slavery policy "to the faded intellect, the petulant passion, and trembling dotage of an old man on the verge of the grave."

**Abraham Lincoln,** lanky lawyer from Springfield, Illinois, who rose to national prominence in 1858 with his "House Divided" speech and the seven debates he engaged in with Democratic senator Stephen Douglas. While in Jonesboro, Illinois, preparing for his third debate with Douglas, Lincoln watched entranced as Donati's Comet, the same comet that amazed watchers in California during the "Year of Archy Lee," appeared in the evening sky.

**Stephen Douglas,** Abraham Lincoln's opponent in the senatorial election of 1858. He won reelection to the Senate but suffered ultimate defeat when Lincoln was elected president in 1860 against the opposition of Douglas and two other opponents.

**William H. Seward,** US senator from New York who, in "The Year of Archy Lee," made his famous prediction about the coming of an "irrepressible conflict."

**Jefferson Davis,** US senator from Archy Lee's home state of Mississippi who, observing the determination of the anti-slavery forces gathering strength across the nation told the Mississippi legislature in late 1858 that, if a Republican was elected president and attempted to interfere in the domestic institutions of a state (i.e., slavery), "let the star of Mississippi be snatched from the constellation to shine by its inherent light, if it must be so, through all the storms and clouds of war."

**Mary Ellen Pleasant,** semi-legendary black woman called "Mammy" Pleasant, who, according to one historian, sheltered Archy Lee in her San Francisco house when his opponents were trying to capture him and put him on a steamer to be returned to slavery in Mississippi.

CHAPTER ONE

# A Slave from Pike County

ARCHY LEE WAS A YOUNG MAN OF AFRICAN-AMERICAN ANCESTRY WHO was born in about 1840 in Pike County in southern Mississippi but lived most of his life farther north in Mississippi's Carroll County. Like so much of the rest of Mississippi, Pike and Carroll Counties were both devoted to agriculture. Founded in 1815 as one of Mississippi's first counties, Pike was a moderate producer of livestock, rice, and potatoes, and a small producer of cotton, much of which was taken to market in New Orleans.[1] Established eighteen years later, Carroll County produced some wool, cowhides that were made into shoes, and large quantities of cotton that were milled locally, packed into bales, and then taken west in large wagons to be loaded onto riverboats for eventual sale and export in busy port towns that lined the Mississippi River. Corn was also grown in both Pike and Carroll Counties for, in the words of Mississippi historian John Hebron Moore, corn was "by far the most important food crop for man or beast. It was grown in all parts of the state during the entire ante-bellum period, on agricultural establishments of all sizes and types, from the simple clearing of the hunter to the sprawling plantation of the great slave owner, in quantities and importance second only to cotton."[2]

Archy Lee worked for a time in a mill in Choctaw County, a county established in the same year as Carroll but located just to its east. The Choctaw mill was owned by the same master who claimed Archy's ownership in Carroll County. But in January 1857 Archy suddenly left both Carroll and Choctaw Counties behind. He headed north into Tennessee, then west into Missouri, and finally across the Great Plains toward

California. The story of his journey, and its dramatic culmination on the Pacific coast of North America, was what gave rise to the joyous hymn sung in the African Methodist Episcopal Zion Church in San Francisco in April 1858 and to the bitter struggle that played out in state and federal courts in California that year. But the circumstances that gave rise to his departure from his Mississippi homeland, and the motives that inspired the hymn sung in his honor, were mysterious, obscure, almost enigmatic. And not surprisingly, for slaves who lived under the whips of their masters in the slave states of the American South in 1858 were only partially recognized as real persons. Their lives were kept to themselves, except when they stepped out of the bounds set for them by whites, when real and sometimes brutal consequences followed.[3]

Real person though he was, and historic though the circumstances that surrounded his journey to California unquestionably were, we have little information about Archy Lee the real human being. No known picture of the man has been found. For all the historical record reveals, he never posed for a photographer and never sat for a portrait artist. This is not surprising, for slaves were rarely recognized as anything more important than work animals before the civil war. They were valuable as items of property, useful for the hard work they could do, bought and sold in slave markets, counted as assets in determining the wealth of their owners, pledged as security for loans, transferred by will on the death of their owners, kept under watch and restraint so they would not run off, and pursued with determination when they did.[4] We know that Archy Lee stood five feet five and a half inches in height and weighed about 140 pounds.[5] He was a strong young man, though subject to many of the same illnesses as the man who claimed to be his master. He was a valuable worker who, if his labor was not needed by his master, could be hired out for income paid to the master.

Archy Lee's origins are subject to the same paucity of evidence as his physical appearance. A letter written many years after 1858 by a woman named Mrs. R. A. Hunt, who then lived in Marshall, Texas, states simply that Archy's mother was named Maria and that Maria was the mother of four children, whose names were Archy, Candace, Pompey, and Quitman. Mrs. Hunt was the daughter of Candace, and thus Archy's niece. Mrs.

Hunt also stated that, in 1858, Maria and her family were slaves owned by a man named Simeon Stovall.[6] It is not surprising that Maria and her children were identified only by their first names. Slaves were rarely identified by anything other than their first names before the Civil War.[7] Archy himself was almost always called "Archy," "Archy the slave," or, more condescendingly, "the boy Archy," even in official court documents. It was after he won his freedom in San Francisco, when his victory over slavery was celebrated in the hymn sung in the Gold Rush city's African Methodist Episcopal Zion Church, that he was identified as "Archy Lee." He was a free man then, and entitled to the same identification as other free men in the United States. It was an honor that would soon be extended to other African-American men and women, even in the American South. But that honor would follow only after slavery was abolished by ratification of the Thirteenth Amendment to the US Constitution at the end of 1865.

Simeon Stovall's family had come into Mississippi in the 1820s from Georgia. Before that, they had been Virginians and, before that, seventeenth-century emigrants from Surrey in England. Simeon was born in Lincoln, Georgia, in 1806. In 1828, he was married in Marion, Mississippi, to a woman named Louisiana T. Jenkins (called "Lucy" in later family records). Simeon and Lucy raised a family that included at least four sons and three daughters. According to the surviving records, their oldest son was Charles Allan Stovall, who was born on November 13, 1831, in Carroll County.[8] Charles Allan (often called Charles A.) was the man who claimed to be Archy Lee's owner after the two got to California and who waged a history-making but ultimately losing battle in 1858 to take him back to Mississippi as a slave.

The Stovall name was common in Mississippi (and in other states) in the years leading up to the Civil War, but historical references to the family of Simeon Stovall are rare.[9] The census records, however, tell us some interesting information. Simeon's name is listed in the US census of 1850 as the owner of thirty slaves: twenty-two males and eight females.[10] One of the males was then ten years old. Since that would have been Archy Lee's approximate age in 1850, it could have been him, but we cannot determine that for certain since the names of the slaves were not given. The census for 1860 reveals that Simeon owned thirty-one slaves in that year, twenty-one males and ten females.[11] Archy Lee's departure from Mississippi in 1857 could have caused the number of Stovall's male slaves to decline from twenty-two in 1850 to twenty-one in 1860, but we do not know for sure. Slaves were freely bought and sold in the years leading up to the Civil War. Some were born on slave plantations, and some died there, thus changing the slave master's ownership from year to year and from census to census.

Simeon Stovall may be described as a moderately large slave owner. There were many slave owners who owned fewer slaves and a few who owned more, but neither thirty nor thirty-one was an inconsequential total. An average slave was valued in Mississippi in the 1850s at about $1,500, so the total value of Simeon Stovall's slaves would have been between $45,000 and $46,500. These were large numbers in the 1850s, when $1,500 was a substantial amount of money, more than enough for an average family to live on for a year or to acquire a house to accommodate them through their lives.[12] In addition to his slaves, the 1850 census revealed that Simeon Stovall was the owner of real estate valued at $12,500.[13] The 1860 census valued his real estate at $12,000, but it added another figure: the value of his "personal estate," which would have included slaves. It was set at $48,600, another substantial number.[14] Land prices in Mississippi, like land prices elsewhere, varied from year to year and decade to decade. Land was valued at about eight dollars an acre in 1850 and as much as eighteen dollars in 1860.[15] Applied to Simeon Stovall's land values as stated in the census records, this would indicate that he may have owned something between 666 and 1,562 acres in Carroll County. He might also have owned land in adjoining counties like Choctaw, where he was not listed in the census records.

Simeon Stovall's occupation was given in the 1850 and 1860 censuses as a "farmer." This, coupled with his slave ownership and the value of his real estate, make it clear that he was what historians now call a "planter" or "plantation owner."[16] And not surprisingly, for his Mississippi property was described as a "plantation" by a witness who had personal knowledge of it and testified in Archy Lee's first California trial in Sacramento.[17] A good number of slaves as well as some extensive land were needed for a productive cotton plantation. Simeon Stovall had both. Whether Archy ever worked in the cotton fields is another bit of intriguing information that history has not preserved. But the fact that he was employed in a mill in an adjoining county indicates that there was other work to do for the Stovalls besides planting, cultivating, and harvesting cotton.

The slaves and the land that the Stovalls owned indicated that they were a prosperous family, as did the educations they were able to give their children. Existing records show that Simeon's eldest son, Charles A., attended Centre College in Danville, Kentucky, in the early 1850s.[18] Centre was a prestigious educational institution, one of the first and most respected schools established west of the Alleghenies and, in the early 1850s, regarded as superior to any schools in Mississippi. After he reached California, Charles told a man there that he had gone to Kentucky for his education because they had "no good education" in the Deep South.[19]

Of course, slaves in the southern states were almost uniformly deprived of the most basic education. They were not taught to read or to write. Most lived their whole lives in illiteracy, unable even to write their own names.[20] Illiteracy was a condition that slave masters believed would make their slaves content with their status. They would not read books or newspapers that included disturbing reports about other parts of the country, or parts of the world, in which men and women were campaigning for the abolition of slavery. The slaveholders knew that written words can be dangerous—they can plant ideas, even hopes, in the hearts of those who read them.

During all this time, Mississippi grew richer and richer. By the 1850s, it was one of the richest states not only in the American South but in the entire Union. And the riches were dependent, not on the entrepreneurial genius of the plantation owners, not on their superior business acumen or market strategies, but on "King Cotton" and the endless labor performed by slaves in the fields, in the mills, and in the villages and towns that grew up to supply the plantations.[21] Slave labor soon made cotton the most valuable agricultural product produced, not just in Mississippi, but in the entire United States, and even the world.[22] The snow-white balls of cotton fiber were "white gold," and cotton itself was elevated to the status of

"King Cotton." As Senator James Henry Hammond of South Carolina said in a speech he delivered in the US Senate in March of 1858—the year that later would be celebrated in California as "The Year of Archy Lee"—the North "dare not make war on cotton. No power on earth dares to make war upon it. Cotton is king."[23]

Dramatically differing accounts of the circumstances under which Archy Lee headed west in early 1857 were offered during his struggle for freedom in California. Some men who had known Archy, or known Charles Stovall, or merely struck up a casual acquaintance with Charles, gave their own versions of what had happened, or what they believed might have happened. Archy's own story of how and why he left Mississippi was one of the most detailed, most revealing, and ultimately most persuasive of all the accounts, principally because of his personal knowledge of what happened. Archy was denied the right to offer any court testimony when he arrived in California—as he would have been almost anywhere in the country in 1857, where blacks were almost uniformly forbidden from testifying against whites in court. But he was not denied the opportunity to tell a reporter for the *Daily Alta California*, one of San Francisco's most respected and widely read newspapers, what had happened, and the reporter recorded what Archy said.

Archy admitted that he was "in the possession of Charles Stovall" in January 1857, but he said that "there was a dispute in the family about the negroes, and about him among others." Charles was then living in Carroll County, while Archy was working in adjoining Choctaw County at the Stovall mill. One night a "colored man" came to Archy and asked him to go to the bridge that separated the two counties, there to see a "Mr. Smiley." "After much objection," Archy agreed to go. Smiley was on the Choctaw side of the bridge when Archy arrived, and Archy said he tried to persuade him "to go to some distant place with him." Archy refused. Smiley then told him to "say nothing of what had passed" between them and that he would give him five dollars (a substantial sum at that time). But after looking in his pocketbook, Smiley admitted that he had no money and invited Archy across the bridge, where he would get some money and give him the promised five dollars. But Archy was quickly seized by Smiley and another man named Carroll Stovall, who Archy identified as a cousin of Charles Stovall. Smiley then told Archy that the sheriff of Carroll County "was there and had an attachment for him." Archy was not persuaded. He told Smiley that he "was not the sheriff," and he attempted to break away. He "drew a knife and stabbed Smiley twice in the left breast, inflicting two wounds." But the wounds were not serious. Archy said he then ran back across the bridge and "was not troubled by Smiley." He was told afterward that the sheriff of Carroll County had refused to take any action against him, that "Smiley got well, and that no legal proceedings were ever taken on account of the stabbing." The next morning, however, a man named Aaron Hart, who had charge of the Stovall mill, told Archy "to go away" and "hide in the bushes." Archy did as he was told, and while he was hiding "a negro took his dinner out to him." In the evening, yet another black man came out and told him that "he must go away from there."

Archy then accompanied the man to the Carroll County town of Middleton. Near there, Charles Stovall suddenly appeared with a buggy, took Archy aboard, and "drove away with him." The two men traveled north through Mississippi and Tennessee to Memphis, where they crossed the Mississippi River in a ferryboat, and then continued traveling north in Missouri. Charles took Archy to the plantation of a man named John Carnes in Cape Girardeau County, Missouri, about 175 miles north of Memphis and some 115 miles southeast of St. Louis. The town of Cape Girardeau had been founded as a trading post in 1793, but the surrounding county was full of agricultural land. Slaves worked both in the town and in the surrounding fields. Carnes was, like the Stovalls, the operator of a slave plantation, and a slave owner himself. He was not, however, Archy Lee's owner or master, for it was never claimed that Charles Stovall had transferred ownership of Archy to Carnes.[24]

Archy's departure from Mississippi was by this time complete. He would never again return to the state, despite the furious efforts to get him to do so that were made in California in 1858.[25] But he had by no means achieved freedom, for Missouri was, like Mississippi and Tennessee, a slave state in 1857. He had gone from one slave state to another and was still subject to the harsh legal restrictions and penalties that slaves were subject to throughout most of the South.

Archy told the reporter in San Francisco that there were other men in both Mississippi and Missouri "who knew the truth about Charles Stovall taking him from Mississippi to Missouri."[26] Archy continued his story by saying that he remained in Missouri for "several months," until one of Charles Stovall's brothers, a man named William D. Stovall, "came and got him."

What happened to Archy Lee after William Stovall "came and got him"? How did he get from the slave plantation of John Carnes in Cape Girardeau, Missouri, to California, where all of the evidence agrees that he arrived early in October 1857 with Charles Stovall?

The statement Archy gave to the San Francisco newspaper reporter did not cover this part of Archy's story, and the statements made by Charles in California were at first cursory and then mysteriously ambiguous. William, who was two years younger than his brother Charles, testified in California that he and Archy were at the "crossing of the North Platte River" some eight hundred miles west of the nearest border of an American state "on or about the 20th day of June AD 1857" when Charles "came up with, and found his said slave Archy."[27] The crossing of the North Platte was a famous site on the overland trails, mentioned in many diaries, memoirs, and other accounts. Both Archy and William had, in other words, traveled several hundred miles to the west without Charles, and Charles had traveled there without them. William said that Charles was traveling "with other persons," all of whom were going to California. One was another of Charles's brothers, a man named Henry, who was nine years Charles's junior. Archy and William were also on their way to the western state, for why else had they traveled so far from Cape Girardeau?

We have no direct evidence indicating how all of these men got to the crossing of the North Platte, though it is not hard to guess. Hundreds of thousands of men—and some women and children—had traveled across the Great Plains on their way west in the fifteen or so years before 1857. Important overland journeys had been made in the early 1840s to both Oregon and California, but after the discovery of gold in California in 1848 the initial crossings increased dramatically. Taken as a whole, almost half a million men, women, and children traversed the overland trails between 1841 and 1869, the year the transcontinental railroad was completed.[28]

The greatest flood of travelers began in 1849. The year 1852, which saw about fifty thousand travelers on the plains, was probably the peak year, but there were an estimated twenty thousand in 1854, about seven thousand in 1855, some two thousand in 1856, and more than six thousand in 1857, the year of Archy Lee's travels.[29]

An overwhelming number of the travelers were, of course, white, but many blacks—slaves as well as free men and women—also made the western journey.[30] Most traveled with companies of whites, for blacks who were traveling alone excited suspicion and were often challenged to prove that they were not slaves, or even worse, that they were not fugitives from slavery in the American South. The prevailing illiteracy of blacks prevented them from keeping the diaries and journals in which many white travelers recorded the important events of their western journeys, or writing the letters to loved ones left behind, and when whites wrote about their travels they almost always avoided mentioning blacks, even when they traveled with them.[31] African Americans, whether slave or free, were akin to beasts of burden, workers traveling with whites only to make the journey more bearable for the whites and not to mark their own accomplishments. They worked as wagon drivers, teamsters, wranglers, herders, and cooks. They stood guard over the wagon trains at night while others slept, and they watched the trains' wagons so livestock did not wander away, or fall into the clutches of thieves lurking nearby.[32] And so whites hardly noticed them, and certainly did not write about them. They generally remained nameless and, if circumstances required that they be referred to, it was by their first names only.[33] It is likely that Archy Lee's travels from Cape Girardeau, Missouri, to the crossing of the North Platte River would never have been remembered if Archy's status as a free man or a slave had not become the subject of a furious legal battle in California in the following year, and the men who traveled with him had not been called on to testify about when and where they saw him, and what he did after he was encountered.

Some of the white men who traveled with Archy and the Stovalls testified that they made their way through Kansas.[34] Organized as a federal territory in 1854, Kansas was sparsely populated by whites in 1857, although there were Indians there, not yet completely removed from the land they had called their home for generations, and there was a sudden rush of slaveholders from neighboring Missouri who were fighting to make Kansas a slave state and thus contribute to the power of southerners and their supporters in Washington. One of the slaveholders' champions was Senator Stephen A. Douglas of Illinois, whose presidential aspirations had prompted him to introduce the controversial Kansas-Nebraska Act in 1854, a federal law that repealed the Missouri Compromise of 1820 and authorized settlers in territories (all white, of course, and all male) to decide by referendum whether a new state would be open to slavery or barred to it. The Kansas-Nebraska Act and the so-called "popular sovereignty" that it authorized were what brought slaveholders into Kansas hoping to establish slavery there; it was what brought bitter abolitionists like John Brown into the state, determined to block the spread of slavery, with violence, if necessary; it was what gave Kansas the gory name of "Bleeding Kansas"; and it was what prompted a lanky lawyer named Abraham Lincoln to forsake his successful law practice in Springfield, Illinois, and challenge Stephen Douglas in Illinois's senatorial election of 1858. The historic debates between Lincoln and Douglas were conducted in 1858, in the midst of "The Year of Archy Lee."

In 1857, westbound travelers who traversed Kansas generally began their journeys at jumping-off points along the Missouri River, where they bought wagons, draft animals, cattle, and supplies that would sustain them as they headed across the plains. There they also obtained the maps that were necessary to identify key routes and take precautions against dangers that lay along those routes. Independence, Missouri, and the nearby river crossing at Westport, formed the favorite jumping-off place for many of the western travelers. Historian Michael Wallis has called Independence "the epicenter of western migration."[35] It was here that the travelers crossed the Missouri, but only after the winter rains and snows had abated, after the roads had firmed up enough to support heavy wagons, and after the grass that was essential to provide feed for animals had begun to grow along the trails.

In the testimony Charles and William Stovall gave in California, they said that Charles "started on the 16th of April AD 1857 to cross the plains."[36] Coupled with the statements about crossing Kansas, it seems likely that the Stovalls and Archy Lee traveled in a northwesterly direction from Independence and Westport following the Big Blue or the Little Blue Rivers through northeast Kansas. Both of these streams flowed toward the Platte River. We have no evidence, however, that Archy Lee "started" his journey through Kansas at the same time as Charles. He was traveling with William, not Charles, and William later made it clear that his brother did not see Archy until June, when he "came up with and found his said slave."

We know from testimony, however, that all of these men were travelers in wagons and that their wagons were organized into companies. This was an almost absolute necessity, for wagons would sometimes become mired in mud along riverbanks, and wheels and axles could be broken when traversing rocky trails and roads. When events of this kind happened, many strong backs and arms had to join together to repair the damage and get the wagons ready again to move on. Food also had to be gathered along the way, oftentimes by hunting, and Indians were still encountered on the western plains, nursing the resentment they felt for the travelers' intrusions into their homelands. Illnesses had to be treated—cholera was a common depredation on the overland trails—and livestock had to be guarded against straying or Indian thefts.[37]

Most overland trails followed rivers whenever possible, for water was essential to sustain the travelers and their animals, and grass along the banks provided food for the cattle, horses, and mules that moved with the wagons. The Platte River was important for western travelers to follow. Called the *rivière plate*, or "flat river," by the French, it was a shallow, meandering stream that extended 310 miles toward the west until it forked into the North and the South Platte Rivers, near the modern-day town of North Platte, Nebraska.

It was here that Charles Stovall encountered Archy Lee for the first time on the western trail. There was no law in that remote part of the western territories that compelled anybody to submit to the degrading status of a slave, nor any law that gave Charles the legal right to be

Archy's master. William Stovall never claimed that he was Archy's master or that Archy owed the duties of a slave to either William or Charles as they traveled west. Despite this, Archy quickly joined Charles's wagon train. Why? Was he afraid that Charles or William would punish him if he did not? Was he afraid that he would be hunted down as a fugitive slave, perhaps restrained of his liberty, and treated like an escapee from Mississippi if he did not travel with the two Stovalls? Or did he simply decide to do so because he and the Stovalls were friends and appreciated the help they could give each other as they traveled west?

In Mississippi, as elsewhere in the slave states, whites and blacks often formed relationships that were not dictated by legal duties or the desire to make money but by personal affection. As Charles S. Sydnor noted in his history of slavery in Mississippi, a slave was not always regarded as a source of profit for his white master, as a "machine for making money." The slave could also be "a person for whom he might have kindly feelings or even true friendship."[38] In his classic study of slavery in the South before the Civil War, Kenneth M. Stampp pointed out that the attitude of slaves toward their white masters "was frequently one of amiable regard, sometimes of deep affection. A slave who lived close to a warm, generous and affectionate master often could not help but reciprocate those feelings, for the barriers of bondage and caste could not prevent decent human beings from showing sympathy and compassion for one another—slave for master as well as master for slave."[39] The relations between Archy Lee and Charles Stovall after they came together on the western trail suggest that they may have decided to travel together simply because they were friends—perhaps very good friends. Supporting this conclusion, a man named John P. Zane, who knew both Stovall and Archy Lee after they arrived in California, testified in San Francisco that Stovall's relationship with Archy was based on nothing but "affection."[40]

Now traveling with Charles, Archy took the reins of the oxen that pulled Charles's wagon. He also cooked for Charles and the other travelers when their train came to rest for the night. All of the men knew where they were headed. It was along the North Platte River, heading into what later became the state of Wyoming, across a corner of what later became the State of Idaho, southward through a corner of what later became the

State of Utah, then following the Humboldt River across the interior of what later became the State of Nevada, then across dry land leading up to the edge of California. It was near the frontier outpost called Fort Hall that the trail forked, with a northern branch heading into Oregon and a more southerly route heading toward California. This was not surprising, for what was known by early emigrants as the Oregon Trail later became famous to generations of travelers as the California Trail, because the number of travelers who were headed to California exceeded those who were headed for the more northern territory.[41] As they approached the edge of California, the travelers reached the place called Carson Valley.

Charles Stovall's oxen—he had three yokes—were so badly weakened by the long rigors of the trail that he determined they could not make it over the high mountains that lay ahead. So he paused long enough in Carson Valley to buy a tract of land—it was later described as a "rancho," in the Spanish style—where he could leave his animals for a while. It consisted of a quarter section (or 160 acres) and had a house on it.[42] Carson Valley was an important supply point and trading station for travelers heading to California, and noted because it was the site of an early Mormon settlement.[43] Later testimony was given that Charles was impressed by the country he saw in the valley and contemplated settling there.[44] But he remembered that his goal was California, and so he decided to push westward, with his brothers and Archy Lee traveling with him.

The travelers now encountered the most challenging physical obstacle of their entire journey, California's Sierra Nevada. In 1857, trails from Carson Valley twisted through the mountains, plunging into passes and avoiding high peaks, the loftiest of which is Mount Whitney, which rises 14,495 feet above sea level and is recognized as the tallest mountain in the lower forty-eight states. Archy Lee and the Stovalls could choose which trail they wanted to follow in 1857. All were physically challenging, but all led gradually down from the highest altitudes through narrow valleys, along rivers and creeks, and into the sprawling Sacramento Valley. We do not know whether Archy Lee and the Stovalls traveled in wagons or horse-drawn coaches when they crossed the Sierra Nevada—both were available in 1857—but we do know that they arrived at the principal population center of the valley, the busy city and state capital of Sacramento, on October 2, 1857.[45]

The travelers had now reached their destination—or had they? According to a claim Charles Stovall later made in court, California was not his real goal. He did not want to remain permanently in the western state, but to sojourn there for a while, after which he would return to his home in the plantation South, with Archy Lee in tow.

Was this claim a true reflection of Stovall's intentions, or a ploy to prevent Archy Lee from leaving him? Events that would follow—and the great legal struggle that would be fought out in California courts in 1858—would provide some of the information needed to answer this question.

CHAPTER TWO

# The Black Heart of the Gold Country

THE CALIFORNIA GOLD RUSH BEGAN WITH THE DISCOVERY IN JANUARY 1848 of a few nuggets of gold in the tailrace of a sawmill on the south fork of the American River. The initial discovery led to other discoveries in the foothills of the Sierra Nevada and in mountain regions to the north and south. News of the discovery reached the rest of the world toward the end of 1848, unleashing a flood of immigrants from all over the United States, and soon from all over the world.[1] The population of the mining area grew from about six thousand at the end of 1848 to more than one hundred thousand in 1852.[2]

No formal records of the total wealth extracted from California's gold fields were ever made, but there have been estimates of its value. Almost a quarter of a million dollars is thought to have been taken out in 1848, ten million in 1849, more than forty-one million in 1850, almost seventy-six million in 1851, and an astounding eighty-one million in 1852. The numbers tapered off slightly after that but still topped fifty-five million in 1855.[3] Remembering that the US government paid Mexico only fifteen million dollars for the acquisition of all of the land captured in the Mexican War, these numbers are astounding. But the wealth created by the Gold Rush was not the sole benefit derived from the metal taken out of the earth. A great flood of new residents followed; business and agriculture grew rapidly; employment opportunities blossomed; and profits that flowed into the hands of investors and entrepreneurs became even more dazzling than the gold itself.

The population of California grew dramatically. There were perhaps 150,000 Indians in the state in the late 1840s and an estimated 15,000 or so residents of Spanish and Mexican ancestry. The Indian population declined precipitously in the following years, due to policies now condemned as racist, even genocidal,[4] but the population of white residents increased rapidly. The state's official population was set at 92,597 by the first US census in 1850, an estimated 255,000 by a state census taken in 1852, and set at 380,015 by the federal census of 1860.[5]

There had been blacks in California before the Gold Rush. Spain's occupation of the land they called Alta California began in 1769 when an expedition of Catholic missionaries and Spanish and Mexican soldiers pushed north from Mexico to occupy the land in the name of the Spanish king. People of African ancestry had mixed with native Indians and pure-blooded Spaniards for more than two hundred years in Mexico, creating a population of mestizos and mulattoes that joined in the settlement of California.[6] Twenty-six of the forty-four original founders of Los Angeles were of mixed African and Mexican origin.[7] While complete racial equality was never achieved in the Spanish or Mexican days, there were opportunities for Mexicans of African descent. One prominent Californian who had both African and Spanish ancestors was a man named Pío Pico, who was born into a pioneer family near Los Angeles in 1801, rose to serve two terms as governor of the Mexican province of California in the 1830s and 1840s, and in later years was regarded as one of California's most prominent Hispanic citizens.[8]

The flood of gold-seekers that entered California from 1849 on inevitably included people of African ancestry. Slave owners from the American South were not immune to the lure of wealth that might be won in the California gold fields, and many brought their slaves with them, sure they were quite as capable of digging for metals in the earth as of cultivating cotton in the fields or loading boats with bales of the precious fiber. Some free blacks also joined in the Gold Rush for California wealth, although not all of those who did so were determined to hunt for gold. Some slaves entertained hopes that they might achieve freedom far from the plantation South.[9] Many realized that the exploding population of California would provide employment opportunities. Blacks, both slave and free, hoped that they might find jobs, or even create jobs for others by starting small businesses. A whole new society was forming at lightning speed, and the opportunities presented to ambitious men—and some women—were almost limitless.

Blacks came to California in the same way that whites did. Most traveled over the Great Plains in wagons, like Archy Lee and the Stovalls. Some came by sea in ships that carried them through the Caribbean to Nicaragua or Panama, where they crossed over the land from the Atlantic side to the Pacific, and then boarded ships waiting to take them north to California. Some were seamen who worked on American ships and, when they heard of the wealth that lay buried in the California mountains, promptly abandoned their shipside duties and joined the stampede to the diggings.[10] Others came from the West Indies, where many blacks lived in British, French, and Dutch colonies.[11] The exact numbers of blacks who came to California in the Gold Rush has never been determined. It has been reliably estimated, however, that between 1.5 and 3 percent of all the overland immigrants to the state were blacks, and that the majority of them came, like Archy, by way of the Platte River trail.[12] In 1852, there were more than two thousand blacks in California, but this was only about 1 percent of the population.[13] More than a thousand were in the gold country, while San Francisco had 444 and Sacramento 338. There were between three and four thousand blacks in California in 1858, but they still constituted only 1 percent of the total population. By 1859, the population of Sacramento was 10,900, but only 426 were blacks.[14]

If southern slave owners valued their slaves' labor, non-slaveholding whites generally resented it. Projecting the same feelings of racial superiority they carried through their lives in the plantation country, white southerners believed that blacks simply had no right to share in California's wealth. God had created gold for the benefit of whites, they believed, not Africans. When they saw blacks, slave or free, working a mining claim, they challenged their right to do so, sometimes by demanding that they pay fees to the whites, at other times by organizing mining districts with rules and regulations that required blacks, or the owners of black slaves, to pay taxes for the privilege of mining. Armed groups of southern whites sometimes went so far as to take over mining claims that were being worked by blacks and summarily order the blacks to leave the area. Whites from non-slaveholding states often shared the anti-black views of the southerners.[15]

Some slaveholders brought their slaves to California with the promise that they would be rewarded with freedom after they had worked a specified period of time.[16] Others told their slaves they could purchase their own freedom after they had collected enough gold to meet their masters' prices.[17] Promises were sometimes made and then summarily revoked. Yet other slave masters brought their slaves to California simply to hire them out.[18] If they commanded good wages, the masters would gladly pocket the money, expending only the most minimal sums to house and feed them.

Some free blacks came to California on their own initiative, at least half from the American Northeast, most from Massachusetts and New York.[19] Others came from slave states in which they had won their personal freedom but hoped to make enough money to buy the freedom of their wives and children who remained behind in slavery.[20]

Historian Rudolph Lapp has written that thousands of blacks "worked at mining gold and had their proportion of lucky strikes."[21] In some places, they joined with whites to form profitable mining companies in which the two races could work together. It was more profitable, these people reasoned, and also fairer, for people to work together than separately, regardless of their racial differences. As one eastern newspaper writer commented: "There are no gentlemen here. Labor rules Capital. A darkey is just as good as a polished gentleman and can make more money."[22] Mining towns here and there were given names that reflected that blacks worked in them. The fact that only one black worked in a town or settlement was sometimes enough to name it Negro Hill, Negro Bar, Negro Butte, or Negro Canyon. Inevitably, the word *Negro* gave way, both in speech and in print, to *Nigger* in names such as Nigger Hill, Nigger Jack Peak, and Nigger Bill Bend.[23]

Some free blacks worked only a short time in the mining districts, after which they left in search of other places where they could find employment. And they soon learned that labor was valuable in towns and cities as well as in mining districts.

Of course, blacks were not the only victims of discrimination and bigotry. Many thousands of gold seekers had come to California from China and from Spanish-speaking countries such as Mexico, Peru, and Chile, and they too were greeted with angry opposition. There was violence in many of the mining camps, stabbings, and rapes of some of the women who had come to live there, some reputed to be prostitutes while others were merely accompanying their husbands. Coming from the southern Chinese province of Canton, then stricken by economic depression and famine to a land they called "Gold Mountain," the Chinese were willing to work for a fraction of the wages whites commanded. In angry response, the whites dismissed them as "coolies" and sought laws that would make it nearly impossible for them to compete for jobs. But the Chinese continued to work, maintaining low profiles so as not to antagonize the opponents who overwhelmingly outnumbered them, and their numbers increased rapidly. From an estimated population of only 660 in 1850, California's Chinese-born population grew to 34,935 by 1860; and it grew to 48,790 by 1870.[24]

American Indians were rarely permitted to work in the mines. Even native Californians were driven out of the mining camps because they did not share the newcomers' language or religion. It mattered not that the land had been their own only a few years before—now it belonged to a new people who did not want to share it with anybody. The consequence of all of this rivalry and bitterness was a kind of lawlessness that, in some places, bordered on warfare. There were brawls and even riots. Hispanics and Chinese workers were lynched. But gold was still drawn out of the earth, carried into the towns and cities, stamped into coins, and used as money in thousands of transactions, some devious and deceitful, others honest and upstanding and productive. Gold coins and bars were regularly loaded onto steamships bound outward from Sacramento and San Francisco for transport to the Atlantic states, where they were used to nourish the growing economy of what was already on the way to becoming the world's richest nation.

The Sacramento that Archy Lee and the Stovalls came to in October 1857 was a thriving accumulation of stores, blacksmith shops, stables, express offices, warehouses, restaurants, banks, schools, boardinghouses, hotels, and official public buildings. The business district faced crowded wharves and docks aligned along the Sacramento River where it is joined by the American River, one of the most important streams that flows down from the slopes of the Sierra. There was a train station in the city, although the tracks extended only twenty-three miles eastward, for the construction of the great transcontinental railroad through the Sierra Nevada had not yet been begun.[25] Sacramento was connected by navigable waters all the way to San Francisco, situated some eighty miles to the southwest at the edge of the mighty San Francisco Bay, so river steamers and sailing ships were constantly coming and going, loaded with passengers, goods, and gold. Sacramento had been the state capital since 1854,[26] so it was not only a commercial center but also home to the governor's office, the state legislature, and the state Supreme Court, in which important official business was conducted.

If the black population of Mississippi was greater than that of the whites, it was very small in Sacramento. But there were opportunities for both races, providing they did not interfere with each other's ambitions or trespass on each other's rights—and providing they could accommodate themselves to the strange mixture of laws that was soon enacted to govern them.

On their arrival in Sacramento, Archy Lee and Charles Stovall had to find lodgings. They boarded for a time at the National Hotel on K Street between 1st and 2nd, where Archy worked as one of the cooks. Although we do not know how much Archy was paid for this work, we know that black cooks were valued highly and compensated commensurately for their work.[27] Stovall apparently regarded himself as a qualified teacher—perhaps his studies in Kentucky's Centre College had given him that confidence—for he almost immediately took steps to open a school for boys and girls. He called on a man named Millman and leased a house on K Street near 7th that included a hall suitable for use as a classroom, then went to the office of a man named Samuel J. Noble, one of the proprietors of a newspaper called the *Sacramento Age*, and placed an advertisement that read:

Private School
For Boys and Girls
By
C.A. Stovall
K street near 7th. To commence on Monday, the
12th of October, 1857.
Terms—$5 per month, in advance.[28]

Students came to the school both from Sacramento and neighboring towns. While he was teaching, Stovall roomed for two months with a man named Copeland, who also became one of his students. Many adults apparently realized that they still had some basic things to learn, and Copeland was persuaded when Stovall assured him that he could teach him more than he would be able to learn in a common school. Stovall told Copeland that he had come to California for his health and that he knew that Archy was a free man and not a slave under California law. But he did not think that Archy would leave him. Stovall's father had requested that he bring Archy with him to act as a body servant, he said, to help him with his journey across the plains, and to cook for him. When Archy came to Stovall with a request that he buy him some new clothes, Stovall refused, telling Archy that he brought enough clothes with him and didn't need any more. Archy was sick for a while and could not work. During that time, Stovall looked after him, fed him, and collected the wages that were due him for work he had already done.[29] Their relationship seemed to be friendly, with Stovall treating Archy well and Archy satisfied with it. Copeland said that Stovall appeared to be contented with his situation and told him that he might remain in California for two or three years.[30]

The state capital had come to rest in Sacramento after having been bandied about for four years between the towns of San Jose, Vallejo, and Benicia.[31] Mexico's *Alta California* had been seized by military force in

1847 and formally annexed to the United States by ratification of the Treaty of Guadalupe Hidalgo in March 1848. The state called California was admitted to the Union only two and a half years later, on September 9, 1850, a date later celebrated as Admission Day. It had become a state so quickly because of the fantastically rapid growth of its population— more rapid than that of any other new state in the nation's history— and because the value of the gold taken out of the mines had been so enormous that it was generally agreed that it could skip the territorial status that other applicants for statehood were required to pass through. The American military governor, Brigadier General Bennett Riley, had summoned a constitutional convention to meet in the old Spanish and Mexican capital of Monterey in September 1849. The delegates there— American immigrants with a small mixture of old Spanish and Mexican Californians blended in—had worked promptly to draft the basic law for an American state, tackling difficult questions like fixing the state's eastern boundary and, more importantly, deciding whether California would come into the Union as a free or a slave state. Not surprisingly, slavery was the key issue, for it had hung like a phantom over the nation's history since its earliest days. It had repeatedly wracked deliberations in the national capital and, because the issue had not been resolved, it still threatened the political stability of the Union. Ambitious politicians had already come into the state from the Northeast, the Midwest, and the South, determined to take charge of the state's wealth and play a part in influencing the future course of American slavery. Most of the ambitious politicians who came into the state were Democrats, and many were from southern states. William M. Gwin, a former congressman from Mississippi who owned several plantations and at least two hundred slaves in that state, became one of the dominant forces in the constitutional convention.[32] His avowed ambition was to become a US senator from California and to make his mark in Washington. Surprisingly, Gwin agreed with those who sought to exclude slavery from the new state. Why he took that position has been debated many times over. Was it because he realized that California's admission to the Union would be delayed, or perhaps even blocked, if it sought to come in on the side of the slaveholding South, which then held the balance of power in Washington, and that he would then be denied his ambition of becoming a senator? Or was it because he believed that California could in the future be divided into two states, one in the North that would be free of slavery and the other in the South where plantations could be planted and slavery would thrive as it had in Mississippi? The Missouri Compromise of 1820 had drawn a line at 36 degrees 30 minutes North latitude, the southern boundary of the State of Missouri, with slavery allowed in new territories below it and prohibited above it. Could that line be extended to the Pacific coast, thus dividing California at its center?[33]

As adopted, the California Constitution's prohibition of slavery was explicit, stating: "Neither slavery, nor involuntary servitude unless for punishment of crimes, shall ever be tolerated in this state."[34] When the Constitution reached Washington, however, the provision became part of a bitter debate that raged for nearly nine months, drawing in the great political leaders of the day. They included Henry Clay of Kentucky, Daniel Webster of Massachusetts, John C. Calhoun of South Carolina, Lewis Cass of Michigan, Salmon P. Chase of Ohio, William H. Seward of New York, Stephen A. Douglas of Illinois, and Jefferson Davis of Mississippi. Differences of opinion on the issue of whether pro-slavery southerners could agree to admit California to the Union with such a strong statement against slavery were so great that many feared that the slave states would secede from the Union and that the nation's unity would be shattered. California historian Kevin Starr has called the debate "a drama of titanic intensity" and declared that "nothing less than the survival of the Union, already so fragile, was at stake."[35] But there were attempts to work out a compromise that both sides could accept, even if grudgingly. Clay and Webster took the lead in these efforts, while Calhoun, rapidly approaching death and too weak to read his own speech on the Senate floor, led the opposition. As a result, Senator James M. Mason of Virginia read Calhoun's speech for him. The death of President Zachary Taylor in the midst of the debate and the accession of his vice president, Millard Fillmore, added confusion and consternation to the dilemma. In the end, a series of measures were adopted that included the admission of California as a free state, prohibition of the slave trade in the District of Columbia (though not slavery itself), permitting the new territories of Utah and

New Mexico to decide for themselves whether to allow slavery within their borders, surrender of Texas's claim to part of New Mexico's land in return for a payment of ten million dollars from the federal government, and the adoption of a new and strict Fugitive Slave Law.[36]

The realization that slaves often seek to escape from their masters was not new or novel in 1850. Horses often run away from their owners unless they are restrained, as do mules and cattle and pigs. Human beings are even fonder of freedom than these animals, and when they are treated as beasts of burden, as items of property belonging to other human beings, they seek new lives of freedom and autonomy. The US Constitution had recognized this fundamental principle when it was ratified in 1789 with a provision stating that "no person held to service or labor in one state, under the laws thereof, escaping into another, shall, in consequence of any law or regulation therein, be discharged from such service or labor, but shall be delivered up on claim of the party to whom such service or labor may be due."[37] Of course, the Constitution consistently avoided use of the terms *slave* or *slavery*, substituting euphemisms such as a "person held to service or labor in one state," but everybody knew what it referred to: persons held in bondage as chattel slaves. But the constitutional provision itself was not self-enforcing, so in 1793 Congress passed a Fugitive Slave Act that provided that "when a person held to labor in any of the United States . . . shall escape into any other part of the said States or Territory, the person to whom such labor or service may be due" was "empowered to seize or arrest such fugitive from labor" and "take him or her before any Judge . . . of the United States . . . or before any magistrate of a county, city, or town corporate, where such seizure or arrest shall be made." The Act continued by providing that "upon proof to the satisfaction of such Judge or magistrate . . . it shall be the duty of such judge or magistrate to give a certificate thereof to such claimant . . . which shall be sufficient warrant for removing the said fugitive from labor to the State or Territory from which he or she fled."[38] Many slaves had escaped in the years following 1793, with some apprehended and some never found because they were able to flee far to the north along what came to be known as the Underground Railroad that led ultimately to freedom in Canada. The number of escapees had been so great, and the support they received from the growing number of abolitionists north of the Mason-Dixon Line had been growing so rapidly, that the defenders of slavery in 1850 demanded a new and even stronger fugitive slave law than that of 1793.

Initially drafted by Virginia's US senator James M. Mason, the new law purported to be an amendment to the law of 1793. In actuality, it created a whole new system of law enforcement whereby slaves (or simply those claimed to be slaves) could be pursued, captured, and hauled back into chattel slavery with almost no opposition or defense. It provided for the appointment of federal officials called commissioners who were authorized to issue warrants for the arrest of accused fugitives and certificates commanding their return to their masters. The cases were to be heard "in a summary manner." The commissioner would receive a fee of ten dollars for every fugitive he returned to a master but only five dollars when he denied the master's claim. The Act passed the Senate by a vote of 27 to 12 on August 23, 1850, and the House of Representatives by 109 to 76 on September 12. It was signed into law by President Fillmore on September 18.[39] It was a law that in 1858 would play a central role in Charles A. Stovall's effort to force Archy Lee to return to Mississippi from California.

California's state government began to operate even before the state was admitted to the Union. The state's political leaders were confident that their authority to enact laws derived from the adoption of the state constitution and that any laws they passed before Congress added the state to the national roster would be valid after that event. And so they started their deliberations without delay and quickly began to assemble a list of state laws that they wished to pass.

From the outset, the political environment of the state was strongly tinged with the issue of slavery. The first crop of political leaders was dominated by pro-slavery Democrats, many from southern states, but some from such Middle Western states as Ohio, Indiana, and Illinois, and others from Pennsylvania and even New York. California Democrats who supported the South and slavery—even those who hailed from north of the Mason-Dixon Line—were called the "Chivalry," or "Chivs" for short, because of their elite backgrounds and aristocratic pretensions, and William Gwin was recognized as their leader.[40] He was elected as one of California's first two US senators in December 1849 because most members of the legislature, who then had the constitutional power to elect senators, were "Chivs." He was a Mississippi slaveholder, and he fit their model of an appropriate senator from the Golden State.[41]

Some Democrats held anti-slavery views similar to those of the short-lived Free Soil Party, which had been formed in Buffalo, New York, in 1848 under the banner of "Free Soil, Free Speech, Free Labor and Free Men." Opposing the spread of slavery into the western territories, the Free Soilers nominated former president Martin Van Buren as their presidential candidate in 1848 and chose Senator John P. Hale of New Hampshire for that position in 1852. The Free Soil Party faded away after 1854, but some Democrats and some Whigs continued to hold free soil views. Those who did so were ideologically opposed to the "Chivs," although they often formed alliances with them for tactical purposes.[42]

Whigs had been the principal opponents of the Democrats nationally, although their influence was quickly waning because of their inability to take a strong position on slavery. Some opposed the institution. Some argued that it was a state issue and that national politicians should not interfere with its resolution. Some simply opposed its spread into the western territories, believing that it would ultimately die if it could not expand. By the middle of the 1850s, the Whigs were generally disappearing as a new, more resolutely anti-slavery party called the Republicans was emerging. John C. Frémont, the legendary explorer of the West whose initial forays into politics included a brief affiliation with the Democrats, was elected to a short, two-year term alongside William Gwin as one of California's first two US senators. When Frémont's term expired, his strong anti-slavery views prevented his reelection, and John B. Weller, a Democrat who had come to California from Ohio with strong pro-slavery views, was sent to Washington as his successor. When the Republicans met for their first national convention in Philadelphia in 1856, they chose Frémont as their presidential nominee.[43]

The first governor of the State of California was Peter H. Burnett, a Tennessee-born lawyer and politician who crossed the Great Plains to Oregon in 1843 and came on to California after the discovery of gold in 1848, bringing with him strongly anti-black opinions. Lieutenant Governor John McDougal, also a Democrat, became governor when Burnett resigned to practice law in early 1851. The Pennsylvania-born John Bigler was elected to succeed McDougal in 1852. Like his fellow-Pennsylvanian, President James Buchanan, Bigler was a northerner who shared strong pro-slavery views and cultivated pro-southern supporters. A short interruption in the reign of the Chivalry Democrats came when the Indiana-born J. Neely Johnson became California's governor in 1856. Johnson was a member of the newly organized American Party, popularly known as the "Know-Nothings" because, when they were asked about their activities, they often answered "I know nothing." The Know-Nothings belonged to a larger movement called nativism, which rested on opposition to immigrants, principally Irish and German Catholics. Powerful for a short while, the Know-Nothings quickly receded before the even greater struggle between the supporters and opponents of chattel slavery.

Chivalry Democrats dominated not only California's governorship and senate positions, but its other elected offices as well, including members of the US House of Representatives. As the editor of the *Daily Alta California* wrote in 1855: "We never send a man to Congress that speaks, acts, and votes with the North. . . . Does a man here from the North aspire to Congressional honors, he must first lay his belly in the dust and endure all the violent and aggressive measures which the South has ever attempted, or he is at once thrust aside to make way for one of chivalrous birth."[44] In 1856, a strongly anti-slavery lawyer from Vermont named Oscar Shafter wrote his family back home: "We have no slavery here, but the State is and ever has been in bonds to the slave power since the hour of its birth."[45]

One of the most important Democrats in California in the early 1850s was a former New Yorker named David C. Broderick. Broderick was to take a leading role in the events of 1858 not only because, after coming to California at the beginning of the Gold Rush determined to take a leading role in the new state's political life, he had become the principal leader of the anti-slavery wing of the new state's Democratic Party; not only because, in that capacity, he had been elected to the US Senate in the same year in which Archy Lee crossed the plains to

California; but most importantly because, in 1858, while Archy Lee was struggling for his freedom in California's courts, he delivered a resounding attack on slavery in the Senate, helping to oppose President James Buchanan's efforts to win approval for the expansion of slavery into Kansas, thus contributing to the nation's inexorable march to secession and military conflict.

Born in Washington, DC, in 1820, the son of two immigrants from Ireland, Broderick had apprenticed to his father's trade as a stone-cutter after he moved to New York, but as he did that he also became active in the rough-and-tumble street politics of the eastern metropolis. He was not able to win important elective office in New York, so when he learned of the discovery of gold in California and of the rush of new residents to the state, he headed west, taking a steamer from New York to Panama and, after crossing over the isthmus, moving on to San Francisco, where he arrived in June 1849. Broderick began working as a private gold refiner, minter, and coiner, and made good money while doing so.[46] But he was also a combative politician who quickly set about the work of organizing his followers in San Francisco much like the directors of Tammany Hall organized theirs in New York.[47] He took an active role in fighting the many fires that scourged the ramshackle buildings of the Gold Rush city, founding a volunteer fire company, organized like those in New York, and winning election as foreman, a position that encouraged many other firefighters to support his political aspirations. Because his avowed ambition was to become one of California's US senators, he was quickly recognized as Senator Gwin's most important rival. In his early campaigns for office, however, he was only able to achieve election to the State Senate.[48]

Most of the Democrats who dominated the new government— joined by a few Whigs and a sprinkling of Know-Nothings—strongly supported slavery, so soon after the organization of the state government they began efforts to exclude blacks from California, or at least to severely limit their participation in its public life. In March 1850 they passed a law that limited the right to vote in California to white males over the age of twenty-one.[49] This followed a provision of the state constitution that contained the same limits.[50] No females, no blacks (male or female), no Indians, and no Asians were to have any voice in how the state was run, or what kind of laws would be adopted. The following month, they passed a law providing that "no black or mulatto person or Indian shall be permitted to give evidence in favor of or against any white person." Every person who had "one eighth part or more of Negro blood" was deemed a mulatto and thus covered by the prohibition, and every person who had "one half of Indian blood" was deemed an Indian and subject to the same prohibition.[51] This law followed the pattern of similar laws in the American South, giving whites license to rob blacks, even murder them, with impunity. A crime committed by a white person against a black or mulatto would thus go entirely unpunished even if dozens of blacks were witnesses to its commission.[52]

In early 1852, the pro-slavery forces passed a law authorizing state commissioners to order slaves who had been brought to California before it was admitted to the Union to be summarily returned to their masters in the South. Modeled on the federal Fugitive Slave Act, the California statute was generally regarded as "California's Fugitive Slave Law." Broderick attempted to block it in the State Senate, but it was passed over his opposition. It initially applied for only one year, but was renewed twice before finally being allowed to lapse in April 1855.[53]

The California law was challenged in two important legal cases. One arose in 1852 when three former slaves, two men and one woman, were arrested by the sheriff of Placer County and taken before a trial judge who ruled that they would have to be returned to Mississippi, the state in which they had formerly been held as slaves by a man named C. S. Perkins. The judge's decision was appealed and taken before the State Supreme Court, where a group of courageous anti-slavery lawyers argued that the California law violated the constitutional provision excluding slavery from the state. The chief justice, a young Know-Nothing named Hugh C. Murray, ruled that the law did not violate the state constitution because it did not make slaves of anybody. It simply recognized that some people were made slaves by other states. "States for their own safety may exclude any obnoxious class of inhabitants," Murray said, noting that the growth of California's free black population had "for some time past been a matter of serious consideration." Blacks were "festering sores upon the body politic." If a black man who was alleged to be a slave was in fact a free man, it was up to the courts in the states he came from to decide that, not California's courts. Thus Murray ordered the three blacks back to Mississippi in the custody of their slave master Perkins.[54]

Another case arose in 1855 in southern California when a Mormon slaveholder from Mississippi named Robert Smith tried to force a group of fourteen blacks, some who had formerly been his slaves and some who were children of the former slaves, to move from California to Texas. Smith had left Mississippi for Utah in about 1848, taking his slaves with him. In 1851, he moved from Utah to the Mormon settlement at San Bernardino in southern California. Then, in late 1855, he attempted to force all of the blacks he claimed as his slaves to go with him to Texas, where slavery was vigorously enforced, and where he might attempt to sell them. One of the blacks, a thirty-eight-year-old woman named Bridget (but commonly called "Biddy") objected strenuously to the move. She managed to get a petition for habeas corpus filed before a district judge in Los Angeles named Benjamin Hayes. In a written decision filed on January 19, 1856, Hayes ruled that "Biddy" and all of the other blacks that Smith claimed as his slaves did not have to go to Texas because California law prohibited slavery. "They are entitled to their freedom and are free forever," Hayes declared.[55] Remaining in Los Angeles, Bridget took the name of "Biddy Mason," worked as a nurse and midwife, purchased some land, became a successful entrepreneur, and accumulated a large fortune from which she made generous gifts to charity. She helped to found Los Angeles's First African Methodist Episcopal Church in 1872, and after her death the city honored her with the creation of a municipal park named in her honor.[56]

Repeated efforts were made by the Chivalry to force the division of California into two states, but these efforts were also opposed by Broderick, who challenged them as indirect efforts to introduce slavery into southern California.[57]

Though small in number and almost continuously beleaguered, the black people in California struggled to better their situations. They worked at whatever jobs they could find, always hoping to find better-paying positions. They petitioned the legislature for relief from the discriminatory laws aimed against them. They gathered in churches, organized along racial lines (as most other institutions were in that time), to summon spiritual strength and offer comfort to their fellows. And they organized public meetings, called Colored Conventions, in which they gathered to share their concerns, discuss methods by which they might ease their common plight, and make plans for a better future.

The first national Colored Convention had been held in Philadelphia in 1817, but by the 1830s similar conventions were held in Ohio, Michigan, and Illinois.[58] The first California convention met in Sacramento's St. Andrew's African Methodist Episcopal Church in November 1855. It was convened "for the purpose of taking into consideration the propriety of petitioning the Legislature of California for a change in the law relating to the testimony of colored people in the Courts of justice of this State," and "to adopt plans for the general improvement of their condition through the State."[59] A second California convention met in San Francisco in October 1857. With delegates attending from eighteen different counties, "measures were discussed and initiated with a view of improving the condition of the colored people throughout the State."[60] Particular proposals were made to extend the benefits of education to all of the state's children.[61]

The Reverend John Jamison Moore (affectionately known as "J. J. Moore") was one of the leaders of the Colored Conventions in California and widely recognized as one of the leaders of the state's black community.[62] Moore had been born a slave in Virginia in 1804 but won his freedom when his mother escaped to the North, taking him with her while he was still a boy. He became the pastor of several important black Methodist churches in the East before coming to San Francisco, where he founded the all-black African Methodist Episcopal Zion Church (often called the A.M.E. Zion Church, the Zion M.E. Church, or just the Zion Church) in 1852. At about the same time, Moore established the first school for black children in San Francisco.[63]

John Wesley, the principal founder of Methodism, had declared his opposition to slavery as early as 1774, thus encouraging free blacks in the United States to seek spiritual solace and protection in the Methodist

Church.[64] His followers continued to oppose slavery until the 1830s when, confronted with the growing wealth and political power of the cotton states, many of them gave way to a reluctant acceptance of the institution. The first A.M.E. Zion Church had been founded in New York in 1821 by African-American worshippers who had been treated badly by the white-led Methodist Episcopal Church.[65] The A.M.E. Zion Church was separate from the much larger African Methodist Episcopal Church that had been founded in Philadelphia in 1787, although the two denominations shared the same Methodist beliefs and teachings. Religious worship was important for African Americans, who sought solace in the teachings of Christianity, in the words of the Bible, and in the hope for ultimate liberation both from the horrors of southern slavery and the cruel discrimination they experienced at the hands of northerners. This liberation was to be the "Year of Jubilee" celebrated in the Bible.[66]

The first African-American church in California was St. Andrew's African Methodist Episcopal Church, established in Sacramento in 1851 by Reverend Bernard Fletcher.[67] Reverend Moore's A.M.E. Zion Church was opened in San Francisco on August 1, 1852, in a modest frame building on Stockton Street.[68] In 1854, Reverend Fletcher came from Sacramento to San Francisco to open an African Methodist Episcopal Church called St. Cyprian on nearby Jackson Street. It soon became the larger of the two African-American churches in San Francisco, although Reverend Moore's Zion church remained the principal gathering place as well as the house of worship for hundreds of San Francisco blacks.[69] As historian Quintard Taylor has noted, the African-American churches formed an important moral and spiritual base for the black population of California, but they also supported orphans and widows with food and money, aided the victims of natural disasters such as floods, and after the outbreak of the Civil War provided aid to black soldiers injured while fighting for the Union.[70]

Mifflin Wistar Gibbs was another leader of the Colored Conventions.[71] Born a free man in Philadelphia in 1805, he had come to San Francisco aboard the steamship *Golden Gate* in 1850. The only work he could initially obtain was as a bootblack, but he worked hard, saved his money, and soon formed partnerships with other black men in the city.

The first was Nathan Pointer, with whom he operated a clothing store called the Philadelphia House. About a year later, he joined Peter Lester to operate a store that sold fine boots and shoes. This store was called the "Emporium for fine boots and shoes, imported from Philadelphia, London, and Paris."[72]

One of the most colorful black residents of Gold Rush San Francisco was Mary Ellen Pleasant, a legendary, almost mythical woman of African-American ancestry who amassed a considerable fortune in Gold Rush San Francisco and fought to establish black rights. Often called "Mammy" Pleasant (although she much preferred to be called "Mistress") she was born about 1814—whether in Virginia, in Georgia, or in Pennsylvania is not clear—and spent her early years in New England. She came to San Francisco in 1852. An intelligent woman with a sense of determination, her entrepreneurial skills enabled her to invest in restaurants and boardinghouses while at the same time advancing the cause of abolition. Some reports say she was also the operator of at least one "house of ill repute" in the city. This would not have been surprising, for prostitution was not then illegal in San Francisco—or other parts of the West—and many lonely men in the bayside city craved feminine companionship.[73]

This was the society Archy Lee entered into in October 1857 and in which he struggled to maintain his freedom in 1858.

CHAPTER THREE

# "I Want It to Come Out Right"

EARLY IN JANUARY 1858 CHARLES STOVALL WENT TO A STEAMSHIP
office in Sacramento and purchased tickets for passage on a river steamer
that would take him and Archy from the capital city to San Francisco.
It was an innocuous enough action. Hundreds, even thousands, of men
and women were doing much the same thing, traveling by water up and
down California's central rivers and out through the delta to San Francisco Bay. While Stovall was doing that, however, hundreds, even thousands, of men and women were traveling from San Francisco and other
towns and cities to Sacramento to attend the inauguration of the state's
new governor and the opening of the legislature's Ninth Session. All the
while, Stovall quietly made plans for a journey that would take him and
Archy, first to San Francisco, then out to sea, and then, via Panama, back
to the slave fields of Carroll County, Mississippi. But the crowds that
were gathering in the capital were excited and noisy.

"A large number of San Franciscans are now in this place," a reporter
for San Francisco's *Daily Evening Bulletin* wrote on January 5, "and one
would almost fancy he was on the streets of the Bay City, so many familiar faces greeting his vision on every side. . . . The Town is full of people,
and the principal streets present a lively appearance."[1] Soldiers paraded
in the streets and crowds gathered in front of the Capitol to hear the new
governor speak. The Democrats had once again dominated the elections,
and California was set for another series of public addresses, events, and
debates that would shape the future of the state whose wealth derived

from gold, not from King Cotton, and Californians were gathering in Sacramento to celebrate.

The new governor was John B. Weller, the ex-Ohioan who had succeeded Frémont as one of California's US senators in 1852 and, with the support of the same pro-slavery Democratic majority, been elected as the state's chief executive at the end of 1857. He delivered his inaugural message on a platform erected in front of the Capitol on Friday, January 8, 1858, but only after his oath of office was administered by David S. Terry, the fiercely pro-slavery chief justice of the California Supreme Court.

Weller spoke in what a newspaper reporter called a "clear, firm, and distinct manner," addressing the state's finances, speaking of the need for faithful enforcement of the laws, and noting the desirability of reforming statutes relating to land holding. When it came to the central issue then wracking the nation and the state, however, he became more specific. He recalled that the people of the state had "with great equanimity" decided that there should be no slavery in California. "No one denies our right so to decide," the governor asserted, "nor do any of our sister States attempt to interfere with this question." But other states had seen it "proper to tolerate slavery," and Weller believed they had just as much right to do that as California had to bar it. The governor then issued a warning:

> The States can never be kept together by force. The tie of affection can alone hold us. Destroy this, and it requires no prophet to foresee that disunion is inevitable. We must live together as friends and as equals in all respects or we cannot live together at all. . . . We cannot be equals unless territories acquired by our common blood and common treasure is [sic] left free to emigrants from the respective States, with their different species of property. . . . May He who controls the destinies of nations preserve and protect our national ship from the impending storm which threatens its destruction.[2]

It was clear that the governor was addressing the coming issues facing the nation—slavery or a breakup of the federal Union. He preferred the Union, but not if it had to be coerced. Each state had the right to decide for itself.

After Weller finished speaking, the legislature convened in the Capitol to begin its business, and guests who had come to Sacramento gathered in a hall fitted up for the inaugural ball. Anyone who could afford the admission price of ten dollars was admitted, and music, dancing, and laughter continued until four o'clock in the morning.[3]

On the same day that Weller was inaugurated as governor, the *Sacramento Daily Union* published a back page story about a habeas corpus petition that had been filed before Judge Robert Robinson of the Sacramento County Court. It centered on a young "colored boy" named "Arch [*sic*]" who had been "claimed as a slave by a young man named Storall [*sic*], a citizen of Mississippi." It seems that "Arch" had been arrested as a fugitive slave in Sacramento's Hackett House and taken to the city jail.[4] Owned and operated by blacks, the Hackett House was a two-story brick building located on Third Street between K and L that was operated as a hotel. It was a first-class operation, the largest African-American business in the city, and the center of the black population's social and political life.[5]

Robinson issued the writ, which ordered the city marshal to produce "Arch" in his court at two o'clock that afternoon. "From what we can learn of the case," the *Union* said, "Arch" left Mississippi against his will and accompanied his young master to California as a body servant. His master was "taking the trip with the view of recovering his health."[6]

The Sacramento paper's story was quickly taken up in San Francisco's newspapers. The *Daily Alta California* reported that "the young master" (whom the *Alta* correctly identified as "Mr. Stovall") had started to come to San Francisco the previous Wednesday, "intending to return to Mississippi and take Archy with him." But when he got to the boat that was to take them away from Sacramento, Archy "had disappeared." Archy made it clear that he "did not want to return to slavery." Stovall found him in the Hackett House and had him taken to the city prison as a fugitive slave.

On Thursday, lawyers Edwin Bryant Crocker and John H. McKune sued out a writ of habeas corpus in Archy's behalf, asserting that he was entitled to his freedom. Although Crocker and McKune were both originally from New York, they had followed different paths to California.

Crocker had come by way of Indiana and then taken steamer passage to Panama and, from there, north to California, while McKune moved through Pennsylvania and Illinois before crossing the plains to California. McKune had arrived in Sacramento in 1850 and Crocker in 1852. Although Crocker was already a prominent Republican and thus dedicated to halt the spread of slavery into the western territories (he became chairman of the newly organized California Republican Party in 1856), McKune was a Democrat with free soil leanings. Crocker had been a member of the Liberty Party in Indiana. It was composed of determined abolitionists who boldly argued that slavery was barred by the terms of the Constitution itself. They ran presidential candidates in 1840 and 1844, but without success. Their most prominent member was the Ohioan Salmon P. Chase, who would become secretary of the treasury in Abraham Lincoln's presidential cabinet in 1861 and three years later succeed Roger Taney as chief justice of the US Supreme Court, thanks to Lincoln's nomination. Edwin Crocker's younger brother was Charles Crocker, an energetic Sacramento merchant who in a few years would become one of the founders of the Central Pacific Railroad and take personal charge of the construction of the transcontinental railroad over the Sierra Nevada. Crocker and McKune had offices in Sacramento's Read Block, only one block from the Hackett House.[7]

It goes without saying that Crocker and McKune were white men. There were no black attorneys in California, almost none in fact in the entire United States.[8] If a man's racial background made him ineligible to vote, if it disqualified him from testifying in court against anyone with a different racial background, it could hardly be expected that he would be entitled to represent other men in court. And if blacks were routinely excluded from schools attended by whites, they had virtually no opportunity to get legal training. Their natural powers of persuasion might be strong, their passion for justice and fairness in the administration of the laws might be equal to that of any other person, but they still could not be attorneys. And so the only attorneys eligible to represent Archy Lee would inevitably be white men.[9] And the only attorneys who would lend their efforts to Archy's case would inevitably be white men with anti-slavery opinions.

In accordance with ancient principles of common law, writs of habeas corpus were available in California to "every person unlawfully committed, detained, confined, or restrained of his liberty."[10] Since Archy was a "person" and writs of habeas corpus were not limited, like other basic rights, to "white persons," he was entitled to apply for the writ. But the city marshal did not agree, for he argued that Archy was a slave and that jurisdiction to decide his status was "vested exclusively in the judicial tribunals of the United States."[11] A dispute was clearly in the offing and, to decide it, Judge Robinson was called on. He announced that he would hear the case the following Monday. "This we believe is the first case of the kind ever broached in California," the *Union* said.[12]

The San Francisco *Daily Evening Bulletin* reported more about the case on Monday. Archy had been arrested as a fugitive from Charles Stovall and lodged in the jail under the charge of City Marshal James Lansing, and the writ of habeas corpus had been applied for by Charles W. Parker, one of the black proprietors of the Hackett House.[13] When the case came up for hearing before Judge Robinson, Stovall argued that the writ was issued without Archy's knowledge or consent and, because Archy was a slave, the only court competent to rule on his status was a federal court.

Robinson proceeded cautiously. He asked Archy if he really wanted the writ to be issued in his behalf; if he didn't, the judge said, "the writ would be dismissed." Archy was apparently unprepared for the question. Blacks, after all, were forbidden, in California as well as in Mississippi and in dozens of other states, from saying anything against whites in court proceedings; they were condemned by the law to utter silence. So the *Bulletin* reported that "Archy made no sign." Robinson was puzzled. Could he order a black man to be freed if the black man did not want to be? After "some consultation," the judge remanded Archy to the marshal's custody and postponed further deliberations in the case. "Considerable interest is manifested in these proceedings," the *Bulletin* added, "by the colored people of Sacramento."[14]

No sooner had Archy been taken back to jail than Judge Robinson ordered his case transferred to George Pendleton Johnston—familiarly called George Pen Johnston—a man who was both the clerk of the

US Circuit Court in San Francisco and the US commissioner who had authority to enforce the Fugitive Slave Act passed by Congress in 1850. Although his business was ordinarily conducted in San Francisco, Johnston happened to be in Sacramento to attend the inauguration of Governor Weller. Born in Kentucky in 1826, Johnston had moved to Mississippi when he was only twenty-one and there begun a successful legal and political career. He was admitted to the Mississippi bar and soon thereafter was elected sheriff of Issaquena County, a cotton-producing county on Mississippi delta land that had the highest percentage of slave residents of any Mississippi county in the 1850s.[15] When news of the California gold discovery reached Mississippi, Johnston joined the Gold Rush to the western state, where he quickly won the favor of the state's pro-slavery Democrats. He won election to the lower house of the state legislature and was quickly rewarded with a succession of federal patronage positions: US marshal, custom house clerk, and US Circuit Court clerk and commissioner.[16]

Robinson transferred Archy to Johnston because a pro-slavery lawyer in Sacramento named James H. Hardy had filed a petition in Charles Stovall's behalf, and Johnston had issued a warrant commanding marshals to arrest Archy and bring him before him.[17] Hardy was an Illinois-born Democrat with a combative personality and fiercely pro-slavery views who had come to California in 1852, established a law practice in Sacramento and, with enthusiastic Democratic support, been elected district attorney of the county in 1854.[18] Many tales were told of Hardy's courtroom battles, some waged with angry words, others with knives. His petition was filed under the Federal Fugitive Slave Act of 1850, and he was prepared to make vigorous arguments that Archy was covered by it. Johnston heard Hardy's petition in Hardy's office, since his own office was in San Francisco.[19] There Archy was represented by Joseph W. Winans, an anti-slavery attorney who had offices in the same building as Crocker and McKune. Winans was known to be a scholarly attorney, and one who had previous experience handling fugitive slave cases.[20]

Answering Hardy, Winans argued that Johnston had no jurisdiction over Archy because Archy was not a "fugitive slave." He had not escaped from his master's custody in Mississippi. He had come to California with

Charles Stovall, and the two had lived peacefully in the city.[21] Hardy made a long and detailed argument against Winans, contending that Archy was a slave and had "no legal rights except those of his master." In support of this point, Hardy cited the US Supreme Court's already notorious decision announced in March 1857 in the case of *Dred Scott v. Sandford*.[22] Johnston was not certain how he should proceed and, as the *Bulletin* noted, he "intimated that he would not render a decision until he had consulted at San Francisco with Judge McAllister of the U.S. Circuit Court."[23] San Francisco's *Daily Evening Bulletin* commented that "so far, there has been little excitement occasioned, but it is altogether likely to prove an exciting topic of conversation."[24]

Judge Matthew Hall McAllister was a Democrat and slaveholder from Georgia who had been born in Savannah in 1800, served as US attorney there, and pursued a political career that included service in the Georgia State Senate, on the Savannah board of aldermen, and as mayor of his city. He mounted a campaign for election as Georgia's governor in 1845 but lost. The lure of the riches in California's hills drew him west in 1850, following the earlier move of his son Hall McAllister, also a lawyer. He settled in San Francisco and pursued a very successful law practice but went home to Georgia in 1853 to make a bid for election as a US senator. This effort, like his earlier gubernatorial bid, was unsuccessful. He returned to San Francisco in 1855 with an appointment from Democratic president Franklin Pierce as judge of the newly created US Circuit Court for the Districts of California. (There were two federal districts in California, one in the south and the other in the north, and McAllister had appellate jurisdiction over both.)[25] McAllister's fame derived not only from his own legal abilities, but because of the social prominence he enjoyed, first in Savannah and then in San Francisco, and also because of the even greater fame of Hall McAllister, who quickly won a reputation as San Francisco's most admired attorney. He had another son besides Hall who helped him enjoy that prominence. Ward McAllister was a budding lawyer who joined his father and his brother in California before going on to New York, where he became the celebrated arbiter of mid-nineteenth-century New York society. (It was Ward McAllister who coined the term *The Four Hundred* to describe the number of people in elite New York society who "really mattered.")[26] During Matthew Hall McAllister's time as judge of the US Circuit Court in San Francisco, he was regarded as the most powerful judge in all of the West.[27] Johnston owed his positions as clerk and commissioner to McAllister's appointment.

After four days of consultation with McAllister, Johnston returned to Sacramento and announced that he lacked jurisdiction to deliver Archy to Charles Stovall. Neither the petition nor the evidence laid before him showed that Archy had escaped from Mississippi, the state in which he had been held as a slave. He had come to California, where no slavery was allowed, the commissioner said, before deciding that he no longer wanted to be the property of Stovall. He was not a fugitive from a slave state, and thus he was not subject to the Fugitive Slave Law. Johnston dismissed Hardy's petition. Archy's future would be decided in the state courts.[28]

Archy and his attorneys may have been pleased by Johnston's conclusion, but not by his failure to order Archy's release from the Sacramento city jail. He was still a prisoner there, still held as a slave, still regarded as a piece of chattel property belonging to Charles Stovall. He had been there for more than two weeks.

Jurisdiction over Archy's case remained with County Judge Robinson, who scheduled another hearing on Saturday, January 23. The *Sacramento Daily Union* reported that the county courtroom was "well filled, many colored people being present," when the judge took the bench at two o'clock in the afternoon.[29] James H. Hardy was again on hand to represent Stovall, and Joseph W. Winans again appeared for Archy.

Hardy had filed an affidavit signed by Charles Stovall in which he set forth the facts that he believed entitled Stovall to Archy's custody: Archy was a Negro slave who owed service to Stovall in the State of Mississippi, the affidavit said. He had escaped from Stovall, who pursued and arrested him "by virtue of his authority as master and owner." Stovall delivered Archy to James Lansing, the city marshal, "for safe keeping" until he could leave the State of California. Lansing filed a return in which he said that he was holding Archy "at the request of C.A. Stovall, his master, and by no other authority."[30]

Hardy opened his arguments before Judge Robinson by asserting that Archy was not asking for his freedom. Archy did not want to stay in California while his master went back to Mississippi. Third parties were trying to take Archy away from his legal owner. Listening to Hardy, Robinson again asked Archy if he wanted to remain in California or return to Mississippi. Archy had had some time to reflect on his earlier refusal to answer the judge's questions. This time he spoke out in terms that the newspaper reporters specifically noted in their stories. "I don't understand what you are speaking of," Archy told the judge, "but I want it to come out right. I don't want to go back to Mississippi."[31]

Winans said he "hoped that the matter would go to the court on its legal merits, as it involved grave questions which would probably be appealed to the Supreme Court." There was no doubt that the court to which Winans referred was the California Supreme Court, whose chambers were only a short distance away from Hardy's office. But there was speculation in the newspapers that the case was important enough even to attract the attention of the US Supreme Court, whose sessions were held a continent away.[32] Hardy said he was willing to do so if Judge Robinson would give both attorneys "a few hours' notice of what his final decision should be." This was a proposition to which all the parties consented.[33] That settled, the court now proceeded to hear the testimony of witnesses.

J. H. Bailey told the judge that he knew Stovall and Archy in Mississippi as well as on the plains, for he had traveled with them. He had heard both men conversing while they were coming west and after they arrived in Sacramento. He knew nothing of Stovall's reasons for coming to California but what Stovall told him, and that was that he was coming to California "on account of his health."[34]

Edward H. Baker (not to be confused with Edward D. Baker, the attorney who later argued Archy Lee's case in San Francisco) said that he knew Charles Stovall and Archy in Carroll County, Mississippi, as well as when they were traveling across the plains.[35] "My understanding was that he was a family Negro," Baker said, referring to Archy. "He belonged to Stovall or the family. I knew nothing to the contrary," although Archy "was in Charles A. Stovall's possession in crossing the plains." Baker knew that Archy's "value" (the price that he could be sold for in a slave market) "was about $1,500." Stovall had left Mississippi "a day or so after the 15th of April" in 1857. "He said he was coming to California for his health. I heard him say he wanted to come across the plains. . . . We had to stop a while because our stock were tender footed." Stovall's stock was "left at Carson Valley."[36]

D. R. Doyle was another witness. He told the judge that he had known Stovall "in Mississippi since he was a boy—in Carroll County." He had also known Archy for several years. Archy "was on a plantation where Stovall made it his home." The men all crossed the plains the previous year; they "traveled together." Doyle heard Stovall say while they were traveling that "the grandest object he had was in coming for his health." He was "under the impression that he did not intend to remain a great while; how long, I can't say; can't say positively that he said he might remain. He might have said that he might remain if circumstances warranted."[37]

Witnesses who first encountered Stovall and Archy in Sacramento were now called to the stand. Charles P. O'Neill was a Sacramento policeman who told Judge Robinson that "Archy had not been treated ill while under arrest"—not of course, "beyond the fact of his imprisonment." John Randall testified that he had rented Stovall a hall on Seventh Street between J and K Streets "for the purpose of teaching school." Stovall "pursued the business of a school teacher in this city." "Stovall did not say to me at the time he rented that he wanted to go home but hadn't the money to go home with." Stovall settled with Randall when his first month's rental ended "and paid me in full."[38]

Robert F. Blakely told the judge that he kept a boardinghouse in Sacramento and knew both Stovall and Archy. "About the first of November I went after the boy (Archy), and Stovall called in the afternoon to see if I wished to hire him. He asked what I'd give." When Blakely told him, Stovall said his offer "was not high enough." But Archy called on Blakely in the evening. Blakely then told him that he was willing to give him the wages Stovall asked for, and Archy "went to work the next day." Archy wasn't hired for a specific time. "I agreed to keep the boy as long as he suited me," Blakely said. "He remained with me about a month. He then left me on account of sickness.... The boy received all but what was due when he was last sick. Stovall afterwards came and got that."[39]

H. D. Campbell next took the stand. He kept a boardinghouse in Sacramento where Stovall had boarded "since about the 15th of October." When he wasn't working, Archy was at Campbell's boardinghouse. Campbell said that Archy "was sick about a week at my house the first time. He was taken sick again and Stovall brought him back. He was sick about eleven days, at my house that time." Stovall got a room in which he could take care of Archy. "Stovall, I expect, pays his board," Campbell said. Stovall told Campbell that he had left his cattle in Carson Valley "because they were tender footed. He asked me at times if I didn't think his cattle would bring a good price in the spring."[40]

Evidence was also received about the advertisement that Stovall had placed in the *Sacramento Age*, advertising his school and stating the fees he charged for instruction.[41]

Judge Robinson announced his decision on Tuesday, January 26. It was a long and detailed opinion, summarizing the arguments made by the parties and the evidence he heard. He concluded that there were three questions he had to answer in making his decision. First, was Archy a "fugitive" from slavery within the meaning of the Constitution and laws of the United States? Second, was there any law of California that would permit Stovall to seize Archy and remove him from the state against his will? Third, would the legal doctrine of "comity" authorize him to send Archy to Mississippi because he was regarded as a slave in that state even though he was not a slave in California?[42]

Comity is an elusive although historically important doctrine under which one state enforces the law of another state even when that law contravenes its own.[43] Judge Robinson put it in simple terms when he said that "comity is simply courtesy; a disposition to accommodate."[44] Archy was a slave under Mississippi law but not under California law. Would "courtesy" require California to respect his status under Mississippi law? Mississippi was, after all, a sister state to California, as much a part of the United States as California.

Robinson answered all of these questions in Archy's favor:

First, Archy was not a "fugitive" under terms of the federal Fugitive Slave Act of 1850, because he had been voluntarily brought into California by his master. "To constitute him a fugitive from labor, under the Constitution and laws of the United States," Robinson said, "he must have fled from one State into another." To emphasize his point, Robinson revealed that San Francisco's US circuit judge Matthew Hall McAllister had already determined that Archy was not subject to the federal act. The determination was apparently made when Commissioner Johnston went back to San Francisco to confer with McAllister.

Second, no law of California authorized a slave master to seize a black man and carry him away into slavery. The California Supreme Court had already decided that point in 1852, in the case of *In re Perkins*.[45]

Robinson acknowledged that the third question was the most difficult to answer. Although California law did not authorize a California citizen to seize a black man and hold him as a slave, the law of Mississippi did. Would California enforce Mississippi's law under the doctrine of comity? If Stovall was a mere traveler going through California, entering it for a short period of time and then leaving, perhaps the doctrine of comity would apply. He would then be a mere traveler, still a citizen of Mississippi, and still entitled to the protection of its laws. But he was much more than a mere traveler. He had come to California for the benefit of his health. He had rented a house in Sacramento, opened a school, and given lessons to students. He had hired Archy out with no limitations as to time. He had become a resident of California, and hence a citizen. He had voluntarily accepted the state's law. He was no longer a Mississippian. He was not entitled to claim any rights that California citizens could not exercise. Robinson continued his conclusion with some force, saying:

> Now, if a man may retain his citizenship in the State of Mississippi, and sojourn here two months, and work his slave, why may he not stay twenty years and work twenty slaves? The principle is precisely the same. The law would not permit a citizen of this State to hold and work a slave against his consent. And what

it does not allow its own citizens to do, it cannot be reasonably expected to sustain strangers in doing. Again, if one citizen of Mississippi sojourns here with his slaves, why not a thousand of them, or ten thousand, and bring all the slaves of Mississippi to work in our mines, and thus drive free labor out entirely, and shield themselves under the plea that they are citizens of Mississippi and only sojourners here for a time? The law of comity does not, and cannot reach that point.[46]

Robinson now concluded: "Upon the facts of this case, and the law applicable to them, I am satisfied the prisoner should be discharged, and it is ordered accordingly."[47]

The courtroom spectators listened attentively. The judge had said that Archy was a free man. He was not a fugitive slave. He was not subject to the law of Mississippi; he was a Californian. He could not be held in jail at the behest of Charles Stovall.

When, early in the proceedings, Robinson had asked Archy if he wanted to remain in California or return to Mississippi, Archy had said: "I want it to come out right. I don't want to go back to Mississippi."[48] Now, according to the judge's ruling, he didn't have to.

*Or did he?* If Archy and the blacks who gathered in Robinson's court to support him felt a sense of exultation when the judge spoke, their feelings would be short, for events would very quickly turn against him.

CHAPTER FOUR

# "The Archy Case"

A SERIES OF ODD EVENTS QUICKLY FOLLOWED ROBINSON'S DECISION.
About an hour before he delivered his opinion, he announced what
the newspapers called "the substance of it." Whether he did this at the
request of one of the attorneys, or with the agreement of both, was not
clear. In either case, the announcement alerted James Hardy and Charles
Stovall to the need to do something, and to do it quickly, for Archy was
about to be released from the city prison. As Robinson read his opinion,
the slave master and his attorney hurried to the office of a nearby justice
of the peace, where they made an affidavit to the effect that Archy was a
slave who was trying to escape from Stovall, who was his master. The justice of the peace, whose name was H. J. Bidleman, then issued a warrant
authorizing the arrest of Archy and his continued confinement in the city
prison. So as the young black man walked out of the County Courthouse,
thinking he was now a free man, he was arrested again by a police officer
and clapped back into prison.[1]

Hardy and Stovall then hurried to the office of the California
Supreme Court where another affidavit was filed and a writ of habeas
corpus was issued by the court's chief justice, David S. Terry. The purpose
of this writ was ostensibly to free Archy from the prison cell into which
he had been clapped by Justice Bidleman's warrant. In what the *Sacramento Daily Union* called "the strangest part of the whole proceedings,"
Stovall filed an affidavit substantially claiming that Archy was improperly
held in prison "although he was thus in custody by the act of Stovall
himself." "We doubt whether a parallel case, in its facts and attendant

circumstances can be found among the entire list reported in the United States since the formation of the government," the *Union* told its readers.[2] The Sacramento paper's comments were promptly copied into the San Francisco newspapers.[3]

The California Supreme Court's office and courtroom were on the second floor of Sacramento's Jansen Building at the corner of Fourth and J Streets.[4] This was not far from Robinson's county courtroom, so it did not take long for Hardy and Stovall to approach Chief Justice Terry. Writs of habeas corpus, as Hardy knew, are useful tools, for they can be used to test legal confinement in a variety of ways. The writ that Charles W. Parker had sought claimed that Archy's confinement in the city prison was illegal because Archy was a free man and his confinement deprived Archy of his freedom. The writ of habeas corpus that Stovall now sought claimed that Archy's confinement in the city prison was illegal because Archy belonged to Stovall and his confinement deprived Stovall of his property. The new writ was issued quickly enough to make sure that Lansing would not set Archy free. The Supreme Court would express its own opinion about Archy's status by holding a hearing on the writ.

There were three justices on the California Supreme Court in 1858. Any one of them could have given James Hardy the writ of habeas corpus he sought, but David Terry was a good man to ask, for he was a skilled judge with a good knowledge of the law and no hesitation in expressing his views.[5] More importantly for Hardy and Stovall, he was known to have strong pro-slavery sympathies.[6] Born in Kentucky in 1823, Terry had moved with his family to Texas while still a boy. There he studied law and became a lawyer. According to some reports, he participated as a volunteer in the struggle for Texas Independence in 1836, although he was then only thirteen years old. He later served for a while in the Texas Rangers. After the outbreak of the Mexican war in 1846, he volunteered to fight on the American side and eventually rose to the rank of second lieutenant. Moving to California in 1849, he practiced law and became active in politics, winning enough support both from California's pro-slavery Democrats and its anti-immigrant Know-Nothing Party to win election as an associate justice of the California Supreme Court in 1855.[7] A tall man with muscular arms, a face that was clean-shaven except for chin whiskers, and hair worn long in the southern style, Terry was noted for making quick decisions and enforcing them with equally quick bursts of temper. His anger was not lightly ignored, for it was known that he carried a bowie knife and was not at all reluctant to use it.[8] In 1856, when a vigilance committee was formed in San Francisco to hang some men the regular law enforcement officials did not believe deserved hanging, Terry had mounted a vigorous opposition to it, and in one of his explosions of temper he had stabbed a member of the committee with his knife. He was arrested, but released from custody when the committee member recovered from his wounds.[9] Terry kept his Supreme Court seat despite his conflict with the vigilance committee and, when the intensely racist Chief Justice Hugh Murray died in 1857, Terry succeeded him in the presiding justice's chair.[10]

Former governor Peter H. Burnett was one of the two associate justices in 1858. He brought strongly racist views with him when he came to California from Oregon, where he took a leading role in the organization of the territorial government. One of the measures he helped to pass in Oregon was a law that banned blacks from any entry into the state.[11] As the western historian Hubert H. Bancroft later wrote, "The exclusion of free negroes was always a hobby of Burnett's."[12] Adopted as part of the territory's fundamental laws in 1844, the anti-black law was incorporated into the state Constitution when it was approved in 1859.[13] News of the gold discovery in California lured Burnett south in 1848. He tried his hand at mining for a short time, then resumed his law practice and indulged his zest for politics. In December 1849, only a month after the adoption of the state Constitution, he was elected as California's first governor.[14] In his new office, he urged the passage of a law like Oregon's that would have banned all blacks from entering the state. Burnett's proposed law readily passed the lower house of the California legislature but was blocked in the State Senate by David Broderick.[15] Burnett served as governor for just over a year before resigning to resume the practice of law and serve for a time as a trial judge. Then, in January 1857 he accepted an appointment to the Supreme Court from the outgoing Governor J. Neely Johnson.[16]

The third member of the Supreme Court in 1858 was Stephen J. Field, a man who was nearly as colorful as Terry and almost as talented in winning political support as Burnett, but in his judicial conduct more skillful than either of his associates. Born in Connecticut in 1816, the sixth son of a distinguished Congregationalist minister, he had moved to Massachusetts with his family while still a boy. Sent to travel in Greece and Turkey as a teenager, he had returned home to study at Williams College, where he graduated in 1837. After reading law in Albany, New York, and practicing for a while in New York City, he left for California in 1849. Uninterested in gold mining, he practiced law in the busy mining supply town of Marysville before serving as an *alcalde* (a Mexican official combining the duties of mayor and judge), winning election to the state legislature in a hard-fought political campaign, and in 1857 being elected to the third seat on the California Supreme Court.[17] Like Terry and Burnett, Field was a Democrat. Unlike them, however, his views on slavery were murky. Years later, he recalled questions that were put to him about his views on slavery when he was campaigning for office in California. He denounced the charge that he was an abolitionist as a "base calumny," explaining that he had a brother in New York who was a Free Soiler and another brother in Tennessee who was a slaveholder, and asking with which one, "in the name of all that is good, were they going to place me?"[18] He also stated that he believed that slavery was a "domestic institution which each State must regulate for itself, without question or interference from others."[19] Did he believe it was right? Or did he believe it was wrong? No answer.

The Supreme Court justices did not hold a hearing on Stovall's writ for thirteen more days, during all of which time Archy remained behind bars. The lawyers, however, were busy, researching the law applicable to the case and preparing their arguments. Hardy continued to represent Stovall and Winans Archy Lee. Finally, on Saturday, February 6, the court hearing began. Hardy spoke first, reciting a familiar argument he had made many times: "There is no question, from the return of the writ and evidence in the case, that the boy Archy was a slave owned and held to service by the petitioner, in the State of Mississippi. Nor is there any pretence [*sic*] of any voluntary or actual emancipation of the slave by his master."

Hardy recalled Winans's claim that Archy was "voluntarily brought to this state by his master," but he vigorously disagreed. Slave property was protected by due process of law, he argued, and that there was "no magic" in the words of the California Constitution purporting to ban slavery from the state. He reminded the judges that the state constitutional provision had not been supported with any penal sanctions. Thus, he argued, it had no effect. Hardy cited the opinion of US Chief Justice Roger Taney in the case of *Dred Scott v. Sandford*, not yet a year old, that seemed to offer constitutional protection to slavery in every state of the Union. But Hardy did not rest with his invocation of the authority of Roger Taney. He appealed to an even higher authority, telling the justices:

Slavery derives its force and dignity from the same principles of right and reason, the same views of the nature and constitution of man, and the same sanction of Divine revelation as those from which the science of morality is deducted. Its effect is the moral and physical improvement of the slave himself.

He asked:

Is "justice" established by the confiscation of a citizen's property because his interest or his pleasure has induced him to visit a sister State? Is "domestic tranquility insured" by an instrument which secures to the citizen of one State the full, free and perfect enjoyment of his peculiar property, but denies the same rights to citizens of other States with their peculiar property?

Hardy told the judges that "the relations of master and servant are like those of guardian and ward, parent and child, or any other relation involving mutual interests, duties and responsibilities. . . . If the Negro is free, let it be asserted in a Court competent to try the matter, and such a Court can only be found in the State of Mississippi."[20]

Winans's argument was neither as long nor as impassioned as Hardy's, but it seemed to be supported by careful research and reasoning. He began by reminding the judges that Stovall had come to California, not for the purpose of capturing Archy and taking him back to Mississippi, but "to be a sojourner here." He carried on business in Sacramento and let Archy out for hire. Doing that, Stovall was "acting in violation of the spirit and meaning of the constitutional prohibition of slavery." But after his arrival in the state, he appeared "to have entertained nothing but a remote undeveloped intention of leaving the State at some future unascertained period."

Winans reminded the judges that Stovall came into California "with a full knowledge of its institutions," then continued: "He commenced the pursuit of business and the acquisition of fortune here in obedience to our laws. He thereby obtained and enjoyed all the advantages of citizenship. Should he not be subject to all the disabilities thereof?"

Winans next addressed the issue of comity that Judge Robinson had discussed, saying: "Comity does not require any State to extend any greater privileges to the citizens of another State, than it grants to its own. As this State does not allow its own citizens to bring a slave here, even in transit, and to hold him a slave for any portion of time, it cannot be expected to allow citizens of another State to do so."[21]

Hardy and Winans continued their arguments for nearly an hour and a half, after which the case was taken under advisement. The decision would be rendered the following Thursday, February 11.[22] Archy would remain in his cell for at least another five days.

The Supreme Court met at four o'clock in the afternoon on February 11 to deliver its opinion. The *Sacramento Daily Union* reported that "the fact that an opinion would be delivered, involving questions in which the community generally has taken a deep interest, . . . induced a large attendance crowding the Courtroom." Some of the spectators were blacks who warmly supported Archy's bid for freedom. Others were supporters of Stovall and his effort to regain physical possession of Archy. The opinion had been written by Justice Burnett, but he did not read it. Justice Terry simply announced that the Court had decided that Archy should be given back to Stovall.[23]

Police were on hand to quickly take custody of Archy and lead him back to their station house. A crowd formed to follow along. Archy was frightened, bewildered. He tried three times to escape, first as he descended the stairs from the Supreme Court rooms to Fourth Street, again when the party escorting him arrived on Front Street between I and J Streets, and lastly when they approached the station house. The *Union* told its readers that the case had "excited embittered feelings on both sides; the sympathizers with the slave being indignant that he should be delivered up to the claimant, and the friends of the latter apparently laboring under the idea that an attempt would be made, by a 'rescue,' to avoid the judgment." But none of this happened. "Of course," the *Union* said, "Archy was safely delivered at and secured in the City Prison."[24]

The Supreme Court's written opinion was inscribed by hand in graceful, flowing script for the Court's official records. For the public, however, it was quickly set in print and set forth in newspapers, where readers all over the state—and soon all over the United States—could read it and begin to comment on it. The case was titled "In the Matter of Archy on Habeas Corpus" in the handwritten opinion.[25] When it was included in the Supreme Court's official reports, it had the same title on the first page but was identified as *Ex Parte Archy* at the top of the subsequent pages. Later references to the case in legal treatises and historical accounts referred to it as *In re Archy*. The decision carried the authority of the entire court, although the opinion, which occupied eleven pages of print in the official reports, was the work of only one of the justices, Peter Burnett.

The former governor reviewed the principal facts of the case. He restated Charles Stovall's argument that he was the owner of Archy, that Archy was a slave, and that he was entitled to Archy's custody. Stovall said that he had taken up residence in Sacramento, opened a school there, and hired Archy out for wages, only because he was "short of means" when he arrived in the city. It was not because he wanted to establish permanent residence there, or remain any longer than would be necessary to get back on his feet and resume his journey back to Mississippi.

Burnett began his discussion of the law applicable to the case by stating that it had "excited much interest and feeling" and that it gave rise to "many questions of great delicacy." "It is not so much the rights of the parties immediately concerned in this particular case," he said, "as the bearing of the decision upon our future relations with our sister States, that gives to the subject its greatest importance."

The justice went on to repeat a statement made in 1820 by a judge of the Kentucky Court of Appeals in a case involving the status of slaves in the Northwest Territory, where slavery was prohibited by the Northwest Ordinance of 1789: "We disclaim the influence of the general principles of liberty," the Kentucky judge had said, "which we all admire, and conceive it should be decided by the law as it is, and not as it ought to be."[26] If this quotation did not disquiet Archy's supporters, Burnett's reference to Roger Taney's widely excoriated opinion in *Dred Scott v. Sandford* should have.[27] "It must be concluded that, where slavery exists," Burnett said, referring to *Dred Scott*, "the right of property of the master in the slave must follow as a necessary incident. This right of property is recognized by the Constitution of the United States."

But it was one thing to say that the right of property in a slave was guaranteed by the US Constitution and another to say that it had to be honored in a state that had banned slavery. The case of *Somerset v. Stewart*, decided in England in 1772, was often cited as authority for the proposition that slavery could not exist anywhere in the Anglo-American world unless it was supported by the local law. In that case, Lord Mansfield, chief justice of the King's Bench, had decided that James Somerset, a slave who had been taken to England from Virginia by his master, a Scot named Charles Stewart, and who had there escaped into freedom, could not be recaptured and compelled to board a ship bound for slavery in Jamaica, because slavery was "so odious, that nothing can be suffered to support it, but positive law." Since there was no positive— that is, statutory—law supporting slavery in England, Mansfield ordered that Somerset could not be forced to go to slavery in Jamaica; he "must be discharged."[28] *Somerset* was widely recognized in jurisdictions where no slavery was allowed by law. But it was also recognized in some slave jurisdictions, one of which was Archy Lee's home state of Mississippi. It was there, in 1818, that the State Supreme Court ruled that three slaves whose owner had taken them from Virginia to live in a part of the Northwest Territory that later became the State of Indiana, where slavery was illegal, were entitled to be regarded as free men when they were then brought to Mississippi, regardless of the Mississippi law authorizing slavery. The court had then stated: "Slavery is condemned by reason, and the laws of nature. It exists and can exist only through municipal regulations."[29] California, like England and the Northwest Territory, had no positive, no written, no "municipal" law supporting slavery; in fact, its constitution explicitly forbade slavery. How then could California force Archy Lee to return to slavery in Mississippi?

Burnett's opinion did not refer to the *Somerset* decision, although it was cited in Joseph Winans's argument.[30] Instead, he rested his decision on the legal doctrine of comity, first discussed by Judge Robinson. Burnett said that comity rested "exclusively in the discretion of each state." In California, it would be guaranteed to slave owners who were passing through the state but not to slave owners who had set down roots there—who had, in effect, become residents. Stovall's residence in Sacramento was not, as his attorney claimed, a mere "delay" in his passage through the state to Mississippi. It was a full stop, a transformation from travel to residence. Stovall could not claim the benefits of comity because he was not a mere traveler. He was a resident of the state who had engaged in business and become a citizen. He was thus subject to the laws of the state, including the constitutional provision banning slavery.

Up to this point, Archy's supporters may have been encouraged by Burnett's words. But their encouragement quickly vanished as they read the final paragraphs of his opinion. "This is the first case that has occurred under the existing law," the justice wrote, and Stovall might have had some reason to believe that the constitutional provision banning slavery "would have no immediate operation." "This is the first case," Burnett repeated, "and under these circumstances we are not disposed to rigidly enforce the rule for the first time. But, in reference to all future cases, it is our purpose to enforce the rules laid down strictly, according to their true intent and spirit." Then Burnett concluded: "It is therefore ordered that Archy be forthwith released from the custody of the Chief of Police, and given into the custody of the petitioner, Charles A. Stovall."[31]

The law was against Stovall, as Burnett had explained at some length—it favored Archy. But the Court's order favored Stovall and was against Archy. Archy was to be released from the city prison, but he was not to be set free. He was to be delivered into Stovall's custody and thus returned to slavery. If anyone wondered why Archy had tried three times to escape while he was being taken back to the city prison, they might now understand. His attorney had won the Supreme Court case on the law, but lost it in the final order delivered by the judges.

Chief Justice Terry did not join in Burnett's opinion, but he was not particularly disturbed by it. He appended a single paragraph at the end of Burnett's long discourse in which he agreed that Archy should be delivered to the custody of Stovall, but differed in the reason why. "I concur in the judgment," Terry wrote, "and in the principles announced in the opinion of my associate; while I do not entirely agree with his conclusions from the facts of the case. I think the delay of the petitioner was unavoidable, and that the fact of his engaging in labor in order to support himself during his necessary detention, did not divest his rights under the law of comity, as laid down in the opinion."[32]

Justice Field took no part in the decision. He did not join in either Burnett's or Terry's opinions. It was widely understood that he had been ill when the case came up and thus could not participate in it.[33] Appellate court decisions do not require that all members of the court participate, and in this era decisions of the California Supreme Court were often issued over the signatures of only two of the three justices, so Field's absence did not occasion particular notice. A few days later, the *Sacramento Daily Union* told its readers: "We have the assurance that Judge Field does not concur with Judge Burnett's decision in this case," and San Francisco's *Daily Evening Bulletin* said it had been told that if Field had been able to write an opinion in the case, "it would have been a fit rebuke to the miserable, partial, illegal one given by Burnett and Terry."[34] Although supporters of Stovall may have been skeptical about the views that Field was reported to have held, Archy's defenders hoped that the *Union*'s report was true. In either case, however, it was of little help to Archy, who was still denied his freedom. He was still a prisoner, whether of the Sacramento city jailer or of Charles Stovall.

The California newspapers lost no time in condemning Burnett's opinion. The *Sacramento Daily Union* analyzed it in some detail and declared it a "double disappointment." Burnett had declared that the law of comity was no protection for Stovall and yet he ordered that, under the law of comity, Archy would be delivered into Stovall's custody. "Can the Court make an order contrary to the law as laid down by itself?" the *Union* asked. "Can it make exceptions to its own legal rules?" By trying to do that, the Court had rendered itself "supremely ridiculous."[35] In San Francisco, the *Daily Alta California* told its readers that it found the Supreme Court's decision "curious in the extreme," adding: "We doubt whether a parallel case, in the facts and attendant circumstances, can be found among the entire list reported in the United States since the formation of the government."[36] The *Alta* thought that Burnett's ruling on the issue of comity had aroused "astonishment and indignation."[37] San Francisco's *Daily Evening Bulletin* called Burnett's decision to release Archy to Stovall "a most lame and impotent conclusion."[38] The *Marysville Express* called the Court's decision "the most extraordinary of all the decisions that were ever delivered by any tribunal upon earth. It caps the climax of all human absurdity."[39] The *San Joaquin Republican* told readers that Burnett had rendered "a very remarkable decision" in which he had stated the law "very clearly and, as it appears, very correctly." But his decision to order Archy into Stovall's custody contradicted the law. "If, as Judge Burnett clearly decides, the boy Archy is free, we should like to know by what authority he, as a Supreme Judge, or otherwise, can remand him into a state of slavery. . . . This is a mockery and a trifling with the law."[40] Back in San Francisco, the *Argus* asked its readers: "How will this decision sound to the judiciary of the country? How in Europe, or wherever civilization exists? To us it ties with the most despotic decisions in the world; and it reflects disgrace upon the spirit of liberty." The *Argus* concluded: "We are clearly of the opinion that Judge Burnett owes it to himself and the people of this State to resign."[41]

Judge Burnett did not resign. He did not modify his fiercely pro-slavery views.[42] Nor did he have to, for there were plenty of men in California in 1858 who agreed with him, who believed that slavery deserved protection in the slave states of the American South and hoped that it might one day be brought west with the flood of gold seekers who were coming to California, and that that one day might not be far off.

Burnett did, however, give up his Supreme Court seat when his term of office ended in early October 1858, at which time he was succeeded by a lawyer named Joseph Baldwin who had come to California in 1854 from Alabama, bringing with him a ready wit and an aggressively anti-black racism.[43] Baldwin was to serve on the California Supreme Court from October 2, 1858, until January 1, 1862. He took no part in the decision of Archy's case, although he did express a perceptive opinion of it, when he said simply: "It gives the law to the North, and the nigger to the South."[44]

## CHAPTER FIVE

# A Struggle on the Water

ARCHY REMAINED IN THE SACRAMENTO CITY PRISON FOR FIVE DAYS after the Supreme Court's controversial decision was announced, held there for Charles Stovall. Then, at about two o'clock in the afternoon on February 16, a wagon pulled up to the prison with Stovall, one of his brothers (probably William), and police officer Charles O'Neill on board. Archy was taken out of the jail and securely placed in the wagon. Newspaper reports about the party's destination varied wildly. San Francisco's *Daily Alta California* reported that Archy was to be taken back across the Sierra Nevada to Carson Valley. The *Sacramento Daily Union* reported that he was to be carried away to some unspecified destination, possibly the nearby city of Stockton. Sacramento's *State Journal* suggested that Archy was headed for Utah, or some other place "where both himself and master will obtain the privileges to which they are entitled." The *Union* confessed "to a dullness of apprehension as to what privileges" the *State Journal* was referring. "Archy was well ironed," the *Union* told its readers, "and the escort well-armed, to guard against an escape or rescue."[1]

Sacramento's black community was understandably concerned by all the conflicting rumors. They posted men along the levee that bordered the river so they could spot any attempt to put Archy on one of the boats that crowded the waterfront. But they did not see any. Reporting on what was happening in Sacramento, the best the *Alta* could tell its readers in San Francisco was: "It is not known what has become of Archy."[2]

On February 26, the *San Joaquin Republican* reported that "the boy Archy" was now in Stockton and had been ever since he left Sacramento.[3]

On his arrival there, he was secretly confined in the county jail, held "awaiting the pleasure of Stovall to conduct him home to Mississippi."[4] In Stockton, Stovall had reportedly tried to purchase passage from the Pacific Mail Steamship Company for himself and Archy to sail to Panama. To raise the cost of the fare, he had offered to "make Archy over" to the company. The offer, however, was declined.[5] According to another report, Stovall had already sent Archy back to Carson Valley with instructions that from there he would be taken across the plains to the eastern states.[6] In Sacramento, the *Union* denied a story told by the *Sacramento Bee* that the express house of Wells, Fargo & Co. had given Stovall a receipt for Archy and agreed to deliver him to New Orleans as an item of "property." He would arrive there in "good order and condition" according to the agreement.[7]

About a week later, the *Alta* informed its readers that Stovall and Archy had left Stockton. They were traveling slowly, the newspaper said, stopping here and there along the road. They went first to the south end of San Francisco Bay, where they passed through the old Mexican town of San Jose, which from 1849 to 1851 had served as California's first state capital. They then proceeded northward into Alameda County, a broad chunk of land that rolled up from the east edge of the bay to a range of wooded hills and faced the city of San Francisco across the water.[8] They spent Thursday night, March 4, in Oakland, the rapidly growing business and population center of Alameda County. Oakland was an important transportation spot, for it was only eight miles across the bay from San Francisco, and the busy harbor in which steamers bound for Panama and the eastern United States were constantly coming and going.[9] Ferries were also crossing the bay from Oakland to San Francisco and back transporting goods, wagons, coaches, carriages, and passengers. News of the excitement provoked by the "Archy Case" had already been transmitted to the Atlantic states. In an article published on March 1, the *New York Times* had told its readers about the case and the controversy surrounding it. Among other things, the *Times* advised readers that Archy was a valuable piece of property in the slave country, worth about fifteen hundred dollars "at home."[10]

Reports had already reached San Francisco that Stovall and Archy were nearby and that Stovall had engaged passage for both on the steamship *Orizaba*, which was scheduled to leave San Francisco for Panama on Friday, March 4. Two Panama-bound steamers were actually scheduled to leave on that date. The Pacific Mail Steamship Company's *Golden Age* made monthly trips to and from the Central American isthmus, carrying mail, freight, passengers, and what people on both the Pacific and Atlantic coasts described as "treasure," a combination of gold, silver, and other precious metals that had been extracted from California's mines.[11] The second steamer was the *Orizaba*, owned and operated by the rival Nicaragua Steamship Co.[12] Both the *Golden Age* and the *Orizaba* transported passengers to Panama, where they were transferred to a train that took them across the isthmus to the Caribbean side. The Nicaragua Steamship Co. had previously taken passengers to a railroad that crossed through Nicaragua, but the railroad there was undergoing repairs and had been replaced for the time being by the Panama route. Both steamships did a good business, although the *Orizaba* had made efforts to increase its passenger traffic by advertising that its rates had been reduced. A ticket for a first-class cabin was now two hundred dollars, a ticket for second class was one hundred fifty dollars, and steerage cost only fifty dollars.[13]

Alerted to Stovall's plans, one of the leaders of the city's African-American community sought the help of two attorneys who were sympathetic to the plight of the blacks. A ship's steward and cook by trade who called San Francisco his home, James Riker was one of the leaders of California's Colored Conventions. He was also a manager of a two-story house called the San Francisco Athenaeum, located at 273 Washington Street. The first floor of the house was the Athenaeum Saloon, a social gathering place for the city's blacks, while the second floor was the Athenaeum Institute, in which meetings were held to discuss initiatives that might be taken to improve the lives of African Americans in the city and state.[14] The attorneys who welcomed Riker and agreed to help Archy's struggle for freedom were Elisha O. Crosby and Walter H. Tompkins. Both Crosby and Tompkins were respected San Francisco attorneys, while Crosby had the additional distinction of having been one of the delegates who framed the California state constitution in 1849. In 1861 he would gain further recognition when President Abraham Lincoln appointed him as the US minister to Guatemala.[15] Crosby and Tompkins prepared an affidavit which Riker signed under oath, then took it to San Francisco County Judge Thomas Freelon. The affidavit reviewed the basic facts of "Archy Lee's" travels to California (both his first and his second names were set forth here) and the difficulties he had encountered in Sacramento. It informed the judge that Charles Stovall claimed Archy as a slave and that Riker believed Stovall was concealed aboard one of the steamships set to sail from San Francisco for Panama. It assured the judge that Archy Lee was a free man and not the slave of Charles Stovall "or any other person." If prompt action was not taken, he would be carried out of the state and beyond the jurisdiction of the court before a writ of habeas corpus could be enforced. In response to the affidavit, Freelon issued a warrant for the arrest of Charles Stovall for kidnapping.[16]

Acting to enforce Freelon's warrant, San Francisco's police chief James F. Curtis took measures to frustrate them. He ordered two of his officers, Isaiah W. Lees and another named Johnson, to try to discover Archy's whereabouts and, "at all hazards" prevent Archy from being taken aboard the steamer. They were to inquire at the steamship office, Curtis said, and to "make the necessary inquiries concerning the matter." Following these orders, the officers remained on alert all night, trying to "trace out the affair." By daybreak, however, they had not been able to discover any information.[17]

In a long story titled "The Denouement of the Archy Case," the *Alta* gave its readers a detailed account of the events that followed. The black population of San Francisco had been alerted to the situation, the *Alta* reported.[18] Ever since Archy was taken out of Sacramento, they had used all of their resources to try to learn where he was being held and to prevent him from being irreparably lost. According to the *Alta*, they "mustered in considerable numbers" at the Market Street wharf, where the *Orizaba* was moored. The *Golden Age* was at the Folsom Street wharf, a few blocks to the southeast, and it was still possible that Stovall would take passage on that ship. So all night, groups of black men stood by the gates to the wharves, watching the police officers and trying to learn if Archy was to be secretly conveyed on board either vessel during the night.

At daybreak, the police officers separated, Johnson stationing himself at the *Golden Age* and Lees at the *Orizaba*. By ten o'clock, according to the *Alta*, "the excitement began to increase," with word spreading that Archy would be "rescued" by the city's blacks. The crowds assembled along the wharves were growing rapidly. "Here and there were seen groups of negroes talking mysteriously together, gesticulating violently, or casting furtive glances at carriages as they wheeled rapidly down to the steamers, piled with baggage, and filled with departing Californians. Closed carriages were particularly the objects of scrutiny."[19]

At eleven o'clock, reports circulated that Archy was concealed at North Beach, or on Alcatraz Island, and that he was to be put on board a steamer from one of these places. Two boats then set out into the bay, with what the *Alta* called "stalwart blacks" aboard. One lay off North Beach, while the other proceeded much farther out toward the Golden Gate, the channel that connected the Pacific Ocean with San Francisco Bay. "What action they intended to take is not known," the *Alta* told its readers, "but no little amount of determination was expressed in the faces of the party."[20]

While all of this was happening, Archy was secreted at some unknown place, either on the east side of San Francisco Bay or on one of the islands in the bay. It was reported that Stovall was accompanied "by three or four of his friends," all of whom were anxiously waiting for the steamer they had booked passage on. On shore, meanwhile, excitement was spreading all over the city. Rumors that there was to be a black "rescue" of Archy lured large crowds to the wharves. But when the hour for sailing arrived, Archy was nowhere to be seen. The police and the observers were puzzled.[21]

At half past twelve o'clock the *Orizaba*, crowded with passengers, cast off its moorings and headed out into the bay. A total of 616 passengers were aboard, and four hundred thousand dollars in "treasure."[22] Stovall and Archy were still nowhere to be seen. But a crew of police officers was on the ship's deck, determined to foil any attempt to take Archy aboard as the vessel headed into the swift moving waters of the bay. Officers Lees and Ellis and Deputy Sheriff DeWitt C. Thompson were among the law enforcement officers. Just before the *Orizaba* sailed, Lees had engaged a couple of privately owned boats at the Pacific Street wharf and directed them to follow the *Orizaba*. Thompson had brought aboard a writ of attachment just obtained from one of the judges in San Francisco. The writ would give him the authority to seize Archy as soon as he could put his hands on him. And Lees had brought the warrant for the arrest of Stovall on charges of kidnapping Archy.[23]

As soon as the steamer cleared the wharf, Lees noticed a couple of men in the vessel's bow who seemed to be acting oddly. One was waving a handkerchief tied to a cane. As Lees approached the men, he heard some remarks that confirmed his suspicion that they were connected with the Archy case. The officer heard no reply to their signal, so he turned and went aft. But a minute or so later, he heard the man who had been waving the handkerchief yell out "There they are." Turning in the direction indicated, Lees saw a boat filled with several rowers approaching the steamer. According to the *Daily Evening Bulletin*, the boat was coming from Angel Island, located six miles north of San Francisco, and it had six men in it.[24] As the boat approached the *Orizaba*, Lees studied its occupants. Based on the description he had been given of Stovall, he quickly recognized the Mississippian. As the boat got nearer, the officers stationed themselves near the gangways on both the port and starboard sides of the steamer. This aroused the attention of some of the passengers, who sensed the impending confrontation and shouted to Stovall and his companions, "Keep off! Keep off! There are officers on board!" But the boat was already alongside, and Lees saw Archy crouching in it.[25]

Stovall and the men with him now struggled to pull their boat away from the steamer, but it was close enough that Lees could jump down and grab Archy. Confusion then erupted aboard the *Orizaba*. The steamer's engines were fueled by coal, which made a tremendous roar, but the observers were now shouting loudly enough to be heard above the din. Some were eager to applaud the boldness of the officers in seeking to apprehend Archy, while others hooted at their "insolence" and condemned their "interference" with Stovall and "his property." Stovall and his supporters protested angrily. Stovall said the Supreme Court had given Archy to him, and "he'd be G-d d—d" if any other court would take him away from him. He glared at Officer Lees, threatening to blow the "top of his head off." But Lees was used to such threats and calmly continued his duties. Archy was trembling when Lees picked him up and passed him up to Deputy Sheriff Thompson like what the *Alta* called "a sack of potatoes." And "in a twinkling," the *Alta* continued, "Archy was in the custody of the authorities."[26]

On deck, Archy began to look around him. He had enough sense to hold his tongue, thinking, as he later recalled that "da white folks was doin' nuff talking for him and demselves, especially da white folks." A general scramble then followed, the crowd "circling around Archy and the officers but no one offering to help the officers rescue Archy." Lees then served his warrant upon Stovall for kidnapping, and Archy was shoved toward the starboard gangway. Lees and Thompson stayed behind Archy, and Ellis cleared the way ahead. The ship's officers and such of the cabin passengers as chose to mingle in the throng were in favor of the policemen, but a large number "were not for letting the negro or his master leave the ship."[27]

The *Alta* reported that "one old lady, with spectacles and extensive crinolines, 'sailed in' and made herself amusingly conspicuous. She pitted her whole force to the shoulder of the negro, pushing him along, now and then raising her voice in triumphant shouts, such as, 'You varmints! We'll see whether free people are to be kidnapped in this way. Yes, yes—Thanks to the Lord—Shove hard, Mr. Officer—That's a good one—Ugh! Don't squash me that way. You good for nothing critter.'" An old Negro, as he saw Archy pass over the side of the boat, shouted, "Hosanna! That's your sort!" Others shouted, "Kill the d—d nigger thief!" Amid the babel and confusion, Archy, his master, the two officers, and the deputy sheriff tumbled and bundled into the boat and pulled away for the shore, followed by a mingled yell and cheer from the steamer.[28]

As they approached the Market Street wharf, the men in the boat were received with cheers from a crowd that had gathered to await their arrival. The *Bulletin* reported that the colored population were "all out" and that Archy was "the observed of all observers."[29] As he landed on the wharf, there was a general rush to see the "kidnapped darkey," and the interested spectators increased in numbers as they proceeded up town. About two o'clock, Archy was safely ensconced in the sheriff's office where, according to the *Alta*, "there was soon a collection of all degrees and shades to see the 'little nigger' about whom so much fuss has been made."[30]

When speaking with the newspaper reporters, Archy "seemed a little stupefied or frightened at all the commotion." He was not much disposed to answer questions, although he said that he was a native of Mississippi and that he was twenty-two years old. Stovall corrected him, saying he was only eighteen. From the sheriff's office, Archy was promptly taken to the county jail, there to await further action by the courts. Stovall was more fortunate. He appeared in court on the kidnapping charge, where two sureties promptly came forward to guarantee his bail of five hundred dollars.[31]

Conversation in the sheriff's office turned to the attorneys who would be called on to represent Archy and Stovall. Plenty of attorneys were available, and there was little doubt that both men would be well represented. "The point at issue is whether the adjudication of the Supreme Court was conclusive or not," the *Alta* said. "If it was, it is difficult to see how that decision can be overruled." Judge Freelon "was obliged" by statute to issue the writ in Archy's favor, but he still had the right to retain Archy in custody. So he did just that.

Archy was now in the San Francisco jail, and Charles Stovall was free on the streets. It had been that way before. Archy was used to being held prisoner. If he could ever establish his freedom, fully and finally, he would be a happy man, as would his many supporters, most of whom were part of San Francisco's black community. To prove their concern, his supporters were already gathering in their church on Pacific Street "in relation to the matter."[32] "Their church" was the African Methodist Episcopal Zion Church.[33]

The evening of the day of Archy's rescue and re-confinement in the jail, a notice was posted in the Athenaeum and at other places where African Americans gathered in the city. It read:

NOTICE!!!—There will be a public meeting of the colored citizens of San Francisco this (Friday) evening, March 5th, at Zion

M.E. Church, Pacific, above Stockton Street. To commence at
8 o'clock. Signed by a Committee.[34]

Long before eight o'clock, the church was brightly lit and filled with
men and women, mostly black San Franciscans, but with some whites
blended in. Peter Anderson was elected as chairman of the gathering and
F. R. Carter as secretary. Anderson said that he was glad to see such a large
crowd, "and conducting themselves with such propriety and decorum."
He assured the crowd that they should not take "any measures under the
excitement and impulses of the moment that might in the future make
their action that night appear ridiculous." Archy "deserved the sympathy
not only of those who are present," Anderson said, "but of the people of
the whole State, white and colored." This was not so much because Archy
had been a slave but because forces were then trying to return him to that
status. Anderson believed that it was "only the intention of the people
to resort to all legal means in their power to resist the encroachments of
the slave power from thrusting its giant-like hands into this free State
at will, and dragging at pleasure into slavery those whom the people of
this State, by their own laws, have declared before high Heaven are free."
With this view, Anderson declared that it was "necessary to create a fund
and procure able counsel to conduct the case."[35]

Reverend J. J. Moore then rose and moved to elect a committee of
several persons, to be appointed by the chair, to collect funds. James
Brown was appointed as chair. Resolutions were introduced requesting
colored churches generally to take up collections to aid the fund. A
motion was then made to strike out the word *colored* and insert *Christian*.
Appeals would be made to Christians regardless of their color. After
discussion among Reverend Moore, Jacob Francis, W. F. Keeling, and
others, the resolution as amended was passed. Moore, a Reverend Mr.
Benton, Mifflin Wistar Gibbs, D. W. Ruggles, and other prominent
members of the black community then rose to speak, urging the colored
people generally "not to commit any overt act, as it might be the means of
withdrawing instead of adding sympathy for the alleged slave 'Archy.'" At
the same time, they all believed that it was their right, and also proper, for

them "to resort to all legal means in their power to assist by their purses in paying whatever expenses might be incurred under the circumstances."

A call was made for a general collection, which realized one hundred fifty dollars. A motion was then made to adjourn, subject to the call of a Committee on Finance, and the assemblage dispersed.[36]

One hundred fifty dollars was a considerable sum in "The Year of Archy Lee." If nothing else, it was enough to buy a second-class ticket to Panama on the steamboat *Orizaba*, or enough to buy steerage for three passengers. And other funds were soon added to it. A report was soon received in Sacramento that the black people of Nevada had raised ninety-seven dollars to help pay the expenses of Archy's case.[37]

Archy was still behind bars, as the people gathered in the Zion M.E. Church were well aware. But it was becoming clearer and clearer to them—and they hoped to the rest of the world—that Archy's future might not yet have been finally decided.

## Chapter Six

# The Opposing Forces

THE OPPOSING FORCES WERE NOW WELL ALIGNED. ON THE ONE SIDE were the Mississippian Charles Stovall, the lawyers who were eager to represent his interests in court, and the great majority of the white population of California, who believed that Stovall was well within his rights in seeking to retain custody of Archy Lee. They believed this because slavery was a time-honored institution, protected by provisions of the US Constitution, honored in scripture, and respected, if lamely, in the decision handed down by the California Supreme Court in the case of *In re Archy*. On the other side was Archy Lee, a young black man who was the focus of all of the struggle about slavery. He owed his service to Charles Stovall because it was so ordained in the law of the State of Mississippi. Aligned with Archy Lee were lawyers, abolitionists, Democrats with free soil leanings, and men and women who believed that slavery violated basic principles of justice and equality and should be hobbled, if not completely eradicated. Stovall had been arrested for kidnapping, and Archy had been clapped back into jail to await the latest court decision on his status. Sacramento was the political capital of California, but San Francisco was its business and commercial center and the home of hundreds of lawyers whose services were readily available to anyone who could afford to pay for them. The congregation of African Methodist Episcopal Zion Church was raising funds to pay lawyers to fight for Archy and his cause, and requests were sent throughout the state to raise more money to ensure that good lawyers would be enlisted on his side.

Where would the next battle be fought? And what law would ordain its outcome? Stovall's supporters believed that they would find a hospitable environment in the federal court, and that the law that US Commissioner George Pen Johnston had failed to invoke when they approached him in Sacramento was still the most favorable for their cause. Perhaps they had not adequately explained the case when it first came up before him. The Fugitive Slave Act of 1850 was still heavily tilted in their favor. To recapture Archy Lee now they would pursue that law again.

The Act of 1850 authorized any person who claimed to be the owner of a fugitive slave to seize and arrest the fugitive, or take him or her before one of the commissioners authorized to administer the law. Evidence establishing that the alleged fugitive had escaped from a slave state into another state or territory could be given either by affidavit or deposition. The commissioner could hear evidence from witnesses but was not required to do so, for his proceedings were to be conducted "in a summary manner." No testimony was to be given by the alleged fugitive.[1] If the commissioner concluded that the alleged fugitive had escaped from a slave state into another state or territory, he was required to issue a certificate authorizing the alleged owner, called the "claimant," to take the alleged slave away with him. Anyone who interfered with the claimant, or with any marshal carrying out one of the commissioner's orders, was subject to severe criminal penalties.[2]

Proceedings seeking to have Archy declared a fugitive slave under the Act of 1850 began on March 17 with the filing of an affidavit signed by Charles Stovall. In the affidavit, Stovall swore that he was a citizen of Mississippi and domiciled in that state; that he was the owner of "a certain Negro slave called Archy" who was held to service under the constitution and laws of Mississippi; and that Archy fled from Mississippi sometime during the month of January 1857 "because of the commission of a certain offense against the laws of the State of Mississippi." Archy fled from Mississippi without Stovall's consent and thereafter "escaped into and now is in this state." Stovall's affidavit ended with a prayer that "a writ issue and said slave Archy be dealt with according to law."[3] Responding to the affidavit, Commissioner Johnston promptly issued a warrant ordering the US marshal "to apprehend and arrest the said slave

Archy, and bring him forthwith before me in my office in the city of San Francisco, then and there to do and receive what may be considered in the premises just and proper."[4] Johnston's office was in the Merchants' Exchange Building on Battery Street, the same building that housed the courtroom presided over by Circuit Judge McAllister.

But the state and local courts were also active. Stovall had been taken to the Police Court on a charge of kidnapping Archy. But a technicality was quickly noticed in the warrant for his arrest. It had been sworn to before a deputy county clerk, instead of a proper judicial magistrate, so Police Judge Henry P. Coon dismissed it.[5] On the same day that Commissioner Johnston issued his warrant for Archy's arrest, Archy was brought before County Judge Freelon, who had issued the attachment by which Archy was arrested as he was taken off the *Orizaba*. The corridors of City Hall, where the County Court held its sessions, were crowded with spectators, black and white. James Hardy had come from Sacramento to represent Stovall with the assistance of a local attorney named George F. James (called "Colonel James"). Archy was represented by Crosby and Tompkins, but Edward D. Baker, who had become one of San Francisco's most highly respected attorneys after he arrived in the city in 1852, had also joined Archy's team.

Typically addressed as Colonel Baker because of his military service in the Black Hawk and Mexican Wars, Edward Dickinson Baker had been born in England but brought to the United States while still a boy. Tall and strikingly handsome, with blue eyes, thinning gray hair that arched dramatically across his high forehead, and a booming voice that made him a commanding stump speaker as well as a formidable courtroom advocate, Baker had had a distinguished legal career in Illinois, where he became such a close friend of Abraham and Mary Todd Lincoln that they named their second son Edward Baker Lincoln in his honor.[6] Like Lincoln, Baker was a politically ambitious Whig, but because political opportunities for Whigs were so few in Illinois, he, Lincoln, and a prominent Whig named John J. Hardin agreed (somewhat informally) that they would share their terms as the Whig congressman from Springfield, each serving a single term and then giving way to the other. After Baker's one term from Springfield ended, he headed north to Galena, Illinois, where he won election to another congressional term.[7] In the interim, he volunteered to lead a regiment of soldiers in the Mexican War, going south first to fight under General Zachary Taylor and then under General Winfield Scott before returning north and resuming his political career. After his term from Galena ended, he went even farther south, this time to Panama, where he helped to organize a workforce that was building a railroad to span the isthmus, before coming on to San Francisco in 1852 and quickly becoming one of the most successful lawyers in the Gold Rush city.[8] Like Lincoln, Baker abandoned the Whigs for the Republican Party in the mid-1850s. His most notable San Francisco case was tried in 1856 when he acted as the attorney for a man who had been charged with murder but who was captured after the trial by a self-appointed "Committee of Vigilance" and hanged.[9]

The vigilance committee organized in 1856—sometimes called the "Great Committee"—marked the second time a group of prominent businessmen had appointed themselves to bring "law and order" to San Francisco. The first had been in 1851, when several hundred businessmen claimed that a band of immigrants from Australia, called the "Sydney Ducks," were setting San Francisco buildings on fire so they could loot them and escaping justice because the regularly elected law enforcement officials were in corrupt alliance with them. The accused criminals were subjected to kangaroo trials and summarily punished— some hanged, some banished, and some deported.[10] The 1856 committee was much larger. It followed Baker's successful courtroom defense of a mild-mannered gambler named Charles Cora, who had been charged with the murder of US Marshal William Richardson in a gunfight on a public street. Baker's defense of Cora, in which he argued that Cora shot Richardson in self-defense, ended in a hung jury, after which Cora was returned to jail for retrial.[11] But an ambitious man named James King of William, editor of a newly established newspaper called the *Evening Bulletin*, loudly complained about the injustice of the trial. (King had added "William," his father's Christian name, to his own to distinguish himself from many other James Kings in his native Washington, DC.) Determined to attract readers to the *Bulletin*, he accused a host of local officials with corruption. He called Judge Freelon "an imbecile," Mayor

James Van Ness a "stupid old ass," and John Weller (then a US senator) a "viper." He said Edward Baker was a "base cur" with a "lying tongue" whose defense of Cora marked him as "a slanderer and a coward" and that the city's lawyers were the "pests of society." He lashed out at San Francisco's large Catholic community, accusing the Irish-born attorney Eugene Casserly (a Catholic who would be elected as one of California's US senators in 1869) of "Jesuitical cunning" and branding the Irish-born Father Hugh Gallagher, rector of St. Mary's Cathedral, a "wily priest." The Irish-American state senator David Broderick was a special target of King's invective. King likened him to the Roman conspirator Catiline, referring to him in print as "David Catiline Broderick," though he knew that Broderick's middle name was Colbert, condemning him as a "consummate wire-puller" and "ungodly swindler" and, in an open letter, asking him: "Who can forget or forgive the crime and immorality you have been the means of spreading over this city?"[12]

James P. Casey, a member of the San Francisco Board of Supervisors, was another of King's targets. Like Broderick, Casey had come to California from New York. Unlike Broderick, he had had a scrape with the law in the Empire State and served some time in Sing Sing prison. When King learned about his conviction, he threatened to publicize it in his newspaper. Casey argued that he had served his debt to society and that his reputation should not again be dragged in the mud. King published the information anyway, after which the two men met on the street. Each was armed with a pistol. Who shot first was never clearly determined, but King fell with a bullet in a fleshy portion of his body. It was not thought to be a fatal wound. He was taken to a hotel where doctors hovered over him for about a week before he finally died. Casey's supporters believed King's death was caused by medical malpractice and not by Casey's gunshot. The Committee of Vigilance disagreed, so twenty-five hundred of their members, heavily armed, took him and Charles Cora from the unresisting sheriff to their headquarters in what they called Fort Gunnybags. They quickly tried both men and publicly hanged them.[13] For three months, the Committee of Vigilance held sway in San Francisco. After Cora and Casey, only two more men were hanged, but dozens were threatened with death and dozens more were banished from the city and state. The men who were banished, under threat of execution if they returned, were primarily followers of Broderick.[14] One was California Supreme Court justice David S. Terry who, two years later, was to join in deciding Archy Lee's case in the state's high court.[15] Though a defender of slavery and a man of obstinately independent thinking, Terry had temporarily joined Broderick in resistance to the self-appointed vigilantes.[16]

The issue now before Judge Freelon was the legality of Archy's confinement in the city jail. Baker and Tompkins were asking the judge to free Archy under a writ of habeas corpus issued on the basis of James Riker's affidavit, and Hardy and James were vigorously opposing it. Hardy argued that Riker was unqualified to make an affidavit because he was a black man and, under California law, blacks could not testify against whites. The California Supreme Court had already decided that Stovall had the right to Archy's custody, Hardy said, and Riker was an "intermeddler" who was now trying to "pervert" that court's decision.

When Baker asked a penetrating question about the law controlling Archy's status, Hardy angrily labeled it a "Yankee question," but then asked Freelon to excuse him for "being excited," explaining that he firmly believed in Charles Stovall's right to hold Archy as his slave and "a venal and corrupt" press was trying to undermine that right.[17] As the argument continued, Baker pressed his demand that Archy be freed. Freelon then asked Hardy if he objected to Baker's request, and Hardy surprised everyone by saying that he did not. Hardy's answer was not inadvertent, however, for no sooner had Freelon ordered Archy's release than the US marshal, Perrin L. Solomon, appeared in the courtroom to arrest Archy on the warrant issued by Commissioner Johnston. Baker examined the warrant, found it in good legal order, and then urged the blacks in the courtroom to leave. As Archy was taken away by the marshal and his assistants, there was what the *Bulletin* called "a Gold Rush and press," and a large crowd followed through the streets as Archy was led toward the marshal's office in the Merchants' Exchange Building. Several blacks were arrested for assault and battery and disturbance along the way, but the *Bulletin* told its readers that no rescue was attempted. "Everybody was excited."[18]

Commissioner Johnston took up Archy's case on March 19. Judge McAllister's courtroom, which had been reserved for Johnston's use, was "excessively crowded" and many people had to be turned away at the door for, as the Sacramento *Union* told its readers, there was "much feeling evinced in this community in regard to the matter of sending Archy back into slavery." The *Union* reporter believed "a great principle" was involved in the question.[19] But a friend of his, a man he identified as hailing "from the Sunny South," felt differently. He said that "it would be better, even if it were wrong and in violation of the fundamental law of this State, to send the Negro back into slavery; because, if he were set at liberty it would be regarded by the free Negroes here as a triumph on their part and, as a consequence, they would become so saucy and put on so many airs there would be no such things as tolerating them." The *Union* reporter countered his friend's opinion by saying that it was "about as logical as most of those advanced by the champions of that comity among States which would require California to send to Mississippi, as a slave, a man who the Constitution of the former State regards as free."[20]

Hardy took the lead in arguing Stovall's case to Commissioner Johnston. In what the *Union* reporter called "a very inflammatory speech," he repeated many of the points he had made in his arguments before Sacramento County Judge Robinson and in the Supreme Court hearing in Sacramento. At one point, Commissioner Johnston, himself a one-time sheriff in Mississippi, was so taken aback by Hardy's manner that he asked him whether he was addressing "the Court or the spectators." Unabashed, Hardy argued that in proceedings under the Fugitive Slave Act, a black man had no right to be represented by an attorney. In fact, he had "no right to a defense." All the commissioner needed, Hardy said, was proof that Archy was a slave, that he owed service in Mississippi, and that he was now a fugitive in California. Once these facts were established, "the Negro should be given to his master and taken back to Mississippi." Then Hardy repeated an argument he had made before the California Supreme Court by asserting that, if Archy was not a slave and did not owe service, "why then Mississippi was the place to decide that question."[21]

Baker asked Johnston for a delay, pointing out that Archy's very freedom was at stake and that he needed more time to prepare his case. In addition, Baker was obligated to appear in a murder case that afternoon in a separate court. Hardy opposed the request, saying that "if there was any virtue in the law in California," Stovall would take Archy aboard the next steamer leaving San Francisco and all the controversy would be over. This comment was greeted by applause in the courtroom, which was quickly put down by Johnston. After considerable discussion, the commissioner agreed to put the case over to the following day.[22]

When Johnston reconvened his court the next day, Hardy was ready for action. He argued that Baker had no right to be heard in the court because proceedings under the Fugitive Slave Law were to be *ex parte*, that is one-sided, and "no counsel had a right to appear for the alleged slave." He repeated his claim that "the only tribunal that could pass upon the right to freedom of Archy were the constituted authorities of the State of Mississippi." "Some people might be horrified at the idea," Hardy said, but Archy had "no right at all to be heard; no more right to be heard than a bale of goods." He was "a chattel" and the "Federal Compact and Constitution of the United States regarded him as such." Hardy continued:

> Now, sir, I am about to express an opinion which I feel conscientious; if I do not believe it, let this arm fall from its socket; let my tongue cleave to the roof of my mouth. Before God and these witnesses, I believe, sir, that there is no right and no law whatever for a defense in this case. I want to show that Archy is a fugitive slave, and that he is in this State, and then I want a certificate to be issued, and Archy sent back to Mississippi. I do not want to enter into a war of words about Archy's freedom. I address myself only to your Honor, as a committing magistrate. If the law and the Constitution were carried out, Archy would now be in the State which gave him birth, and pursuing those duties which God and his nature intended that he should perform. All I want to do is to present my prima facie case, that Archy is a fugitive slave, without opposition.[23]

Baker was ready to reply. He agreed that if Archy was a slave owing service to Stovall, he could be sent back to Mississippi. But what might happen if Stovall swore that *Hardy* was his slave and owed *him* service in Mississippi? The Fugitive Slave Law did not say that the fugitive had to be black. In such a case, would Hardy have a right to be heard in his own defense? Would he have a right to present facts showing that he was not a slave? Would he have a right to the assistance of an attorney in presenting those facts and arguing their legal consequences? Baker did not claim that Archy had a right to a jury trial, but he did claim that Archy had a right to present facts showing that he was not a slave and a further right to the help of an attorney in doing so. "If Archy was a horse claimed by another person," Baker commented, "there would be a right to a trial by jury." But since Archy was a man, "he could not be heard by a jury. Such was the law," Baker commented; "it might be a curious one, but he was not disposed to deny it or complain about it."[24]

Hardy admitted that Archy had a right to a jury trial. "But where?" "In the State of Mississippi," he insisted.[25]

In support of his argument that Archy was entitled to be represented by counsel, Baker referred to a sensational fugitive slave case that had been decided in Boston three years earlier. A slave named Anthony Burns had escaped from Virginia in 1854 by stowing away on a ship that brought him north.[26] Captured in Boston as a fugitive slave and put on trial before a US commissioner there, Burns had lost his bid for freedom and was returned to slavery in Virginia. But he was represented in the proceedings before the US commissioner by one of the most esteemed lawyers in the United States: Richard Henry Dana Jr., famous not only as the author of *Two Years Before the Mast*, the classic account of life at sea, but also for his resolute efforts to improve the rights of merchant seamen and oppose the horrors of the Fugitive Slave Act.[27] Burns eventually found his way back to freedom when the pastor of one of Boston's black churches traveled south and purchased his freedom with thirteen hundred dollars raised by the church members.[28]

Commissioner Johnston decided that Archy should be heard by counsel—but "*in a certain way*." He did not want legal points to be argued, he said, for he would decide the case only "upon the facts."[29] Tompkins then read aloud the original affidavit Stovall had filed in the case Johnston had dismissed in Sacramento, and Baker made a long and detailed argument that the affidavit was insufficient to show that Archy presently owed service to Stovall. Baker made several motions to dismiss the case, but they were all denied. He then offered a comprehensive statement of the facts of the case that he said showed that Archy did not owe service to Stovall, that he was not a slave but a free man, and he submitted a long and detailed affidavit sworn to by a San Francisco man named John P. Zane to support it.

Zane's affidavit, based largely on statements Stovall had made to him, argued that Archy was not a slave and that he did not escape from Mississippi into the State of California. He came to California "with the full knowledge and consent and in company with the said Stovall." Zane swore that the evidence establishing those facts could be obtained from a group of witnesses who were then in Sacramento, and another then residing in the city of Sonora in the Sierra foothills, whose name Zane did not know. Zane's affidavit recalled that Stovall had purchased "a farm in Carson Valley" and left cattle there. He had established residence in Sacramento and engaged in business there. Stovall told Zane that he came to California "for the purpose and with the intention of making the said State of California his permanent residence and home." Stovall had told him that he was "fully aware of the force and effect of the laws of the State of California; that by that law he knew that he had no right to the custody or control of the person of the said Archy Lee; that the said Archy Lee was not a fugitive slave; that he depended for his control over the said Lee solely upon his affection."

Baker offered an additional affidavit made by Archy himself in which he swore that he had heard all of the facts alleged in Zane's affidavit (since he was illiterate he could not have read it) and that they were all true.

The case was then continued to Monday, March 29. Archy remained in jail, of course—he was getting used to that environment—but excitement and activity still swirled around the many cases that involved him.

CHAPTER SEVEN

# "Jehovah Has Triumphed"

A CIVIL LAWSUIT HAD BEEN FILED IN ARCHY'S NAME AGAINST CHARLES Stovall claiming damages of two thousand dollars (by some accounts twenty-five hundred dollars) for Archy's wrongful detention and for the manner in which he was roughed up as he was taken off the *Orizaba*.[1] At about the same time, newspapers in both San Francisco and Sacramento surprised readers by reporting that Stovall had left San Francisco on March 22 without Archy in tow. He departed on the Pacific Mail Company's steamship *Sonora* bound for Panama. Many people wondered why his departure had been so secretive; he had, after all, become a familiar figure through much of San Francisco and Sacramento when the newspapers reported his efforts to capture Archy and take him back to Mississippi. A rumor surfaced that Stovall had sold his interest in Archy for one thousand dollars—a substantial discount from the fifteen hundred dollars he was reputed to be worth back in Mississippi—but this was quickly disputed.[2] Many people supposed Stovall left because the evidence he would have given before Commissioner Johnston "would have shown, absolutely, that Archy is not a fugitive slave." Another report was heard that Stovall had left a power of attorney with an aggressively pro-slavery politician from San Joaquin County named Samuel H. Brooks, authorizing him "to receive and ship Archy" if and when Johnston declared Stovall was his master. In Sacramento, the *Union* speculated that Stovall feared a criminal prosecution would be instituted against him. Grumbling complaints were heard in both San Francisco and Sacramento that Stovall was allowed to leave California

81

without being charged with perjury, which many thought was apparent in one or the other of the two affidavits he submitted to Johnston. But the *Union* told its readers that it was "rumored that he had received an advance of one thousand dollars on Archy and therefore did not feel much pecuniary interest in the disposition of the alleged slave."[3] The *Sonora* was not free of "pecuniary interest" when Stovall shipped aboard it, however, as it carried valuable bags of US mail and newspapers, 280 passengers, and "treasure" valued at $1,661,928.[4]

Meanwhile, the black citizens of California were continuing their efforts to help Archy. A public meeting was held on March 25 in the African Methodist Episcopal Zion Church in which a committee was appointed to publish a newspaper notice (called a "card") setting forth the views of the colored people of the city and "their true position in relation to the slavery under which we live." The notice read:

> There has been a disposition manifested by a portion of the press in this city, to misrepresent us, by characterizing us as a rebellious and turbulent class of persons, who disregard the laws of our country, when we come in contact with them, or when they happen to oppose our particular views. Now we wish to inform our friends and the public generally, that we are a law-loving, and law-abiding class of persons, who have always quietly submitted to the unjust enactments that have been imposed upon us, in this our common country, from time to time. We have been the subjects of innumerable wrongs without any just cause, yet we have borne up under them with scarcely a murmur, and can appeal with pride to our character and standing throughout this entire State, and point to our industry, integrity, and moral worth.
>
> It has been publicly asserted that we had counseled and determined to rescue the boy "Archy," from the custody of the officers who had him in charge, and that we had no confidence in the legal tribunals of this State—or in the United States Commissioners, before whom he is to be tried.
>
> All of this we pronounce an unqualified falsehood, gotten up by our enemies for the purpose of making political capital against

us in the community. As a class, we are a liberty-loving people, who are deeply interested in whatever pertains to the welfare of mankind. In the case of Archy, we feel that we are maintaining the laws of the State of California, and ask for his liberation upon just and legal grounds, believing that he is rightly entitled to his freedom, which we are interested in securing according to law, and which we will leave no proper means untried to accomplish. We are well satisfied that the reflecting portion of the people are disposed to act justly by us in this case, and award us all that we merit—that of being a quiet and orderly class of people.[5]

Commissioner Johnston reconvened his court on March 29. The US marshal brought Archy into the courtroom, which was filled with a large audience. Colonel Baker, Elisha O. Crosby, and W. H. Tompkins were again on hand to represent Archy, while attorneys James H. Hardy and Colonel George James were there for Stovall. Hardy surprised the spectators by advising Johnston that he intended to ask for a delay of the proceedings until the end of May or the early part of June, explaining that his client had not left San Francisco on the *Sonora* because he had given up his efforts to recover Archy; he had gone back to Mississippi to obtain documentary evidence proving that Archy Lee was his slave.[6] Johnston said he would listen to testimony before ruling on Hardy's request, then decide whether to grant the delay or decide the case on the evidence already heard.[7]

The evidence presented by Hardy included an affidavit that Charles Stovall signed just before he left San Francisco, in which he offered "an explanation of the original affidavit" he had submitted to Commissioner Johnston. This new affidavit included the information about Archy's affray with Smiley and the fact that he and Archy had left Mississippi at much different times, coming together only when they came to the crossing of the North Platte River. Charles admitted that he had spent some time in Sacramento trying to make money, and that Archy had worked there. But he swore that he was still Archy's master and that Archy still owed him service in Mississippi.[8]

Hardy offered another affidavit signed only three days earlier by Charles Stovall's brother William, detailing the story of Archy's encounter with Smiley, Charles's journey to California on account of his ill health, and his recent departure on the steamship *Sonora* bound for Panama. William swore that his brother was returning to Mississippi to procure a certificate from the circuit court there proving that Archy was a slave and that he in fact escaped from there.[9] Affidavits were also received from Edward H. Baker (not to be confused with Edward D. Baker) and D. R. Doyle, men who had testified before Judge Robinson in Sacramento.

Hardy called Charles O'Neill as a live witness. O'Neill was the policeman who had guarded Archy in the Sacramento jail and frequently conversed with him. Archy had admitted to O'Neill that he was the slave of Stovall in Mississippi. He also admitted that he had "cut" a white man there with a knife. O'Neill had asked Archy why they didn't hang him. "I thought they hung niggers in Mississippi for stabbing white men," he said. Archy answered: "God bless you, I didn't give 'em time." Archy made it clear to O'Neill, however, that he did not want to "go home." He did not want to return to a life of slavery in Mississippi. Tompkins cross-examined O'Neill, asking him if Archy hadn't said that the stabbing affray was caused by a difficulty in the Stovall family about their slaves and if Charles Stovall hadn't told Archy that he "did right." O'Neill replied that Stovall had never said "anything of the kind to him."[10]

When Tompkins tried to call a witness to testify in Archy's behalf, Hardy objected. He said that the fugitive slave had no right to offer any evidence. Johnston quickly overruled this objection. A witness named Nicholas Millman then testified that he had known Charles Stovall in Sacramento and that he was the man who had rented Stovall the hall in which he taught school. Stovall told Millman that he had bought a ranch in Carson Valley and left some cattle there. R. F. Blakeley testified that he knew Stovall and Archy in Sacramento and that he had hired Archy to work for him there. He paid all of Archy's wages except $5.50 directly to Archy; but he paid a small amount to Stovall after Archy became sick.

C. C. Freeman was next to testify. He said he had become acquainted with Stovall near Fort Bridger, a trading post on the westward trail, in July 1857 and that they had traveled a good distance together. Stovall never said anything to him "about Archy's running away." John Copeland then testified that he had roomed with Stovall for two months in Sacramento and that he had enrolled for a while in Stovall's school. Stovall told him that he came to California "for his health." At his father's request, Stovall had brought Archy along as his "body servant." Stovall told Copeland that if he could make his time in Sacramento profitable, "he would remain in town two or three years." Tompkins then offered in evidence the original affidavit of Charles Stovall that had been presented to Commissioner Johnston when he first considered Archy's case back in Sacramento.[11]

Johnston convened the case again on March 30. Hardy presented live testimony from William D. Stovall, who confirmed that Archy was not with his brother Charles when he left Mississippi for California and that the two did not come together until they arrived at the crossing of the North Platte River. On cross-examination, Colonel Baker asked William if there was "a difficulty in the family about the estate at the time Archy disappeared." A long argument followed, at the end of which Johnston ordered William to answer. He still refused, saying that "the court had nothing to do with the private affairs of the family." When Hardy directed the witness not to answer, Baker said he would try to prove that there was a dispute in the family about their slaves, that Archy was "in dispute," and that because of the dispute "there was a quarrel in which Archy fought for his master." Charles Stovall then "carried Archy away to Missouri." But William still hesitated to answer. After Hardy withdrew his objection, Tompkins told William "your counsel has given you permission." But Hardy turned on Tompkins and said: "That's not true, and you knew it when you said it."

"What's that?" Tompkins asked.

"It's not true," Hardy answered, "and you knew it when you said it. You lie."

"You are a liar," Tompkins countered.

Hardy's southern temper was now boiling. He jumped up from his chair and "started to get at Tompkins." Tompkins arose, and every person in court got up. Half a dozen persons started to get hold of Hardy. He was "working about with his arms," and some observers thought he was trying to draw a pistol.

"Let him draw his pistol!" Baker exclaimed. "Let him draw his pistol if he wants to." Commissioner Johnston then left his seat to prevent a fight and, "after a little struggling on the part of Mr. Hardy, he saw the folly of his conduct and sat down." Order was soon restored, and Tompkins addressed Johnston: "I beg your pardon for my offense."

"If I had power I should send you both to prison for your conduct," the commissioner said. "It's an outrage against common decency, as well as an insult to the court. But I do not know whether I have the power." Hardy then apologized, after which Baker made some remarks "trying to show that Mr. Hardy was to blame, the remark of Mr. Tompkins being a proper one."[12]

It was on March 30 that a reporter for the *Alta* managed to speak to Archy for a few moments. Archy repeated the story of his birth in Pike County, Mississippi. He recalled the effort of "Mr. Smiley" to take him away from Carroll County, and he told the reporter about the stabbing incident that followed. He admitted that he had stabbed Smiley twice in the left breast, inflicting two wounds, but they were "not of a serious character" and the sheriff did not try to arrest him. He spoke about his buggy trip with Charles Stovall through Memphis to Cape Girardeau County, Missouri. Archy assured the reporter that "Mr. Carnes and Mr. Hunter, in Missouri" knew the truth of what he was saying about Stovall taking him from Mississippi to Missouri.[13]

To give the attorneys an opportunity to prepare their closing arguments, Johnston continued the case again to April 7. Hardy did not appear in court on that date, as he had gone to Sacramento, but an attorney named George J. Whelan was on hand to represent Stovall. Edward Baker began by delivering what the *Alta* called "a long and eloquent speech on behalf of Archy."[14]

Baker was known as a powerful orator. He liked to speak extemporaneously, not using notes or a written text, and he spoke more from the heart than from the brain. He was, however, a well-informed attorney who knew the law well and could express his ideas with force and eloquence.[15] He began by summarizing the long and tortuous history of Archy's case. He cited legal authorities that supported his arguments. He told Commissioner Johnston that slavery was "not recognized by the law of nations. It only exists by local law, and is confined to the limit of the state or territory where such laws are enacted." He reminded Commissioner Johnston that there was no "local law" in California supporting slavery. The Fugitive Slave Act was "in derogation of the common law," he said, and had to be "construed strictly." Here Baker was echoing the famous statement of Lord Chief Justice Mansfield in the *Somerset* case that slavery is "so odious, that nothing can be suffered to support it, but positive law."[16] In response to a suggestion that he had once made a speech in Congress that was inconsistent with his present views, Baker said it was eight years since he made that speech and his conscience was now "clear of all offenses against the cause of freedom." The *Alta* described Baker's speech as "one of the most eloquent efforts that we have ever heard" and told its readers that "more than one eye in the room was moist with tears."[17]

Hardy's substitute, George Whelan, then complained that he was "unwell" and would have to file a brief setting forth Hardy's arguments in behalf of Stovall. He remarked, however, that the commissioner's authority under the Fugitive Slave Law was severely limited and that it was not his duty "to try the right of property, or to determine the question of freedom or slavery." He was "simply to examine whether the claimant makes such a claim as is described in the law, and in that case he must render judgment for the claimant."

Baker replied that, "according to that interpretation of the law" the commissioner was to "try no fact at all," but once a claim was made, simply "to cut off all examination and give up the alleged fugitive at once." Johnston asked Whelan to explain his argument, but when he had finished the commissioner expressed his own opinion that Whelan was advocating "a monstrous doctrine" on the basis of which one affidavit would be enough to send a man off to another state as a slave, with virtually no opportunity ever to establish his rights as a free man. He would be "under the hammer at a moment's notice," Johnston said.[18]

Both Hardy and Baker filed written briefs. Hardy's was longer and more impassioned than Baker's. He argued that the mere fact that an affidavit had been filed claiming that Archy was a slave and that he had escaped from his master into California was enough to prove that he was a fugitive. He cited the US Supreme Court's decision in *Dred Scott v. Sandford* and argued that it established that "slavery exists in all of the national territories." Stovall had found Archy in Nebraska "by accident" and decided to push on to California with Archy in tow because he had no other choice. "What was he to do?" Hardy asked. "Turn back he could not." Hardy placed great reliance on the decision of the California Supreme Court, which declared that Archy should be treated as a slave and returned to Mississippi with Stovall. The only people who did not accept that decision, he said, were "those who love 'not the Court less but Negroes more.'"[19]

Johnston closed the proceedings, promising to render his decision on the following April 13. On that date, he delayed the proceeding one more day, finally making his announcement on April 14. Taking the bench in the afternoon, he read a long opinion which was summed up in the *Union*:

> As there are no satisfactory proofs to demonstrate the escape of Archy from Mississippi, and the evidence is clear that he was brought into the State voluntarily by his owner, and as the testimony clearly ascertains that, after coming into the State, the claimant hired out Archy and went into business on his own account, thus disaffirming the fact that claimant was merely passing in transitu through the State with his captive runaway, an order for the discharge of Archy from the custody of the United States Marshal must be made.[20]

Colonel Baker came out of the courtroom into the hall where a number of black persons were collected. There he informed the black men Peter Anderson and James Riker of the result. With the consent of the US marshal and Police Chief Curtis, they then went to the county jail, where not less than two hundred people had gathered. They were mostly blacks, eager to greet Archy when he made his appearance. The jail keeper was presented with a notice signed by Marshal Solomon stating: "SIR— In accordance with the order I have from the U.S. Commissioner, you will please release the boy Archy from your custody, and this shall be your voucher for so doing." The keeper then went to Archy's cell, unlocked it, and said: "Archy, my boy, you're all right. You are a free man now. Pick up your duds and be off. Your friends are waiting for you outside."[21]

Archy lost no time in "making his toilette" and heading for the exit. As he stepped outside, a large group of friends gathered around him. One man sang out: "Three cheers!" But nobody responded. All efforts to get up an excitement were discontinued by the blacks. Archy's hand was shaken. He was "pulled, and hauled, and congratulated," but the blacks there maintained an uneasy quiet.

A carriage that had been waiting at the corner of Broadway and Kearny now drove up in front of the jail. Colonel Baker and Marshal Solomon arrived at the same time. Baker was pleased to see his client looking so well. Archy and three others got in the carriage, but as it pulled away the observers still remained quiet. They were concerned that Archy might be arrested again as a fugitive from Mississippi. He had stabbed a man in that state, and the governor there might send a request for his extradition. As the carriage pulled away, the spectators watched it disappear with some apprehension. Many thought that Archy could not remain in San Francisco, for he would be in danger there as long as he stayed.[22]

In the evening, a large meeting of blacks congregated in the A.M.E. Zion Church on Pacific Street. They talked of the danger they felt living in California and considered the possibility of emigrating to some more hospitable land or territory, possibly to Vancouver Island in the British colonies or the State of Sonora in Mexico. But no decisions were made.[23]

The very next evening, an even larger congregation gathered in the Zion Church. The *Bulletin* reported that some five hundred persons were present. After the organization of the meeting, Archy Lee was presented to them, and there was what the *Bulletin* called "great commotion and cheering, and some speech making." When the excitement subsided, the president of the meeting, Jacob R. Gibbs, announced that there was a deficit of four hundred dollars in the Archy fund, for the payment of the attorneys and other expenses, and only fifty-six dollars had yet been collected. "Contributions would be in order."

While the collections were going on, Mr. Keeling read the following hymn, which was sung by the whole congregation:

## The Year of "Archy Lee"
## A Song of Rejoicing for Archy's Deliverance

Blow ye the trumpet! Blow!
The gladly solemn sound.
Let all the nations know,
To earth's remotest bound,
The year of Archy Lee is come;
Return ye ransomed Stovall home.

Exalt the Lamb of God;
The sin-atoning Lamb,
Redemption by the blood,
Through all the land proclaim,
The year of Archy Lee is come!
Return, ye ransomed Stovall home.

Ye slaves of sin and hell,
Your liberty receive;
And in Jesus dwell,
And blest in Jesus live,
The year of Archy Lee is come;
Return, ye ransomed Stovall home.

The gospel trumpet hear—
The news of pardoning grace;
Ye happy souls draw near;
Behold your Savior's face,
The year of Archy Lee is come;
Return, ye ransomed Stovall home.[24]

As reported in the *Bulletin*, "the money came down thick and fast" while the hymn was being sung.

Soon thereafter another hymn was sung. This was an adaptation of a song by the celebrated Irish poet, songwriter, actor, and singer Thomas Moore, titled "Miriam's Song." This was the adaptation:

> Sound the glad tidings o'er land and o'er sea—
> Our people have triumphed and Archy is free!
> Sing! for the pride of the tyrants is broken;
> The decision of Burnett and Terry reversed.
> How vain was their boasting—their plans so soon broken;
> Archy's free—and Stovall is brought to the dust.
> Praise to the judges and praise to the lawyers!
> Freedom was their object, and that they obtained.
> Stovall was shown it was time to be moving;
> He left on the steamer, to lay deeper plans.
> But there was a Baker, a Crosby and Tompkins
> Before Pen Johnston and did plead for the man.[25]

Moore's song was adapted by Thomas P. Freeman, a black shoemaker in San Francisco and a creative member of the Zion congregation.[26] If Freeman's adaptation was not as poetic as "The Year of Archy Lee," it was appropriate for the occasion, for Thomas Moore was a champion of freedom in his native Ireland and many other countries as well. And, based on a visit to the United States in the early years of the nineteenth century, he was also a stern critic of American slavery. "Miriam's Song" had concluded with the inspiring words "Jehovah has triumphed—his people are free."[27] In San Francisco, the words fit the scene.

CHAPTER EIGHT

# "Send Them to the Devil"

CALIFORNIA'S BLACK POPULATION HAD GOOD REASON TO CELEBRATE
Archy Lee's victory in the court of George Pen Johnston. But they had
equally good reason to fear for their future in the state, for they knew
they were surrounded by a hostile population of whites who were outraged by Johnston's decision and determined to do whatever they could
to reverse it. If the courts would not help the whites do that, they could
seek assistance from the California legislature, where their friends greatly
outnumbered their foes.

The legislature that took office in Sacramento on January 4, 1858,
was overwhelmingly Democratic. Of the thirty-five members of the
Senate twenty-seven were Democrats, and of the eighty members of the
State Assembly sixty-six were Democrats. The opposition in the Senate
consisted of three members of the fast-expiring Know-Nothing Party
and five members of the still-infant Republicans, while the opposition
in the lower house, called the Assembly, included four Know-Nothings
and only nine Republicans.[1] Not all of the Democrats were fervent
supporters of slavery and opponents of the black presence in California,
for some held free soil views and opposed the spread of slavery into the
western territories. Most, however, were ardent supporters of the peculiar
institution that had transformed southern cotton into "white gold" and
fierce opponents of the free blacks and white abolitionists who believed
that California's constitution meant what it said when it declared that
"neither slavery nor involuntary servitude, unless for the punishment of
crimes, shall ever be tolerated in the State."[2] And Governor Weller was

an outspoken ally of those who sought to make sure that slaves who were brought to California from states remained slaves.[3]

Archy's struggle in the courts was the obvious inspiration for legislative action, for pro-slavery Democrats were at first apprehensive that "the boy" from Mississippi might prevail there, and finally shocked to learn that he actually would. It was on January 12 that Democratic assemblyman A. G. Stakes of San Joaquin County, a pro-slavery lawyer who had been born in Virginia and served in the Texas military before coming to California, introduced the first legislative bill designed to thwart the aspirations of blacks like Archy Lee.[4] It was a proposed law "concerning slaves escaping from their masters while traveling or sojourning in this State."[5] Six days later, Stakes laid out the text of his proposal. It provided that if "any person or persons who may owe service, or be held to labor in any of the States of the United States," should be brought to California by its owner or master "for the purpose of traveling through this State, or in good faith sojourning in this State with such person so held to service," and if the person owing service attempted to escape, he would be "delivered up to the owner or master upon demand and proper evidence of the fact that such person does so owe service and has escaped therefrom."[6] Any judge who received a petition for the return of such an escaped fugitive was required to hear the case "in a summary manner" and issue a certificate to the master or owner. Stiff penalties of fine or imprisonment were to be imposed on anybody who obstructed or hindered the master's rights to recapture the fugitive. To add special force to these penalties, any judge who refused to issue the appropriate certificate was required to pay five hundred dollars to the master. A Republican assemblyman from San Francisco named S. W. Holladay quickly objected to a second reading of Stakes's bill, but he was outvoted by two-thirds of the remaining assemblymen, who sent the bill to the Judiciary Committee for consideration.[7] This took place only five days after US Commissioner Johnston first denied jurisdiction over Charles Stovall's petition for the recovery of Archy under the federal Fugitive Slave Law and only five days before Judge Robert Robinson agreed to consider Archy's case in the Sacramento County Court.

Anti-slavery newspapers greeted Stakes's proposed law with contempt. In Sacramento, the *Union* told its readers that "no such law, so far as we recollect, has ever been enacted in a free State, and we do not see why such a law is required in California." A master like Charles Stovall, the *Union* said, "might bring a dozen Negroes to the State with the intention of *sojourning* for a year or two, and work them all the time he was sojourning in the mines, and then return with them. In this way thousands might be introduced into the State by their owners, who only intended to sojourn long enough to make a pile, with the assistance of their slaves." The *Union* went on to remind readers that "it is hardly worthwhile to raise objections to the bill, as the Constitution prohibits its passage in express terms."[8]

Stakes's first bill was still in the Judiciary Committee when, on February 2, he gave notice of another proposed law that would prohibit the immigration of "free negroes and other obnoxious persons" into the state.[9] If slaves could not be recaptured after they were brought into the state, Stakes reasoned, perhaps it would be enough to make sure that no free blacks ever set foot inside its borders. But the *Union* was unimpressed by his effort, saying that his proposed law was "an old one revamped" and that it had "probably been blown up by the recent 'Archy' breeze."[10]

On the day after Stakes's second bill was introduced, a Democratic senator from El Dorado County named Samuel Johnson presented a petition from the citizens of his county asking for the repeal of "all laws in the State prohibiting Negroes and mulattoes from giving testimony against white persons." Johnson explained that he opposed such a repeal, but at the request of his constituents he had presented their petition to the Senate. The *Union* commented on the "number of petitions recently presented, asking the repeal of the law excluding Negro testimony," and reported that it had "excited the suspicion of certain ardent supporters of the Administration that their political opponents are moving in the matter." But their suspicion was unwarranted, for Stakes's second bill was promptly referred to the Senate Judiciary Committee and as promptly forgotten.[11] It would be years before the law prohibiting black testimony against whites was repealed.[12]

Stakes's bill to prevent blacks from entering the state was a different matter. It was given new life at the end of March when Democratic assemblyman J. P. Warfield of Nevada County reported it out of committee and urged the Assembly to amend it. Warfield's amended bill repeated Stakes's blanket prohibition of the immigration of all blacks and mulattoes into the state, but it added teeth to the prohibition. Any person who came into the state in violation of the law would be subject to a fine or jail sentence. Sheriffs were authorized to convey the offending person out of the state, but if the offending person could not pay the costs of conveyance—and of his or her criminal conviction—the sheriffs could hire the offending person out to private employers until he or she had earned enough money to pay for the conveyance. County recorders were required to open registry books, in which all blacks and mulattoes over the age of fifteen were required to register themselves. Anyone who brought a black or a mulatto into the state for the purpose of freeing him would be guilty of a crime and either fined or jailed. Employing any black person with knowledge that the person had not been registered would subject the offender to penalties. The law proposed exceptions for blacks who came into the state on ships doing business in San Francisco Bay, and those who were "driven by shipwreck or other unavoidable necessity" into the state, but only if they left the state "as soon as possible."[13]

Warfield wanted his amended law to be subject to immediate consideration by the full Assembly without referral to a committee, and asked that the rules be suspended to permit that. By a vote of thirty-one to nine, his colleagues concurred. Then followed a tumultuous debate in which assemblymen revealed their feelings about blacks in their midst. Democratic assemblyman William Hill of Nevada County provoked laughter when he asked "if a man must have a certificate from a nigger whom he hires of the sheriff of a county." Republican assemblyman J. W. Cherry of San Francisco retorted: "I would ask if this bill does not propose to compel Negroes to submit to involuntary servitude."

Warfield answered: "Yes, sir, are not white men in our jails and prisons undergoing involuntary servitude?"

Assemblyman W. W. Shepard, a Republican from San Francisco, said: "I understand that that bill provides for the 'transportation' of niggers."

"Yes, sir," Warfield replied. "We must adopt some means to rid ourselves of these nuisances if they force themselves into the country."

Republican assemblyman Caleb Burbank of San Francisco noted that the proposed law did not direct that the blacks be hired out at reasonable prices, or in a reasonable manner, or put to reasonable labor. In such a case a black man might simply refuse to work, Burbank said.

Assemblyman George Crane of Monterey County characterized the proposed law as "an unparalleled attempt at outrageous legislation" and said there was nothing like it anywhere in the country, "unless it be some of the provisions of the Lecompton Constitution." (The Lecompton Constitution was then the focus of a furious national debate about the future of slavery throughout the nation, as will be discussed in the next chapter.)

Assemblyman David Buel, a Democrat from El Dorado County, said: "I want to know where we are going to send these niggers. We have got no country for convicts or obnoxious persons, and I know that Canada refuses to be a receptacle for any more runaway or cast away niggers." (Buel's statement would soon prove to be quite wrong.)

Democratic assemblyman George Young of the same El Dorado County replied: "Send them where they come from, of course."

"How are you going to find out where they come from?" asked Assemblyman Charles E. De Long, a Democrat from Yuba County.

Almost immediately, an unidentified voice from somewhere in the chamber shouted: "Send them to the devil!"[14]

Assemblyman Shepard speculated that there were five or six thousand blacks in California (his estimate was only slightly exaggerated) and that they owned about six million dollars worth of property. He said that many white people wanted to get them out of the state because they feared their competition. "They black my boots," Shepard said, "they wash my shirts, and do jobs for me of that kind, and I pay them for it. Now, I never felt any apprehension concerning their running in competition with me. . . . I have been brought up to business habits, and I am a white man, and I do not wish to crush a black man to the earth. . . . It may be a matter of taste."

"Taste of a nigger?" De Long maliciously retorted.

Shepard then launched into an impassioned statement. "The most contemptible, the most despicable tyranny—that which most degrades humanity, disgraces humanity and ruins the moral character of the white race, is that tyranny which is exemplified by an assumption on the part of those who have the power to grind into the dust their inferiors, who have no opportunity, or who, for one reason or another, cannot speak for themselves." Shepard admitted that he had "a personal prejudice against a nigger." But when it came to the current bill, "which contradicts the great foundation principles of humanity and right, I would sooner have my right arm withered than I would engage in the commission of such injustices."[15]

After some further parliamentary maneuvers, the bill was brought up for final consideration on April 7, unleashing another round of debate. One of the most impassioned condemnations of the bill, one that was printed on the front pages of the leading newspapers in both Sacramento and San Francisco, was delivered by a Republican assemblyman from San Francisco named J. B. Moore. Observers may have been aware that April 7 was the same day on which Colonel Edward D. Baker delivered his "long and eloquent speech" in behalf of Archy Lee in the San Francisco court of US Commissioner Johnston.[16] If they did not then know it, however, they would soon realize how closely the events were related. In a lengthy address to his fellow lawmakers, Moore said that the proposed law was "the result of that mean, abject tendency in man to oppression simply because he has the power; that groveling enjoyment of tyranny which sometimes steals into the most merciful bosom in company with the feeling of power." "I should feel that I had not done my duty to humanity did I not expose the error of this measure," Moore continued, "nor my duty to its authors, did I not censure their folly . . . Mr. Speaker, this bill is so ridiculously inappropriate to this country and this age, that I will not use any arguments at all upon it. . . . Pass it by all means, as an index of the united intellect of this House!"[17] And, as if following Moore's command, the Democrats promptly proceeded to pass it.[18]

The proposed law was taken up in the State Senate on April 13, where it promptly received a committee recommendation for passage.[19] But after Democratic senator Alfred Taliaferro from Marin, Sonoma, and Mendocino Counties sought to indefinitely postpone it and Republican senator Samuel Bell from Alameda and Santa Clara Counties moved to send it back to committee, the bill effectively died. It was April 23, only three days before the legislature's adjournment and one week after Commissioner Johnston declared Archy Lee a free man.[20]

It was clear to almost all observers that the California legislature's efforts to suppress the rights of blacks in California, whether by branding them as fugitives from slavery or simply barring them from entrance into the state, were tied to Archy Lee's struggle for freedom. The future of slavery in America was an issue that was not confined to California, but was wracking the entire nation. Although news from California was slow in reaching the eastern states—some was carried in overland coaches with mail deliveries but most came on steamers via the Panama route—when it reached the Atlantic states, readers took notice. News reports about Archy Lee's case were printed in the *New York Times*, the *New York Tribune*, the *Brooklyn Daily Eagle*, the *Berkshire County Eagle* in Massachusetts, and the *National Era* in Washington, DC. Abolitionist journals such as *The Liberator* in Boston, the *True Northerner* in Paw, Michigan, and the *Anti-Slavery Bugle* in Lisbon, Ohio, gave it special notice. Newspapers in slave-holding states were reluctant to talk about anti-slavery activities in other parts of the country, although the *Louisville Daily Courier* in Kentucky did tell its readers about Archy's struggle. An article published in the *National Era* on July 22, 1858, referred to the anti-black legislation in California and linked it directly to Archy Lee, and noting that he had become "the famous 'Dred Scott' of California."[21]

The nation was listening.

Pío Pico, his wife, and two nieces. Born near Los Angeles in 1801, Pico was a prominent *ranchero*, businessman, and political leader of mixed African and Hispanic heritage who twice served as governor of Mexican California. He was an example of the status afforded people of African-American ancestry in California before it became part of the United States.
AUTHOR'S COLLECTION

"The Runaway." Stereotype cut used in many notices seeking the capture of slaves who escaped from their masters. From the *Anti-Slavery Record*, published by the American Anti-Slavery Society in New York in July 1837.

Holy Bible.
*Thou shalt not deliver unto the master his servant which has escaped from his master unto thee. He shall dwell with thee. Even among you, in that place which he shall choose in one of thy gates where it liketh him best Thou shalt not oppress him.*
*Deut XXIII-15-16.*

**Effects of the Fugitive-Slave-Law.**

Declaration of independence.
*We hold that all men are created equal, that they are endowed by their Creator with certain unalienable rights, that among these are life, liberty, and the pursuit of happiness.*

"Effects of the Fugitive-Slave-Law." Published in New York, this lithograph illustrated the plight that African Americans, some slaves and others free, suffered under the Fugitive Slave Act passed as part of the congressional Compromise of 1850. African Americans were pursued and captured under terms of the Act, even in the free state of California, where Archy Lee struggled for his liberty in 1858. LIBRARY OF CONGRESS PRINTS AND PHOTOGRAPHS DIVISION

Mifflin Wistar Gibbs. Born a free man in Philadelphia, he came to San Francisco aboard a steamship from Panama in 1850 and, through determination and pluck, became a successful store owner, an active member of the African Methodist Episcopal Zion Church, and a leader of California's African-American community. He went to British Columbia with other blacks at the same time that Archy Lee and others were there. His career there and in Arkansas after he returned to the United States was detailed in his autobiography, *Shadow and Light,* published in 1902 with an introduction by the pioneering black educator Booker T. Washington.

PORTRAIT BY CHARLES MILTON BELL, C.M. BELL STUDIO COLLECTION, LIBRARY OF CONGRESS PRINTS AND PHOTOGRAPHS DIVISION

John Jamison (J. J.) Moore. Eloquent preacher and founder of San Francisco's all-black African Methodist Episcopal Zion Church, in which the congregation celebrated Archy Lee's freedom by singing the hymn to "The Year of Archy Lee." He went to British Columbia with Archy and other African Americans from California, but later returned, first to California and then to the Atlantic states, where he became a bishop and, in 1884, published *A History of the A.M.E. Zion Church in America*. Frontispiece from *A History of the A.M.E. Zion Church in America*.

Peter H. Burnett. Born in Tennessee in 1807, he crossed the plains to Oregon in 1843 and came on to California in 1848, bringing pro-slavery views with him. He served a brief term as the first governor of the State of California in 1849 and was one of the three justices of the California Supreme Court when the case of *Ex Parte Archy* came before it in February 1858. He wrote the widely condemned opinion that, in the words of a subsequent Supreme Court justice, "gave the law to the North, and the nigger to the South." COURTESY OF THE OREGON HISTORICAL SOCIETY

Stephen J. Field. Born into an accomplished family in Connecticut in 1816, he came to California early in the Gold Rush, practiced law in the town of Marysville, was elected to the legislature, and became a judge. He was one of the three judges of the California Supreme Court when the controversial case of *Ex Parte Archy* came before it. He took no part in the decision (probably because of illness) but later said that he did not concur in it. His views on slavery were ambiguous, but he was appointed to the US Supreme Court in 1863 by President Abraham Lincoln and continued to serve in that position until his resignation in 1897, when he earned the distinction of having served longer on the Supreme Court than any justice up to that time. AUTHOR'S COLLECTION

David S. Terry. Chief justice of the California Supreme Court who, in February 1858, delivered the widely condemned decision in *Ex Parte Archy* (written by then–associate justice Peter Burnett) ordering Archy Lee back to slavery in Mississippi. Born in Kentucky in 1823, he became a lawyer in Texas and an active lawyer and politician after his arrival in California in 1849. A belligerent man willing to use knives to vent his anger, he killed anti-slavery US senator David C. Broderick in an 1859 duel only to be killed himself when, in 1889, he attempted to physically attack US Supreme Court justice Stephen J. Field and was shot to death by Field's bodyguard. AUTHOR'S COLLECTION

Jansen's Building

Jansen's Building in Sacramento. The California Supreme Court had chambers on the second floor of this building at the corner of Fourth and J Streets. Here the controversial decision in *Ex Parte Archy* (called "California's Dred Scott case") was announced on February 11, 1858, ordering Archy Lee to return to Mississippi as a slave. Image published in 1857.

Merchants' Exchange Building on San Francisco's Battery Street. The Federal Court maintained a courtroom in this building, in which Archy Lee was tried before US Commissioner George Pen Johnston in April 1858. The courtroom was filled, but only with whites, as blacks were excluded. Photograph by George Robinson Fardon, published in 1856 in his *San Francisco Album: Photographs of the Most Beautiful Views and Public Buildings.*

San Francisco's City Hall on Kearney Street. Immediately after Archy Lee was rescued from the steamship *Orizaba* in San Francisco Bay, he was brought before a county judge who held court in this building pursuant to an attachment obtained by attorneys representing Charles Stovall. The proceedings there were dismissed and Archy was taken to the federal court in the Merchants' Exchange to stand trial before US Commissioner George Pen Johnston. Photograph by George Robinson Fardon, published in 1856 in his *San Francisco Album: Photographs of the Most Beautiful Views and Public Buildings.*

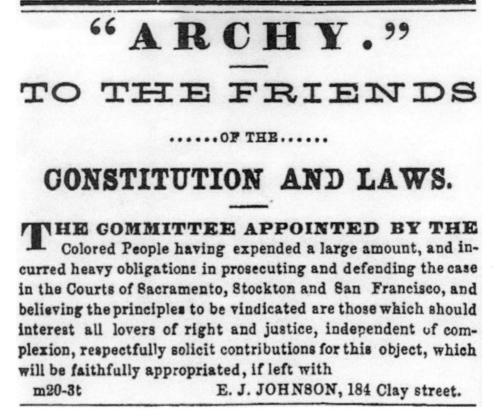

# "ARCHY."

## TO THE FRIENDS

......OF THE......

## CONSTITUTION AND LAWS.

THE COMMITTEE APPOINTED BY THE Colored People having expended a large amount, and incurred heavy obligations in prosecuting and defending the case in the Courts of Sacramento, Stockton and San Francisco, and believing the principles to be vindicated are those which should interest all lovers of right and justice, independent of complexion, respectfully solicit contributions for this object, which will be faithfully appropriated, if left with

m20-3t                    E. J. JOHNSON, 184 Clay street.

Newspaper notice soliciting contributions to help pay for the expenses of defending Archy Lee's freedom in the courts of Sacramento, Stockton, and San Francisco. San Francisco's *Daily Evening Bulletin*, March 20, 1858.

Edward D. Baker. Lawyer, politician, and colonel in the Mexican War. In April 1858, he was the attorney for Archy Lee in the San Francisco courtroom of US Commissioner George Pen Johnston, where after a hard-fought battle he won a decision declaring Lee a free man. He went on to become US senator from Oregon, to personally introduce Lincoln at his inaugural on the steps of the US Capitol in Washington, DC, and on October 21, 1861, to die while leading a regiment of Union troops at the Civil War battle of Ball's Bluff, thereby becoming the first and only sitting US senator to die in military combat. Lincoln described Baker as his "dearest personal friend." A marble statue of him stands in the US Capitol, and a state holiday honoring him was authorized in Oregon in 2011.
AUTHOR'S COLLECTION

Mary Ellen Pleasant. Semi-legendary black woman called "Mammy" Pleasant who, according to one historian, sheltered Archy Lee in her San Francisco house when his opponents were trying to capture him and put him on a steamer to be returned to slavery in Mississippi. She was a proprietor of at least one "house of ill repute" but also noted as a fighter for equal rights and preferred to be called "Mistress" rather than "Mammy." Mary Ellen Pleasant, "Memoirs and Auto-biography," *The Pandex of the Press*, January 1902, p. 5.

Steamship *Orizaba*. Charles Stovall and his supporters attempted to seize Archy Lee after he was declared a free man and take him away from San Francisco aboard this side-wheel steamer, which was owned and operated by the Nicaragua Steamship Company. In 1865, the vessel was sold to the California Steam Navigation Company and operated on the San Francisco-Portland-Victoria run. She continued service on the Pacific coast until broken up in 1887. AUTHOR'S COLLECTION

Steamship *Commodore*. Built in New York in 1850, this side-wheel steamship sailed around Cape Horn in 1851 to do service in the San Francisco to Panama trade as the SS *Brother Jonathan*. George T. Wright purchased the vessel in 1857, renamed it the *Commodore*, and put it into service between San Francisco and Victoria in British Columbia. Archy Lee and a large group of blacks left San Francisco aboard the vessel on April 20, 1858, and arrived in the Crown Colony of Victoria on April 25. Sailing under different ownership and resuming the name of *Brother Jonathan*, the vessel struck an uncharted reef in a storm off the northern California coast in 1865 and sank, plunging more than two hundred of its passengers and crew to a tragic death in the sea. PEN-AND-INK DRAWING BY BRIAN McGINTY

David C. Broderick. Born in New York in 1820, he came to California during the Gold Rush and rose to leadership of the anti-slavery branch of California's Democratic Party. Elected to the US Senate in 1857, he took to the Senate floor in March 1858 and delivered a stinging rebuke to President James Buchanan's pro-slavery policies. The following year, just outside San Francisco, he was killed in a duel with David S. Terry, the pro-slavery judge who had delivered the controversial California Supreme Court opinion denying Archy Lee's bid for freedom. Archy Lee's attorney Edward D. Baker gave a long and impassioned eulogy over Broderick's body. Photograph by Julian Vannerson. LIBRARY OF CONGRESS PRINTS AND PHOTOGRAPHS DIVISION

James Douglas. Born in 1803 in what later became known as the British Colony of Guyana, he made his career in North America with the powerful Hudson's Bay Company and became governor of the Crown Colony of Victoria after gold was discovered on the Fraser River. He welcomed Archy Lee and other blacks who came north from California, in part because he had some African-American ancestry and in part because the Fraser River gold rush depleted the pool of workers he needed in the northern colony. He was later knighted by Queen Victoria. BRITISH COLUMBIA ARCHIVES

Donati's Comet. A celestial body first observed on June 2, 1858, in the night sky over Florence, Italy, by the astronomer Giovanni Battista Donati. On September 14, 1858, it appeared over the town of Jonesboro, Illinois, where it fascinated Abraham Lincoln during his debates with Stephen Douglas. It was also seen in California where Archy Lee's attorney, Edward D. Baker, extolled its beauty. It was the first comet ever photographed, by many accounts the most beautiful comet ever seen in the nineteenth century, and a celestial object that was an emblem of social and political ties that would soon be felt all over the world. Stereo photograph of Donati's Comet over London in 1858. FROM WEISS, BILDERATLAS DER STERNENWELT, 1888

Archy and the Comet. OIL PAINTING BY BRIAN McGINTY

CHAPTER NINE

# "All One Thing, or All the Other"

As "The Year of Archy Lee" continued, Archy Lee's struggle for freedom—and that of millions of his fellow African Americans—continued on the national stage.

California's representation in the US Congress in 1858 was, like its representation in the state legislature, solidly Democratic. The Tennessee-born ex-Mississippian William M. Gwin was the leader of the Chivalry, or strongly pro-slavery faction of the party, while David C. Broderick, the Washington, DC–born, New York–bred Irishman was the powerful anti-slavery leader of Gwin's opposition. California had only two members of the House of Representatives. Both Charles L. Scott and Joseph C. McKibben were Democrats, although the Virginia-born Scott was closely bound to Gwin's Chivalry while the Pennsylvania-born McKibben was a Broderick supporter with free soil inclinations. Scott and McKibben were elected at large, as California had not yet been divided into separate congressional districts. Gwin had been serving in Washington since 1851, while Broderick had taken his seat on March 4, 1857, the same day that James Buchanan was inaugurated as the fifteenth president of the United States.[1]

Broderick had dominated the senatorial elections in early 1857, both by securing his own occupancy of a seat that had a full six years to run and by extracting an agreement from Gwin that he would surrender his patronage rights to Broderick in exchange for a return to a shorter term that had only four years to run. The election was conducted in a joint session of the legislature in Sacramento. Broderick's victory there was striking, not so much because of his anti-slavery views but because of his mastery of political tactics, and his followers were delighted. There were Republicans, however, who admired Broderick's principles as well as his political know-how. One was James McClatchy, editor of the pro-Republican *Weekly Times* of Sacramento, who called Broderick "the staunchest of the many good and true Republicans" in the Democratic Party. "The battle had been long and hotly contested," McClatchy said. "Federal power and patronage—money and the promise of it—office and the promise of it—slander, secret misrepresentation and open calumny—all have been used against him but he has triumphed."[2]

Broderick had gone to Washington believing he could work with President Buchanan, and intending to do so. Both were Democrats, and party loyalty was one of the cardinal rules of political success. Soon, however, a mutual dislike erupted between the men. Broderick wanted to fill federal offices in California with his own followers—men who shared his free soil views—while Buchanan wanted to fill them with the same pro-slavery men he had appointed when Gwin held power in the state. Broderick called on Buchanan at his home outside Lancaster, Pennsylvania—a large and imposing federal-style mansion called Wheatland—to pay his respects, but he was daunted by the reception he received there. "It was cold outside the house," Broderick later said "but it was ice within."[3]

Buchanan believed that the slavery controversy then casting a grim shadow over the nation could only be solved by following the doctrine of "popular sovereignty." This would permit each state to decide for itself whether it would have slavery or not, and the federal government would be barred from prying into the matter. Under the Missouri Compromise of 1820, Missouri had been admitted to the federal Union as a slave state, but slavery was prohibited in all of the territory acquired in the Louisiana Purchase north of 36 degrees, 30 minutes North latitude, the line marking Missouri's southern border. The Compromise of 1850 had badly weakened the Missouri Compromise line by permitting voters in the territories of New Mexico and Utah to decide for themselves whether they wanted to allow slavery or ban it, but they could do so only when they applied for statehood. The opinion issued by US chief justice Roger Taney in the *Dred Scott* decision on March 6, 1857, was a different matter. Taney had first decided that the Missouri slave known as Dred Scott was not entitled to bring a suit in federal court because people of African descent were "so far inferior that they had no rights which the white man was bound to respect" and were thus ineligible for citizenship.[4] But he had gone beyond that issue by arguing that slaves were property protected by the Fifth Amendment to the US Constitution. Thus the Missouri Compromise provision that restricted slavery in the western territories was unconstitutional and void.[5] Slave owners could take their slaves anywhere in the country and demand, and receive, constitutional protection as they did so. But Taney's opinion only expressed his personal views. Eight other opinions were issued by Supreme Court justices, six agreeing with Taney's conclusion but disagreeing with his reasoning and two disagreeing with both his conclusion and his reasoning. Taney's views were the most widely disseminated of all of the justices' and the most enthusiastically endorsed by fervent friends of slavery. James Buchanan thought the *Dred Scott* decision had settled the slavery question once and for all. In fact, it had raised it to a new level of controversy.[6]

The territories of Kansas and Nebraska were organized in 1854 under terms of the Kansas-Nebraska Act, which sanctioned "popular sovereignty" by authorizing the voters in those territories to decide for themselves whether they wanted to enter the Union as free or slave states. Democratic senator Stephen A. Douglas of Illinois, acting as chairman of the Senate Committee on Territories, had shepherded the law through Congress; California's two pro-slavery Democratic senators, William Gwin and John Weller, had warmly supported it; and Democratic president Franklin Pierce, supported by his secretary of war, Jefferson Davis of Mississippi, had signed it on May 30, 1854.[7] Pierce, like his successor Buchanan, was a "Northern man with Southern principles" and anxious to win the support of southern slaveholders. Acting pursuant to the act, pro-slavery residents of Kansas Territory—all white and all men—had gathered in the town of Lecompton and framed a pro-slavery state constitution which they submitted to Congress for its approval in December 1857. But Stephen Douglas recognized that many of the votes cast in favor of the constitution were fraudulent and that most of the residents of Kansas actually opposed slavery, so he argued strongly against its approval. Buchanan, as eager to win southern support as Pierce had been, supported Lecompton. Douglas acquiesced in Taney's *Dred Scott* decision—it was, he pointed out, a decision by the highest court in the land and thus entitled to the highest respect—but he strongly opposed the Lecompton Constitution. Violence had erupted in Kansas, as forces against slavery gathered to oppose the pro-slavery advocates, and Kansas had already acquired its reputation as "Bleeding Kansas." Buchanan, however, made support for Lecompton a test of Democratic Party loyalty. Democrats who joined him in supporting slavery in Kansas would get his full cooperation, and patronage for their supporters. Those who did not would be treated as party outcasts.[8]

When David Broderick returned to Washington for the first session of the Thirty-Fifth Congress in December 1857, he was ready to join Douglas and Democratic senator Charles E. Stuart of Michigan in opposing Lecompton. They were the only Democrats in the Senate who opposed it. All the others, including California's Chivalry senator Gwin and Mississippi's Jefferson Davis, who had taken his seat as a senator from Archy Lee's home state, were supporters. Broderick delivered a speech in the Senate on December 23 in which he allied himself with Douglas and Stuart and took careful aim at the president, saying that Buchanan was "alone responsible for the present state of affairs in Kansas," adding: "I do not intend, because I am a member of the Democratic party, to permit the President of the United States, who has been elected by that party, to create civil war in Kansas."[9]

The debate continued in the early months of 1858, absorbing most of the energies of both the Senate and the House of Representatives. Then, on March 22, California's Senator Broderick rose to deliver another and more impassioned speech. He expressed disagreement with Republican senator William H. Seward of New York, who had said he regretted Kansas-Nebraska's repeal of the Missouri Compromise. Broderick said it was the repeal that gave birth to the Republican Party. Under the Missouri Compromise, most northerners had conceded the territories south of the line to the slaveholders. Now that the slaveholders were trying to push slavery north of the Missouri line, the Republicans were aroused to give battle. Broderick then expressed his disagreement with the Supreme Court's *Dred Scott* decision, saying:

> Slavery is old, decrepit, and consumptive; freedom is young, strong, and vigorous. The one is naturally stationary and loves ease; the other is migratory and enterprising. There are six million people interested in the extension of slavery; there are twenty million freemen to contend for these Territories, out of which to carve for themselves homes where labor is honorable. Up to the time of the passage of the Kansas-Nebraska act, a large majority of the people of the North did not question the right of the South to control the destinies of the Territories south of the Missouri line. The people of the North should have welcomed the passage of the Kansas-Nebraska Act. I am astonished that Republicans should call for a restoration of the Missouri compromise. With the terrible odds that are against her, the South should not have repealed it if she desired to retain her rights in the territories.[10]

Broderick referred to a recent speech given by Senator James H. Hammond of South Carolina, an immensely wealthy man whose holdings included more than three hundred slaves. Hammond had extolled the virtues of slavery, declaring that "cotton was king," and condemning the laborers in the North as "white slaves" and the "mudsills of society."[11] Broderick contradicted Hammond by asserting that "gold is king." The men who came to California and dug into the earth for the precious metals were not too proud to labor with their hands. "There is no State in the Union, no place on earth, where labor is so honored and so well rewarded," Broderick said; "no time and no place since the Almighty doomed the sons of Adam to toil, where the curse, if it be a curse, rests so lightly as now on the people of California. . . . Has it never occurred to southern gentlemen that millions of laboring free men are born yearly, who demand subsistence and will have it; that as the marts of labor become crowded they will spread into the Territories and take possession of them? . . . Would a dissolution of the Union give these southern Territories to slavery? No, sir. . . . Wherever there is land for settlement, they will rush in and occupy it, and the compulsory labor of slaves will have to give way before the intelligent labor of free men."[12]

Broderick recalled his early life as a working man, his "apprenticeship of five years at one of the most laborious mechanical trades pursued by man." (He worked as a stone-cutter, the trade followed by his father.) And he assured the other senators that "the class of society to whose toil I was born, under our form of government, will control the destinies of this nation. If I were inclined to forget my connection with them, or to deny that I sprang from them, this Chamber would not be the place in which I could do either. While I hold a seat here, I have but to look at the beautiful capitals adjoining the pilasters that support this roof, to be reminded of my father's talent, and to see to his handiwork."[13] (Broderick's father, Thomas Broderick, had done much of the stone-cutting work necessary for the erection of the Capitol in the 1820s.)

Broderick concluded his speech by predicting that the Lecompton Constitution would pass the Senate and saying that, if it also passed the House of Representatives, the South would "rejoice at another triumph." But the triumph would "constitute her defeat." Before concluding, he could not resist the urge to renew his condemnation of James Buchanan, saying: "I hope in mercy, sir, to the boasted intelligence of this age, the historian, when writing a history of these times, will ascribe the attempt of the Executive to force this constitution upon an unwilling people to the faded intellect, the petulant passion, and trembling dotage of an old man on the verge of the grave."[14] (Broderick was then thirty-eight years old, the second youngest member of the Senate, strong and vigorous in appearance. Buchanan was approaching his sixty-seventh birthday, with snow white hair that covered a head always cocked to one side and a stooped back that hinted at fatigue if not just old age.)

According to one of Edward D. Baker's biographers, Broderick's opposition to "the outrageous attempt of President Buchanan and the pro-slavery party to force the Lecompton Constitution upon the unwilling people of Kansas" was his "greatest distinction," and the speech that he delivered in the Senate on March 22, 1858, won him plaudits "all over the North and West."[15]

Broderick's predictions about the fate of Lecompton were not exactly right, however. There was so much controversy in both the Senate and the House of Representatives that a compromise measure was adopted. It authorized the people of Kansas to again vote on the constitution. The popular vote took place in August 1858, and the count was overwhelmingly against Lecompton.[16] In fact, Kansas would have to wait until 1861 to achieve statehood, and by that time it was clear that it would be a free state.[17]

After the Senate's adjournment on June 14, Broderick again boarded an ocean steamer to return to California via Panama. He had important political business to attend to there, for the 1858 elections were approaching and as the leader of the state's Democratic Party he wanted to exert his influence. Stephen Douglas had to return to Illinois, where he also wanted to plunge into the brewing political battle. Douglas was regarded by many as the most powerful national leader of the Democratic Party, for he had opposed Buchanan on the Lecompton issue and won, and it was generally understood that he was ambitious to receive the presidential nomination of the Democratic Party in 1860. Before he could seek the presidency, however, he had to fend off a senatorial challenge in Illinois mounted by Abraham Lincoln.

Lincoln had made an earlier, unsuccessful effort to win a senatorial seat in 1855. He lost that effort to the Democratic candidate, Lyman Trumbull. Now, however, Lincoln was animated to make another senatorial effort, in part because he was a politically ambitious man and in part because of his views on slavery. Douglas was opposed to the Lecompton Constitution and Buchanan's support of it, but he was not categorically opposed to slavery. He had no moral objections to the institution, believing simply that voters in each state should exercise their "popular sovereignty" rights to decide whether they favored or opposed it. Lincoln, however, was opposed to slavery itself. He had abandoned the dying Whig Party and joined the Republicans, who were organized for the specific purpose of opposing the spread of slavery into the western territories. Accepting the Republican senatorial nomination at a convention held in Springfield on June 16, 1858, he had delivered a speech that would help to raise his political profile and express his views on slavery.

In the speech, Lincoln reminded the convention delegates that they were then "far into the *fifth* year, since a policy was initiated, with the *avowed* object, and *confident* promise, of putting an end to slavery agitation." But the agitation had not ceased; it had *"constantly augmented."* Lincoln said: "In *my* opinion, it *will* not cease, until a crisis shall have been reached, and passed." He then quoted a familiar line from the Bible, saying: "'A house divided against itself cannot stand.' I believe this government cannot endure, permanently half *slave* and half *free*. I do not expect the Union to be *dissolved*—I do not expect the house to *fall*—but I *do* expect it will cease to be divided. It will become *all* one thing, or *all* the other. Either the *opponents* of slavery, will arrest the further spread of it, and place it where the public mind shall rest in the belief that it is in course of ultimate extinction; or its *advocates* will push it forward, till it shall become alike lawful in *all* the States, *old* as well as *new*—*North* as well as *South*."[18] Lincoln condemned Douglas's defense of "popular sovereignty" as "a mere deceitful pretense for the benefit of slavery."[19] Douglas did not care whether slavery was "voted *down* or voted *up*," but Lincoln did. Lincoln asserted that Douglas was part of a conspiracy to nationalize slavery that included President Buchanan, former President Pierce, and Chief Justice Taney. It was not Lincoln's first reference to Taney's *Dred Scott* decision—he had criticized it in a speech in June 1857—but it was one of his most forceful.[20]

On July 24, Lincoln wrote Douglas, requesting that he meet him in a series of debates.[21] Douglas was not inclined to share his celebrity with Lincoln—his reputation was national while Lincoln's was local—but he did not want to seem cowardly, so he set dates on which he would meet Lincoln in seven of Illinois's congressional districts.[22] Slavery was the principal subject in all of the debates. While Lincoln expressed his opposition to slavery, Douglas revealed his deep-seated racism and essential indifference to the southern states' peculiar institution. In the debate at Charleston, Illinois, on September 18, he said that, in his opinion, "a negro is not a citizen, cannot be, and ought not to be under the constitution of the United States," adding that "this government was created on the white basis. It was made by white men, for the benefit of white men and their posterity forever, and never should be administered by any except white men."[23] Douglas defended "popular sovereignty," saying that if a state chose to "keep slavery forever, it is not my business, but its own; if it chooses to abolish slavery, it is its own business—not mine. I care more for the great principle of self-government, the right of the people to rule, than I do for all the negroes in Christendom."[24]

Lincoln made some very racist statements of his own. In the debate at Charleston, Illinois, on September 18, he said: "I am not, nor ever have been in favor of bringing about in any way the social and political equality of the white and black races[.] . . . I am not nor ever have been in favor of making voters or jurors of negroes, nor of qualifying them to hold office, nor to intermarry with white people; and I will say in addition to this that there is a physical difference between the white and black races which I believe will forever forbid the two races living together on terms of social and political equality."[25] These statements were prodded by Douglas's race-baiting and by Lincoln's knowledge that racism was rampant in Illinois—in much of the North, as well. But he made it very clear that slavery was wrong, that it should not be permitted to spread into the western territories, and that it should be placed "in the course of ultimate extinction."[26] At Galesburg, Illinois, on October 7, he said that he regarded slavery "as a moral, social and political evil."[27] At Quincy, Illinois, on October 13, he affirmed his belief that the blacks were "entitled to all the rights enumerated in the Declaration of Independence—the right of life, liberty and the pursuit of happiness," and that they were "as much entitled to these as the white man." If the black man "is not my equal in many respects," Lincoln said, "in the right to eat the bread without leave of anybody else which his own hand earns, he is my equal and the equal of Judge Douglas, and the equal of every other man."[28] (Lincoln consistently called Douglas by his early judicial title, for he had served a short term on the Illinois Supreme Court.) Lincoln acknowledged that there was a great difference of opinion in the country about slavery, but he said that "the difference of opinion, reduced to its lowest terms, is no other than the difference between the men who think slavery is wrong and those who do not think it wrong."[29]

Douglas supported the *Dred Scott* decision because it was "delivered by the highest judicial tribunal on earth, a tribunal established by the Constitution of the United States for that purpose, and hence that decision becomes the law of the land, binding on you, on me, and on every other good citizen, whether we like it or not."[30] Lincoln, in contrast, believed that the *Dred Scott* decision was based on false premises and that those false premises gave rise to its false conclusions.[31] He did not suggest that Americans should resist the *Dred Scott* decision. He did not "propose that when Dred Scott has been decided to be a slave by the court, we, as a mob, will decide him to be free." But he did oppose the Supreme Court's decision "as a political rule which shall be binding on the voter," and he declared that he and the Republican Party proposed "so resisting it as to have it reversed if we can, and a new judicial rule established upon this subject."[32]

When Illinois's voters went to the polls on November 2, 1858, the statewide candidates of the Republican Party received more votes than their Democratic opponents, but the electoral districts were so malapportioned that more Democrats were elected to the legislature than Republicans, and Lincoln knew he had lost to Douglas. He was initially depressed, writing a friend: "I am glad I made the late race. It gave me a bearing on the great and durable question of the age, which I could have had in no other way; and though I now sink out of view, and shall be forgotten, I believe I have made some marks which will tell for the cause of civil liberty long after I am gone."[33] But he was not to sink out of view, nor to be forgotten. He had made some marks for the cause of civil liberty, but he was to make even more. He prepared a compilation of his debates with Douglas for publication in book form, which was issued in 1860 as *The Political Debates Between Hon. Abraham Lincoln and Hon. Stephen A. Douglas*.[34] It became a very popular book, raising Lincoln's political reputation to a national level, encouraging northerners who hoped to find some way to put an end to slavery in the United States, and adding to the seething rage that was approaching a boiling point in the South. All of this was due to the Lincoln-Douglas debates conducted in "The Year of Archy Lee."

When William H. Seward left the Senate in June of 1858, he went home to New York where, in October, he delivered a speech in Rochester in which he said that the antagonistic systems of free labor in the North and slave labor in the South were coming into closer and closer collision. He coined one of the most memorable phrases of "The Year of Archy Lee" when he said:

> Shall I tell you what this collision means? They who think that it is accidental, unnecessary, the work of interested or fanatical agitators, and therefore ephemeral, mistake the case altogether. It is an irrepressible conflict between opposing and enduring forces, and it means that the United States must and will, sooner or later, become either entirely a slave-holding nation or entirely a free-labor nation.[35]

After the Senate's adjournment, Senator Jefferson Davis first went north to New England to recuperate from a strange eye illness that was causing him great suffering. Then he went home to Mississippi. He was proud of his Senate service—he was a supremely self-confident man who rarely expressed a moment's self-doubt. But he was not pleased by the events that had taken place in Washington nor by the statements made in such northern states as New York and Illinois. On November 16, he addressed the state legislators in Jackson, the capital of Archy Lee's home state, saying that it was probable that "abolitionists and their allies" would have control of the next House of Representatives and that, if the 1860 presidential election did not produce a clear majority for any candidate, the abolitionists might try to throw it into the House for a final decision. They might also attempt to amend the Constitution to ban slavery. "Whether by the House or by the people, if an Abolitionist be chosen president of the United States," Davis said, "you will have presented to you the question of whether you will permit the government to pass into the hands of your avowed and implacable enemies. . . . In that event, in such manner as should be most expedient, I should deem it your duty to provide for your safety outside of a Union with those who have already shown the will, and would have acquired the power, to deprive you of your birthright and to reduce you to worse than the colonial dependence of your fathers." He continued:

> It requires but a cursory examination of the Constitution of the United States; but a partial knowledge of its history and of the motives of the men who formed it, to see how utterly fallacious it is to ascribe to them the purpose of interfering with the domestic institutions of any of the States. But if a disrespect for that instrument, a fanatical disregard of its purposes, should ever induce a majority, however large, to seek by amending the Constitution, to pervert it from its original object, and to deprive you of the quality which your fathers bequeathed to you, I say let the star of Mississippi be snatched from the constellation to shine by its inherent light, if it must be so, through all the storms and clouds of war.[36]

The year 1858 was drawing to a close. Edward D. Baker had won Archy Lee's case in the court of US Commissioner Johnston in San Francisco. California's legislature had failed in its stumbling attempt to reverse the results of that victory in Sacramento. California's Senator David Broderick had extolled the virtues of free labor and condemned the evil of slavery in Washington, DC. Abraham Lincoln had warned the people of Illinois and the nation of the evils of a "House Divided against itself." In New York, Senator William H. Seward had sounded the alarm of an "irrepressible conflict" that was fast approaching, and in Mississippi Senator Jefferson Davis had expressed the South's willingness to defend slavery even through "the storms and clouds of war."

Archy Lee remained in San Francisco after his victory in George Pen Johnston's court, but it was an uneasy time for him, and also for Johnston. On April 30, the commissioner attended an evening ball in San Francisco's Apollo Hall where he was accosted by a man who was outraged by his decision in favor of Archy. He was Samuel H. Brooks, the pro-slavery politician from San Joaquin County who held a power of attorney from Charles Stovall authorizing him to capture Archy and return him to Mississippi. Johnston was talking with a lady when

Brooks approached and called him a "Black Republican" and said that he had "robbed Stovall of his nigger." When Johnston asked him what he meant, Brooks repeated the accusation. Johnston then replied that the charge was false, prompting Brooks to pull out a bowie knife (a favorite weapon of pro-slavery activists in California) and attempt to attack the commissioner. Bystanders interfered to separate the two men and stop the dispute, but Brooks's point was made.[37] Johnston, who was quick to avenge insults, might well have challenged Brooks to combat outside the ballroom, but there is no record that he did so.

The practice of challenging opponents to duels, and accepting their challenges, was ancient and generally condemned, yet it still found practice in the United States, most frequently among people with southern backgrounds. The California Constitution specifically condemned it and disqualified violators from holding public office or voting.[38] William Gwin had strongly supported the prohibition in the constitutional convention in 1849, but many of his supporters did not. When George Pen Johnston was in the State Assembly in 1855, he had championed a stringent statute designed to suppress dueling. Approved by Governor John Bigler on April 27, 1855, Johnston's statute provided that any person who fought a duel "with a rifle, shot-gun, pistol, bowie-knife, dirk, small-sword, back-sword, or other dangerous weapon" would, upon conviction, be imprisoned in the State Prison for up to seven years if his opponent was killed or died within one year of a wound received in the duel."[39] The *Alta* later characterized the law as "one of the most stringent statutes that we have."[40]

Notwithstanding the anti-dueling law he had sponsored, Johnston was not unalterably opposed to dueling, as events would soon demonstrate. He was, after all, the object of many insults, both for his political affiliation with the Chivalry Democrats and for his decision freeing Archy Lee from the claims of Charles Stovall. He ignored most of the insults because, as he explained, they were not made "in his presence." Then, on June 12, a former employee of the US Custom House named Algernon Smith published a notice in the *Morning Call* newspaper that Johnston considered too offensive to ignore. It said that Smith had challenged Johnston to a duel but that Johnston had again ignored the challenge.

And for ignoring the challenge, Smith labeled Johnston a "poltroon, liar, and coward." Johnston replied the following day in the same newspaper, saying that he would have accepted Smith's challenge if Smith was not guilty of seriously fraudulent transactions with the government. "The terms 'poltroon, liar, and scoundrel' are bitterly offensive, under some circumstances," Johnston wrote, but "they lose all their venom and sting when they fall from the lips of a creature who, but for the mistaken charity and magnanimity of the Custom House authorities at this port, must have been convicted, by a jury of his country, as a common thief, guilty of stealing moneys, which came into his hands while employed in that department, as the records will prove whenever referred to." Johnston had "let Smith have it," not with a pistol but with printed words, for all the evidence reveals a duel between the two men was never fought.[41]

In August, however, Johnston's reluctance to engage in dueling broke down. On August 18, he found himself in the Bank Exchange Saloon, one of San Francisco's most popular drinking spots, talking with State Senator William I. Ferguson from Sierra County. Ferguson had once lived in Springfield, Illinois, where he became good friends with both Edward D. Baker and Abraham Lincoln and, following their example, began the practice of law.[42] Johnston and Ferguson had originally been engaging in light banter. After the discussion turned to politics, however, it took an ugly turn. According to later accounts, Ferguson accused Johnston of "being owned by Senator Gwin, or something of that sort." When the discussion turned to Mrs. Gwin, Johnston became indignant and said no one should drag a lady's name into a barroom conversation. The argument became so angry that, two days later, Johnston challenged Ferguson to a duel, and Ferguson accepted. They met on Angel Island in San Francisco Bay on the afternoon of August 21. More than a hundred spectators came to witness the confrontation. When the pistols were fired, both men received wounds. Johnston's was painful but not fatal, but Ferguson received a serious wound in his leg and died about three and a half weeks later.[43]

Both the *Alta California* and the *Union* condemned the Johnston-Ferguson duel, although the *Alta*'s condemnation was the more severe of the two. The San Francisco paper reminded its readers that Johnston had sponsored the stringent 1855 statute condemning duelers to the state prison. It reminded them of "the eloquence expended by Mr. Johnston against dueling" and expressed outrage that he of all people should engage in one of the contests he had so roundly condemned. "Here is a law that declares the act of fighting a duel, a crime of great magnitude, and if attended with a fatal result to either party, the survivor is punishable by imprisonment in the State Prison," the *Alta* wrote, adding that "he who makes a law declaring a certain act to be a felony, seems to us to be doubly guilty, if he himself is among the first to break it."[44] The Sacramento paper was more temperate in its criticism of the duel, writing: "Sober-minded people will look upon the affair as the relic of a barbarous age, and as foolish trifling with human life. The duel settles nothing, and the original cause of it remains without change or alteration. The chivalry of the South, however, was equally met this time by the nerve and coolness of the North."[45] If Ferguson represented the "coolness of the North," his "coolness" was little compensation for his ultimate reward, which was death.

Johnston was arrested under the anti-dueling statute and put on trial in Marin County, just north of San Francisco, but after doctors testified that Ferguson's death was caused by the failure of attending physicians to promptly amputate his leg and not by Johnston's gunshot, he was acquitted.[46] Johnston was arrested again in San Francisco on the same charges, but the case against him there was dismissed when he proved that he had already been acquitted in Marin County.[47]

Johnston's encounters with Brooks, Smith, and Ferguson—and perhaps some other men as well—proved that he was a very contentious figure in San Francisco and that his decision in favor of Archy Lee had done nothing to reduce the controversy that surrounded him. It also showed, if indirectly, that controversy over slavery's future in California, and in the rest of the nation, was not calming—it was growing in intensity. It was still "The Year of Archy Lee," and the nation was still hurtling toward a bloody conflict.

## CHAPTER TEN

# North to Freedom

ARCHY HAD SPENT MOST OF THE FIRST THREE MONTHS OF THE YEAR IN jail, but now he needed somewhere else to rest and find shelter. Although there were many blacks in San Francisco who would have been glad to take the young man into their homes or places of business, there is no clear evidence as to where he stayed. Many years later, Delilah Beasley, an avid student of the history of blacks in California, wrote that the mysterious Mary Ellen ("Mammy") Pleasant "hid Archy Lee in her home" to protect him from the whites who were trying to kidnap him.[1] Beasley's story has been repeated many times over, even though Helen Holdredge, the best-selling author of *Mammy Pleasant*, a semi-fictional biography published in 1953, asserted that Mammy Pleasant and her husband left San Francisco for New York via Panama on April 5, 1858, on their way to help John Brown plan his 1859 raid on Harper's Ferry, Virginia. If Holdredge's assertion is correct, Mammy Pleasant would not have been in San Francisco when Archy needed shelter.[2] There is little doubt, however, that Mammy Pleasant would have been willing to take him in, for she was dedicated to the cause of protecting African-American rights. But Holdredge's assertions are supported by no better evidence than those of Delilah Beasley, as there is no proof that Mammy Pleasant helped Brown prepare his raid, knew anything about it before it started, or left San Francisco for New York early in April 1858.[3] The best that can probably be said about whether Mammy Pleasant hid Archy Lee in her home is: perhaps she did and perhaps she didn't. This conclusion is similar to so many facts about Mammy's long and eventful life that it fits with the pattern. She was an enterprising woman who did much of her work in the shadows and left behind her an intriguing but mysterious trail as to what actually happened and when.

San Francisco's black population realized that the hostility of the pro-slavery whites extended not only to Archy but to virtually the entire black population of the city. If Archy could be kidnapped and put on a steamer bound for Panama and slavery, what was to protect other blacks from similar fates? At the meetings held in the Zion Church, there was celebration for Archy's courtroom victory but also serious discussion about the need to find some other place for the blacks to live in safety.

Mexico had abolished slavery in 1829, and it was generally believed that there was room for immigrant settlements in the Mexican state of Sonora, southeast of California.[4] Some of the San Francisco blacks favored the move to Sonora, declaring emphatically that they would not remain in California to be degraded by their "own American Countrymen."[5] But Sonora had some serious problems. American insurrectionists had in recent years invaded the state and neighboring areas in an effort to transform them into slave lands. A Tennessee-born, San Francisco–based medical doctor and lawyer-turned-journalist named William Walker had led makeshift armies that invaded Sonora and Baja California in 1853 and Nicaragua in 1855 and attempted to establish governments in both places, all for the purpose of spreading slavery in North America. Another effort to establish slavery in Sonora, and perhaps even to annex the Mexican state to the United States as a slave-holding territory, had been led by Henry Crabb in 1857. Crabb was a young man from Tennessee who had practiced law in Mississippi before coming to California in 1848, resuming his practice, and winning election to California's legislature as a pro-slavery Democrat. After he left the legislature, he led a band of armed men into Sonora to capture the state and establish slavery in it. His expedition was initially successful, but the Mexican governor was able to mount a counter-attack to overthrow him and execute him and his men. The insurrectionists who invaded Sonora, Baja California, Nicaragua, and neighboring territories were often called "filibusters" because of their resemblance to the freebooters (pirates) who roamed the seas searching for ships to board and plunder.[6] Considering the possibility that Sonora could be transformed into slave country by invaders from the north, it did not seem a safe place for San Francisco's blacks to move to.

The Zion congregants gave no thought to emigrating to Oregon, even though it was on paper slave-free, because its laws (promoted by Peter Burnett when he lived there) firmly barred the entry of blacks— even free blacks—into the territory and provided stiff penalties for any who came there in violation of the law.[7]

Some thought was also given to Haiti, although that destination was not seriously discussed,[8] and to Panama, which was then part of a country called New Granada. Blacks who came to California via Panama had some acquaintance with the isthmus and had seen other blacks living and working there. A letter was sent there asking "about the inducements offered by that country to colored immigrants." A reply was eventually received from one General Bosques, who was himself of African ancestry. In his letter, Bosques identified himself as the president of the Senate of New Granada, telling the San Francisco blacks to "come on" and assuring them that a black man had "the same political and social rights as a white man in that latitude." Before Bosques's letter arrived, however, a different destination had already been selected.[9]

The location that attracted them the most was the British-held land north of the Washington Territory, for slavery had been abolished in all of the British Colonies by an Act of Parliament passed in 1832 that took effect in 1834.[10] What's more, news had been received early in 1858 of the discovery of gold on tributaries of the Fraser River, an important waterway that extended north and east of the Crown Colony of Vancouver. Although Britain laid claim to the vast expanse of land that bordered the Pacific coast north of the Washington Territory, the only authority actually exercised there was that of the fur-trading Hudson's Bay Company. This company was so powerful that some said "H.B.C." meant "Here Before Christ."[11] Almost immediately after the Fraser River news reached California, crowds of gold-hungry men boarded steamers in Sacramento and San Francisco and headed north.

James Douglas was the nominal authority in the northern land, for he was the chief factor of Fort Vancouver, owned and run by the Hudson's Bay Company. Born in 1803 in what later became known as the British Colony of Guyana, he was the son of an influential Scottish sugar planter and a mixed-race mother from the Caribbean island of Barbados.[12] His uncle was Sir Neill Douglas, the lieutenant-general of Scotland. Educated in Scotland before sailing for Canada and becoming a clerk for the fur-trading North West Company in 1819, he transferred to the Hudson's Bay Company after the two companies merged in 1821. Rising through the ranks, Douglas became governor of Vancouver Island and its dependencies in 1851. He had received reports about the black people's plight in California early in 1858 and, aware of his own mixed-race heritage, hoped that the blacks might become part of the labor supply needed to deal with the population drawn north by the gold rush.[13]

Jeremiah Nagle, an Irish-born shipmaster who regularly carried passengers and freight between San Francisco and Victoria, a small British settlement on the southern tip of Vancouver Island, also offered help to San Francisco's imperiled blacks. Nagle had a good knowledge both of the unfolding events in California and of the burgeoning Fraser River gold rush.[14] He attended a meeting in the Zion Church on April 16 that was attended by more than two hundred blacks. In that meeting, he told them about the opportunities that would be available to them in the northern land. They in turn peppered him with questions, which he was glad to answer. He said that boats and canoes could be obtained at Victoria at a cost of ten to twenty dollars when he left there, but owing to the rapid inflation characteristic of a gold rush they had probably doubled that price in the interim. The distance from the mouth of the Fraser River up to the gold mines was 135 miles, and the diggings were from ten to twenty miles from the river. Vessels drawing twenty feet could go up as far as Fort Langley, thirty-two miles from the mouth of the river. The Indians who lived there were not hostile, although provisions were "dear and scarce." Nagle assured the blacks that settlers had "great inducements to locate in the country." Historian Crawford Kilian has expressed the opinion that James Douglas very likely sent the invitation that Captain Nagle presented to the blacks in San Francisco.[15] In its report of the April 16 meeting, the *Alta California* told its readers that a substantial group of blacks intended to leave for Victoria the following Tuesday, April 20.[16]

Two steamers, the *Columbia* and the *Commodore*, left San Francisco on schedule on April 20.[17] The wharves were crowded with spectators, excited to see some eight hundred passengers, almost all white but with a large group of blacks mixed in, crammed aboard the vessels.[18] The *Union* told its readers that "many an old miner, with his pick, shovel and pan, was on hand, confident and hopeful."[19] Archy Lee was one of a group of blacks who were aboard the *Commodore*. Before he left, Archy was apparently in a good mood, for he told a reporter for the San Francisco *Times* that after he reached the northern country "it might have a colored correspondent." Sensing an opportunity for humor, the *Union* told its readers: "While we hope that Archy will always be able to raise the color in the mines, we hope he will not too highly color his description of the diggings there."[20]

The voyage north was not pleasant for all of the passengers. A letter writer later reported that there was "much difficulty in keeping order and peace among the steerage passengers." After the vessel got out to sea, some sixty stowaways were found on board. They had no money and did not pretend that they had paid for their passage. "These, with others who did pay, were violent and pugnacious on the voyage, insulting and abusing the more orderly class of passengers." "San Francisco is well rid of the scum and wretched who went up on the *Commodore*," the letter writer said. "The same class of rowdies abused the colored people who went up on the steamer, and in sheer wantonness kicked over their pans containing their food, and otherwise indulged in malicious acts." About half of the passengers landed at Victoria and the other half at Port Townsend, an American settlement in Washington Territory about thirty-five miles southeast of Victoria.[21]

The *Commodore* arrived at Victoria on Sunday, April 25.[22] One of the white passengers wrote a letter back to San Francisco. "The good people of Victoria were at church when we arrived," he wrote, "and were perfectly astounded when they came out, and beheld between 400 and 500 Yankees, armed with revolvers and bowie knives. At first, they thought we were the vanguard of a filibustering army coming to take possession of Victoria Island." "But our conduct soon proved we were not the fire-eaters that we appeared to be," the letter continued, "and they soon became reconciled to our presence, especially when we began to spend the quarters which, no doubt, were very acceptable." The letter writer said that the local residents' "next trouble was how to supply this goodly multitude with provisions, and that was a puzzler. However, with the dint of scraping and gathering together from their country larders, and raising the prices, we succeeded in getting enough to eat." The writer said that "the colored people" found shelter in "an unoccupied house, and formed a mess of themselves." But they appeared to be "delighted with their new homes," and some had already purchased land they intended to cultivate. "I believe it is their intention to send for their beloved brethren as soon as possible; they have nearly all got employment, and are going to become free and enlightened subjects (not citizens) of Queen Victoria."[23]

The letter writer went on to describe conditions in Victoria. He had spoken to some people who had been in the mining country and told him that gold was "abundant" but that there was "a great scarcity of provisions, and a difficulty in getting up the Fraser River, in consequence of a rise in the water." He was told that the diggings were "near the surface." One miner said he had not seen any diggings "deeper than six feet." The owner of the *Commodore*, a Captain John T. Wright, had made arrangements with James Douglas to take passengers from his steamer at Victoria up the Fraser River, landing them at Fort Langley, at the rate of five dollars per head. "If that arrangement can be carried out (and I have no doubt about it)," the letter writer continued, "it will save the miners an immense deal of time and trouble, as well as risk of life."[24]

The *Commodore* returned to San Francisco on May 5, bringing with it reports of the "abundance of the 'precious metal'" in the northern land and assurances that employment opportunities there were good. The biggest drawback, however, was "the rugged nature of the country through which the path to the mines passes," which made it "a great difficulty to get to the diggings with passengers and provisions."[25]

One of the earliest reports from Victoria came from a man named Wellington Dabney Moses, one of the black people who had gone north. Moses told the people back in San Francisco that on the day of his arrival he had called on James Douglas (then called "Governor Douglas," although he had not yet received that official title). Douglas received him "in the most friendly manner" and answered the questions he asked "with apparent pleasure." He agreed with reports that there was plenty of gold in the diggings along the Fraser River and that it was difficult to reach there because of the high stage of water in the river. He told Moses that no license was required for working in the mines, nor for carrying on any other trade or business except selling liquor. There were as yet no taxes of any kinds imposed on the miners. Government land could be bought at low prices, and fish were plentiful in the waters surrounding Victoria. Moses had a very favorable impression of opportunities in the northern land, although he advised everyone coming there "to bring provisions with them, for most kinds are selling at high rates."[26]

Not all of the reports from the northland were favorable. A letter written in Port Townsend on May 11 said that food was very expensive along the Fraser River. Flour was being sold at two hundred dollars per barrel, bacon at two hundred fifty dollars per pound, and "everything else in proportion." There were some two hundred men who were then living on the beach at Port Townsend, "subsisting on clams." Some of the people who had "started a Negro colony at Vancouver" had left there, reportedly "disgusted with British liberty." The writer declared that anyone planning to come north now "must have at least $200 to insure a safe transit without starving."[27]

Back in San Francisco, the black population carefully considered the reports received from Moses and others. Some three hundred of them gathered for another meeting in the Zion Church in the evening on May 7. They were impressed with the easy availability of land around Victoria, with the freedom from taxes, and with the cordial greeting the blacks there had received from James Douglas. Most importantly, they were impressed with Douglas's assurance that they would have the right to vote, to sit on juries, and to exercise all the rights of citizens after they had lived there for nine months.[28] How long would they have to wait to receive similar rights in California? Nine years? Or perhaps forever?

The blacks convened in the Zion Church again on May 11 to consider making plans to move the entire population north. They considered the costs of transportation, which were high, and even considered purchasing a vessel in which they could all be carried to Victoria. They found the reports of conditions in the north so favorable that they decided they should make an early start for Victoria.[29] They adopted a series of resolutions embodying their views. One of the most serious expressed their unhappiness with the hostility against them in California and the much more favorable treatment they could expect in the British colony:

WHEREAS, We are fully convinced that the continued aim of the spirit and policy of our mother country is to oppress, degrade, and outrage us; we have, therefore, determined to seek an asylum in the land of strangers, from the oppression, prejudice and relentless persecution that have pursued us for more than two centuries, in this our mother country. Therefore, a delegation having been sent to Vancouver's [sic] Island, a place which has unfolded to us in our darkest hour, the prospect of a bright future. . . .

RESOLVED, That in migrating to British territory, our principles and continued aim shall be to promote intelligence, Christianity and industry, which never fail to secure prosperity to any country, and happiness to a people.

RESOLVED, That we advise our people in their migrating to this God-sent asylum for the oppressed colored American to immediately invest some of their capital in land. . . .

RESOLVED, That in bidding adieu to the friendship, early associations, and the thousand ties which bind mankind to the places of their nativity, we are actuated by no transitory excitement, but are fully impressed with the importance of our present movement, and with our hearts filled with gratitude to the Great Ruler of the Universe, who has provided this refuge for us, we pledge ourselves to this cause, and will make every effort to redeem our race from the yoke of American oppression. . . .[30]

Another party of men—white as well as black—left San Francisco on the *Commodore* shortly after the Zion meeting. A letter back to California reported that the ship had reached Victoria on May 16, that the voyage had been uneventful, and that "there were a number of colored men on board." "All of the colored people here are delighted with the place and the treatment they receive," the reporter wrote. "Archy Lee is here, engaged in making pickets, and is said to be doing well."[31]

Another report reached California early in June, advising readers that "many of the colored people who are here, Archy Lee amongst them, purpose remaining. They are delighted with the social equality and fraternity accorded them."[32] Vancouver Island was a "place which has unfolded to us in our darkest hour, the prospect of a bright future," and Victoria was "one of the garden spots of this world." Part of the "bright future" was, no doubt, the law under which the immigrants would now live. After nine months as landowners, they would be eligible to vote and to serve as jurors, and they would be eligible to become British subjects after seven years of residence.[33] All of this compared wonderfully with what they had endured in California.

The blacks were of course anxious to find a church in which they could worship, and the most readily available was the Anglican chapel presided over by the Reverend Edward Cridge, chaplain to the Hudson's Bay Company. Cridge welcomed them to his services, but his congregants were not quite as welcoming. A letter published in the *Victoria Gazette* in August 1858 expressed some of the white dissatisfaction with the blacks in their midst. "Last Sabbath was an unusually warm day," the letter stated. "The little Chapel was crowded as usual with a 'smart sprinkle' of blacks, generously mixed with in the whites. The *Ethiopians perspired!* They always do when out of place. Several white gentlemen left their seats vacant, and sought the purer atmosphere outside; others moodily endured the aromatic luxury of their positions, in no very pious frame of mind."[34] Members of Reverend Cridge's congregation soon asked for a segregated black gallery, but the minister refused to give it to them. Many whites then withdrew from his church.[35]

A distinguished British visitor came to Victoria in 1858 and expressed some dissatisfaction with the black presence in the colony. He was Kinahan Cornwallis, a London-born lawyer, member of the British colonial civil service, and published author who would soon join American journalists in New York City. For now, however, Cornwallis, expressed discomfort with the blacks in Victoria. He wrote: "I observed that the coloured people, i.e. 'niggers,' collected here, many of whom were 'real estate' owners, conducted themselves in a manner rather bellicose than otherwise which, of course, excited derision; and one of their number, I heard, attempted to take his seat with white people at a boarding house table in town, but was expressed in a manner as prompt and merciless as the style of doing the thing was ludicrous." Cornwallis reported that negroes had been appointed to act as local police, but that they were "heartily despised by the Americans" who were there.[36]

Some of the blacks from California still seemed to be doing well in Victoria. Archy Lee was one. Another was Reverend J. J. Moore, highly respected founder of San Francisco's African Methodist Episcopal Zion Church, who had also come north. Yet another was Mifflin Wistar Gibbs, the San Francisco businessman who had exercised much of the leadership in the Zion Church and in California's black community in general. Gibbs had left San Francisco for Victoria in early June 1858, taking passage with about seven hundred passengers on the steamship *Republic.* Good businessman that he was, he took along some supplies he could sell to the fledgling miners in the north: stores of flour and bacon and a good supply of blankets, picks, and shovels.[37] On his arrival, he bought a lot and house in Victoria and met with James Douglas and other local officials, who welcomed him warmly. He soon learned that in the British colony he would be entitled to vote and to testify in court. These rights had been denied him under the "American Eagle," he said, but granted under the "British Lion." In an autobiography he wrote many years later, Gibbs recalled that "three or four hundred colored men from California and other States, with their families, settled in Victoria, drawn thither by the two-fold inducement—gold discovery and the assurance of enjoying impartially the benefits of constitutional liberty. They built or bought homes and other property, and by industry and character vastly improved their condition and were the recipients of respect and esteem from the community."[38]

In 1859, Gibbs returned to the United States to claim a woman to share his life with: Maria Alexander, a young black woman who lived in Kentucky. They were married there, then proceeded to visit some of Gibbs's friends in Buffalo, New York, and to call on the famous black activist Frederick Douglass in Rochester. They then boarded a steamship in New York City for a four-thousand-mile-long voyage back to their home in Victoria.[39] Many years later, Gibbs recalled that in passing through the United States in 1859 he felt a spirit of unrest everywhere. "The pulse beat of the great national heart quickened an impending danger," he wrote. He recalled that the *Dred Scott* case was still wracking the nation, that people were worrying more than ever before about the "irrepressible conflict" William H. Seward had warned them of in 1858, and that the great debates conducted in 1858 between Stephen Douglas and Abraham Lincoln were on many people's minds.[40]

The blacks continued their lives in British Columbia, but not without distress. A report sent back from Victoria by a reporter for the *Pacific Appeal*, a black newspaper published in San Francisco, included some unfavorable comments about the lives that the blacks were then living in Victoria. It said there was "as much prejudice and nearly as much isolation in Victoria as in San Francisco." In fact, the social and political positions of the colored people were more favorable in some ways in the California city than in the northern land. There were a number of whites (including some Jews) who had come north from the United States and held very unfavorable opinions about the blacks then living in the north. The reporter noted that the blacks had ready access to churches and schools there, although their "leading men had to fight hard to obtain their rights in both." The reporter mentioned Peter Lester, Mifflin Wistar Gibbs, and Jacob Francis, who had "battled manfully to keep churches and schools free from caste," and he attributed the equality in those institutions to their efforts. The equality was, however, "grudgingly and unwillingly awarded." The *Appeal* noted that the black people in Victoria had the right to vote, but that was "all the political privilege they do possess." Naturalized men were eligible to take seats in the city council, but not in the provincial parliament. A law was then being passed to exclude from the province all except subjects of the British empire by birth. This law, according to the *Appeal*, was passed to prevent blacks from winning seats in the legislature. Although about one hundred and fifty blacks and only four whites had taken the oath of allegiance to the crown, blacks were still barred from membership in the parliament and the council. "It is not very probable a colored person will ever be elected to either body," the *Appeal* stated. "Two attempts have been made, and although, in each case, the candidates were as capable and as worthy as any in the colony, they were both defeated. Prejudice is too strong in Vancouver Island; we have brighter prospects of political elevation under our own government, than in any British colony on this coast."[41]

Archy Lee and other blacks had gone north seeking fairness and justice. They were not sure, however, that they had attained those things.

## Chapter Eleven

# "We Feel the Impulse"

THE FLIGHT OF ARCHY LEE AND SEVERAL HUNDRED OF HIS FELLOW-blacks from California to the Crown Colony of Victoria in the far northland dominated the news along the Pacific coast for much of the year 1858. Other events occurring in the same year, however, were also signaling the growing distress that Americans were experiencing. Reports from California and other parts of the country, sent from Sacramento and San Francisco to cities along the Atlantic coast and even abroad, told many observers that the United States was heading toward a conflict that would affect profound changes in the nation. There was an epic legal battle in San Francisco over one of the most valuable mines in the state—perhaps in the world—that fueled much of the economic activity that made California such a valuable part of the United States. There was the successful completion of a telegraph cable that evidenced America's hunger for technical and scientific progress and foretold a major breakthrough in communication, first across the Atlantic Ocean, and soon thereafter all over the world. And there was the appearance of a comet, one of the most brilliant seen in the nineteenth century, that was taken by many on the Pacific coast, in the Middle West, in the Atlantic states, and even as far away as Europe, as an augur of heavenly approval of the telegraph. In San Francisco's Zion Church, 1858 was "The Year of Archy Lee." In much of the rest of the country and the world, the same year was a harbinger of profound legal, social, and political changes, some that many Americans would welcome and others that a part of the country would resist even to the death.

Most of the people who lived in California in 1858 had come there because of the vast deposits of gold that lay buried in the ground. The "treasure" that was carried aboard the steamers that regularly left San Francisco destined for delivery to New York and other cities along the Atlantic coast amounted every year to many millions of dollars. The businesses that had been created in the state, the hundreds of thousands of jobs that had become available, the towns that had suddenly appeared along the rivers and in secluded canyons in the mountains, and the great cities of Sacramento and San Francisco that had become both the financial and the political centers of the western United States, all owed their existence directly or indirectly to the yellow metal. But gold was not the only mineral that created great wealth in California, nor was it the first that had been discovered. Quicksilver, also known as mercury, had been the first precious metal discovered in the state, and in 1858 it was one of the most valuable—and politically controversial.

A bitter battle over the New Almaden quicksilver mine, located in hilly country about fifteen miles south of San Jose, was fought out in the US district court in San Francisco in 1858. Discovered hundreds of years earlier by the Ohlone Indians who lived in and around San Francisco Bay, New Almaden was then being operated by British investors who claimed ownership under a Mexican land grant made in 1847 to a Mexican army officer named Andres Castillero.[1] New Almaden derived its name from the legendary Almadén mine in the Sierra Morena of south-central Spain, which had yielded immensely valuable deposits of quicksilver since Roman times. Quicksilver was as valuable as gold— perhaps even more valuable—because, placed in the bottoms of pans, sluice boxes, or other containers, it amalgamates with gold, making it possible to recover even the tiniest particles of the precious metal. The value of the quicksilver extracted from New Almaden in the 1850s was so great that President James Buchanan directed his attorney general, Jeremiah Black, to send a Pennsylvania-based attorney named Edwin M. Stanton to California to establish that the mine was actually on publicly owned land and not on the Mexican grant, and that its profits belonged to the government and not to private investors. Stanton had just finished the McCormick Reaper trial in Cincinnati, Ohio, a high-profile patent infringement case in which he had very rudely snubbed Abraham Lincoln, who had come to the Ohio city from Springfield, Illinois, to join him in the case.[2] In California, Stanton came into conflict with the hard-driving Henry Wager Halleck, a West Point graduate and former US Army major who had become a San Francisco–based attorney specializing in land titles and also happened to be the British investors' manager of New Almaden. By 1858, the mine was yielding quicksilver worth millions of dollars every year—more than any single gold mine in California, possibly more than was extracted from any mine of any kind anywhere in the world. Stanton and Halleck battled fiercely in San Francisco, developing a simmering personal enmity that continued well into the Civil War, after Lincoln (ignoring Stanton's Cincinnati rudeness) made Stanton secretary of war and appointed Henry Halleck as general-in-chief of all of the Union armies.[3]

As Stanton was preparing his case in San Francisco, the US Supreme Court in Washington was reviewing another private claim to New Almaden, this asserted by a man named Charles Fossat, who claimed ownership of New Almaden under a Mexican grant that conflicted with Castillero's. The Supreme Court announced its decision on April 30, 1858, ruling that Fossat's grant was valid but that its boundaries were not described with sufficient precision to determine whether he was entitled to ownership of the mine.[4] Newspapers in New York and California joined in proclaiming the importance of the case. The *Daily Alta* told its readers that it was "seldom a case of such magnitude comes before the Supreme Court, on which there is such an array of eminent counsel." The *New York Times* described the controversy as "one of the most remarkable civil trials in this or any other country."[5] Meanwhile, the Castillero claim was being examined in a lawsuit filed in the US Circuit Court in San Francisco, in which it was claimed that the British investors had no right to hold or work the mine and that the damage to the United States resulting from their operation of it was "irreparable."[6] The *Daily Alta California* told its readers: "There is a degree of importance attached to this case, that renders it of uncommon interest at the present moment, involving, as it does, legal questions that will have an important bearing in future decisions upon land titles of a similar nature."[7] After a fiercely fought trial, US Circuit Judge Matthew Hall McAllister, joined by San Francisco's US District Judge Ogden Hoffman Jr., announced a decision on October 29, 1858, that there was sufficient doubt about the validity of the Mexican land grant to issue an injunction against further operation of New Almaden. The *Alta* described the case as "one of immense importance" and said that the mine had "for some time, been producing a large portion of all the quicksilver used in the world."[8]

Litigation over the ownership of the New Almaden mine continued for several years after 1858. The western historian Hubert H. Bancroft said that, "in magnitude of interests involved, and bulk of record," its importance was "second to none decided previously by any tribunal."[9] Ownership of the mine was regarded as so vital to the Union war effort that, in May 1863, President Lincoln ordered the US marshal in California to take possession of the mine and hold it for the United States.[10] It was not finally resolved until 1864, when the holders of the Fossat claims won title to the mine and, after a settlement was reached with the United States and the other claimants, they sold their interests for $1.75 million.[11] Under its new ownership, the New Almaden mine continued to produce quicksilver as late as World War I, although its profitability declined after 1890, when it was discovered that cyanide could be used as effectively as mercury in refining gold.[12]

Edwin Stanton's duties in San Francisco in 1858 included an effort to defeat the land claims asserted by a Frenchman named José Yves Limantour, who had conducted business for many years in both California and Mexico and was now asserting ownership of a Mexican land grant that embraced more than a half-million acres around San Francisco Bay. Limantour's claim excited not only lawyers and investors but also ordinary San Franciscans and the government back in Washington, because it included most of the land that then comprised the bayside city. Stanton combed the Mexican archives in California and presented convincing proof to Judge Ogden Hoffman that Limantour's claim was fraudulent. So on November 19, 1858, the judge struck it down. "Farewell to Limantour!" the *Alta* told its readers on November 20. "He was completely demolished yesterday by Judge Hoffman."[13] Stanton sent the news back to President Buchanan and Attorney General Black with obvious satisfaction. "The Year of Archy Lee" was proving itself important to government officials in Washington as well as crusaders for racial justice in California.[14]

The successful completion of a telegraph cable that linked a village on an island off the southwest coast of Ireland to a fishing settlement on the southeast coast of Newfoundland was another momentous event that took place in "The Year of Archy Lee," and though it happened thousands of miles away from California it was acclaimed there with an unprecedented celebration.

The idea of laying a telegraph cable across the Atlantic Ocean had been nursed at least since 1844, when a portrait artist and inventor named Samuel F. B. Morse successfully transmitted a telegraphic message from the US Supreme Court chamber in Washington, DC, to the Mount Clare Station of the Baltimore & Ohio Railroad in Baltimore. Many men had hoped to lay a telegraph cable across the ocean, knowing how profoundly it would change communications between North America and Europe and how much fame it would bring to them for doing so. The ultimate honor for the completion of the line, however, was to be given to a man named Cyrus West Field, who happened to be one of the younger brothers of Stephen J. Field, the California Supreme Court justice who had just weeks earlier disapproved the decision in the controversial "Archy Case" without taking part in it, and who would soon move to Washington, DC, as a US Supreme Court justice by appointment of President Abraham Lincoln.

Unlike his older brothers, Stephen J. Field and David Dudley Field Jr., who both pursued legal careers (David was a successful New York lawyer and the author of the famous Field Codes that modernized civil procedure in courts all across the country), Cyrus Field chose a business career, in which he was so successful that he became a rich man while still in his thirties.[15] In conjunction with a Canadian engineer and an American naval officer and oceanographer, he began in the early 1850s to explore the possibility of laying a telegraph cable on the floor of the Atlantic Ocean. His wealth enabled him to persuade investors in both the United States and Britain to join him in his efforts to lay hundreds of miles of wire cable covered with gutta-percha (a form of latex derived from trees in Malaysia) to protect it from the sea water on the ocean floor. Using British ships, Field made three unsuccessful attempts to lay a complete cable line across the ocean before finally achieving success on August 5, 1858.[16] The cable stretched nearly two thousand miles across the ocean and descended to a depth of more than two miles beneath the surface.[17] On August 17, Queen Victoria and President Buchanan exchanged a congratulatory message in Morse code: "Europe and America are united by telegraph. Glory to God in the highest."[18]

News of the completion of the telegraph line spread rapidly, first to London, then to Paris, then to New York City and Washington, DC, and after a slight delay, to California. Celebrations were held in all of these places. In New York, the lawyer and diarist George Templeton Strong wrote that the newspapers there "vie with each other in gas and grandiloquence. Yesterday's *Herald* said that the cable (or perhaps Cyrus W. Field, uncertain which) is undoubtedly the Angel in the Book of Revelation with one foot on sea and one foot on land, proclaiming that Time is no longer. Moderate people merely say that this is the greatest human achievement in history."[19]

An official celebration of the cable's completion took place in San Francisco on Monday, September 27. Its planners described it as "the greatest demonstration San Francisco has ever witnessed."[20] Colorful banners flew from the masts of ships gathered along the waterfront and a multitude of small flags flew from the third-story windows of the Montgomery Block, the city's largest and most important commercial building—designed and built by the New Almaden mine's general manager, Henry Halleck. A jewelry store was decorated with "a judicious caricature representing John Bull and Brother Jonathan, with the mottoes: What's that pulling on the wire? Oh, that's the little giant California." Crowds gathered to decorate the sides of buildings and to prepare a platform in front of the Oriental Hotel at the corner of Battery and Bush Streets, where speakers would address a huge throng. Marchers paraded with brass bands, drummers, carriages, wagons, and fancy coaches adorned with ribbons and flowers. Rockets were shot into the sky. Bonfires were lit on the hillsides surrounding the city and cannons were discharged into the bay.[21] The official orator of the event was none other than Edward D. Baker, the brilliant lawyer who just a few weeks earlier had successfully argued Archy Lee's case before US Commissioner George Pen Johnston. Baker's long and eloquent address in front of the Oriental Hotel was so enthusiastically received that it was printed in full in the *Daily Alta California* and later included in a separate volume of inspirational addresses. He began by telling his "fellow-citizens" that "the great enterprise of the age has been successfully accomplished," then continued—waxing poetic as well as eloquent:

> Thought has bridged the Atlantic, and cleaves its unfettered path across the sea—winged by the lightning and guarded by the billow. Though remote from the shores that first witnessed the deed, we feel the impulse and swell the paean; as in the frame of man, the nervous sensibility is great at the extremity of the body so we, distant dwellers on the Pacific coast, feel yet more keenly than the communities which form the centers of civilization, the greatness of the present success, and the splendor of the advancing future.[22]

In the same address in which he extolled the completion of the Atlantic cable, Baker referred to another phenomenon that was commanding the attention of California and the nation in "The Year of Archy Lee." It was a comet—one of the most visible ever seen in the nineteenth century—that was streaming through the sky before and after sunset, leaving in its wake a spectacular dust tail, long and curved like a scimitar. It was to be formally named Donati's Comet, after Giovanni Battista Donati, the Italian astronomer who first observed it through a telescope in Florence on June 2, 1858.[23] For centuries, if not millennia, comets had been regarded by humans as omens of approaching danger or disaster, or as augurs of heavenly commendation, marking approval of an earthly event or accomplishment. The appearance of Donati's Comet at around the time of the completion of the Atlantic Telegraph prompted many observers to link the two together. On September 20, the *Sacramento Daily Union* told its readers that in the Sierra Nevada mining town of Placerville for two evenings before September 18, "the northwestern heavens have been illuminated by the sweeping train of a splendid comet. There is, of course, a vast deal of speculation in relation to their fiery stranger, but it is generally conceded to be a sort of celestial torchlight demonstration in honor of the great Submarine Telegraph."[24] Around the same time, the San Francisco-based *California Farmer and Journal of Useful Sciences* reported that the comet was "now visible every clear evening, and thousands are seen at the corners of the streets and upon the hills, looking at this phenomenon in the heavens. Is it not a little singular that the Comet should appear just at this time, as if to herald the completion of the Ocean Telegraph?"[25]

Advances in photography had made it possible for a photographic image to be taken in Italy in September, thus making Donati's Comet the first such heavenly body ever to be photographed.[26] It came closest to the sun on September 30 and closest to the earth on October 9.[27]

The comet was highly visible in the sky over southern Illinois on September 14, when Abraham Lincoln arrived in the small town of Jonesboro to prepare for his third debate with Stephen Douglas, which was set for September 15. After supper, he sat outside in front of his hotel with two journalists who had come with him to cover the debates for the *Chicago Press and Tribune*. Horace White, one of the journalists, later wrote: "The only thing I can recall at Jonesboro was not political and not even terrestrial. It was the splendid appearance of Donati's comet in the sky, the evening before the debate. Mr. Lincoln greatly admired this strange visitor, and he and I sat for an hour or more in front of the hotel looking at it."[28] A popular twenty-first century novelist later suggested that Lincoln's famous statement that "A house divided against itself cannot stand" could have been inspired by the comet and thus may have contributed to the ultimate downfall of slavery in the United States.[29] The statement was not originally made at Jonesboro but in Springfield, Illinois, on June 16, 1858. It was, however, a subject of argument between Lincoln and Douglas in the Jonesboro debate (Douglas referred to Lincoln's statement several times), so it may not be unreasonable to suggest there was some connection between the comet and Lincoln's powerful contribution to the ultimate end of slavery in the United States.

In San Francisco on September 27 the comet was seen as a sign of heavenly blessing and an inspiration for Edward Baker's Atlantic Telegraph oration. Baker knew that the comet had visited the earth in an earlier time and assumed that it was now coming back to congratulate mankind for its great technical accomplishment. "We see, in the predicted return of the rushing, blazing comet through the sky," he said, "the march of a heavenly messenger along its appointed way and around its predestined orbit."[30]

The Atlantic cable completed in 1858 was not Cyrus Field's final triumph. Stressed by an engineer who mistakenly sent too high a charge of electricity through the wires, the cable functioned for only three weeks after August 5, 1858, and then shut down.[31] Disappointment followed the news of the failure, but the disappointment was largely forgotten when, some eight years later, the persistent Field succeeded at last in laying a permanently functioning cable from Newfoundland to Ireland.[32] By then it was 1866—"The Year of Archy Lee" was past. The great American Civil War was over, and Americans could all share Edward Baker's joy in "the greatness of the present success, and the splendor of the advancing future."

## Chapter Twelve

# The Year Lives On

THE EVENTS THAT FOLLOWED 1858 WERE DRAMATIC AND TEMPESTU-ous. The United States had been building toward a confrontation over slavery for its whole history, but the confrontation, once approaching slowly and gradually, was now accelerating. California's struggle over the future of Archy Lee was not the only cause of the acceleration—far from it—but it contributed to it. The western state was too big and too dynamic, its population was growing too fast, and its contribution to the national wealth was too important, to be ignored. Slavery had been banned from California in 1849, but it was now crying for a return, if not in the same form it had taken in the plantation states of the Deep South, then with statutes and court decisions that reinstated many of its characteristics. If black Americans could not be bought and sold in slave auctions in Sacramento or San Francisco as they could be in Richmond, Virginia, or in Jackson, Mississippi, they could be denied rights in much the same manner that blacks were oppressed in those cities. They were barred from voting, forbidden to testify against whites in courts of law, as they were in South Carolina and Mississippi and Texas. They could be forced to work for whites without compensation, as they were in Louisiana and Texas, and jailed if they failed to obey the orders that whites gave them. If some whites protested against the discrimination that blacks were subjected to, many others were satisfied to continue the discrimination, even to increase it. If some whites were demanding that slavery be abolished throughout the land, others were expressing outrage at the demand and matching it with demands that the institution be allowed to spread into every state and territory that slave masters wanted to move to or travel in. And the blacks were protesting, resisting, and even fleeing into a foreign country to seek freedom.

David Broderick had been one of the most powerful opponents of slavery in California. He did not call himself an abolitionist; he made no effort to challenge the claims of southern plantation owners to maintain their peculiar institution in their home states. He did, however, oppose the efforts of slavery's defenders to expand it into the West. He condemned the fraudulent Lecompton Constitution that James Buchanan and his supporters were seeking with such determination to accept, and he supported the so-called "Freeport Doctrine" announced by Illinois's Senator Stephen Douglas in his second debate with Abraham Lincoln, under which the people of a territory or state could ban slavery from their midst by popular vote, "for the reason that slavery cannot exist a day or an hour anywhere, unless it is supported by local police regulations."[1] Abolitionists were not pleased with the "Freeport Doctrine," for it did not absolutely ban slavery for all time, but pro-slavery Democrats and Chivalry candidates for office in California were absolutely outraged by it.

Broderick had returned to San Francisco after the adjournment of Congress in March 1859 to help his supporters prepare for the upcoming elections. He worked with the Republican Edward D. Baker, Archy Lee's defender in the court of George Pen Johnston, to forge a single slate of candidates to oppose the Chivalry candidates who supported the Lecompton Constitution. His efforts were not successful—the Chivalry candidates swept their opponents—but he demonstrated that the Republicans and his free soil–leaning supporters shared a political philosophy.[2] But supporters of Lecompton, including California's Chivalry leader Senator William Gwin, mounted sharp attacks against him. Baker ran for a seat in the House of Representatives as a Republican, concurring with Broderick's opposition to Lecompton, but he lost very badly, as did Broderick's supporters. The campaign was so hard-fought that Broderick's biographer called it the "most bitterly fought in the history of California."[3] Anger rose so rapidly that a Chivalry Democrat named David

Perley challenged Broderick to a duel, but the senator declined to accept the challenge, prompting some to accuse him of cowardice.[4] He then received a challenge from David S. Terry, the knife-wielding Chivalry Democrat who had been one of the Supreme Court judges who ordered Archy Lee back to Mississippi. Terry and Broderick had been allies in opposition to the Vigilance Committee of 1856, but they were now political opponents. In the election of 1859, Terry had attempted to win another term as a Supreme Court justice, running as a pro-Lecompton Democrat, and his failure to win election raised his anger to a boiling point. Broderick made efforts to conciliate his differences with Terry, but Terry spurned them, issuing a peremptory challenge to a duel in September 1859. At the same time that he issued the challenge, Terry wrote out a resignation from his seat on the Supreme Court.[5]

Broderick felt he could not decline Terry's challenge, so the two men met on a farm adjoining a lake on the boundary line between San Francisco and San Mateo Counties. Edward Baker, who had become a close friend of Broderick, stayed up with the senator the night before the confrontation, for Broderick could not sleep. The senator was a crack pistol shot, but he was exhausted by the intense election campaign and could not be sure how the duel would end. When the two men faced each other and fired their pistols, Broderick's bullet spent itself in the ground about nine feet in front of him, but Terry's struck Broderick in the right chest, fracturing his sternum and perforating his left lung. Baker took the wounded Broderick to a house where doctors tended him. But they could not save his life, and he died three days later, on September 16.[6]

Broderick's body was taken to downtown San Francisco, where Baker delivered an impassioned eulogy before a crowd estimated to include thirty thousand people, the largest ever assembled in California up to that date. Many blacks—men and women who had remained in California even after Archy Lee led the exodus to Victoria in British Columbia—joined in the crowd. Baker revealed that Broderick's last words were: "I die because I was opposed to a corrupt administration and the extension of slavery." Baker himself said that Broderick died "having written his name in the history of the great struggle for the rights of the people against the despotism of organization and the corruption of power."[7]

A funeral procession estimated to be a mile long accompanied Broderick's body to a grave on Lone Mountain, a prominent eminence west of the city, where it was buried. But Father Hugh Gallagher announced that Broderick could not be buried in consecrated ground, for he had not been faithful in his attendance at Catholic Mass, so the senator was buried among non-Catholics. Broderick was the only sitting senator in the history of the United States who died in a duel.[8] Terry was charged with murder and tried—but not convicted.[9]

Broderick's death did not erase his memory. A prominent street in San Francisco was named for him, as was a rugged mountain peak in the Sierra Nevada.[10] At an elevation of 6,706 feet above sea level, Mount Broderick stands near the edge of the Yosemite Valley in Yosemite National Park, one of the oldest and most admired national parks in the United States. Although a Democrat, Broderick's opposition to slavery earned him the respect and affection of the Republicans after his death at the hands of David S. Terry. When the Republicans gathered for their national convention in Chicago in 1860, they adorned the entrance to their newly built Wigwam Convention hall with a portrait of the late senator, reminding the many thousands of men and women who came through that the California senator had been "murdered for his opposition to the Slave interest," adding: "Nothing more appropriate could be conceived, than that the portrait of such a man should adorn the walls of a Republican Convention."[11] After the fighting broke out between the North and the South, Broderick became what Lincoln scholar Milton Shutes called "a symbol of devotion to the United States."[12] In November 1863, California's Senator John Conness called on President Lincoln with a group of admirers and presented him with a cane made of California live oak. The handle of the cane carried a gold plate inscribed "Broderick to Conness" and under that a newer plate inscribed "Conness to the President." Conness presented it to Lincoln in gratitude for his issuance of the Emancipation Proclamation. The *Washington Chronicle* reported that Lincoln gratefully accepted the cane, while the *Cincinnati Gazette* described his emotional response to the gift somewhat more extensively. According to the Cincinnati paper, Lincoln thanked Conness and his supporters "with much emotion" and said that "he never personally knew the Senator's friend, Mr. Broderick, but he had always heard him spoken of as one sincerely devoted to the cause of human rights. . . . Whether remaining in this world or looking down upon the earth from the spirit land, to be remembered by such a man as David C. Broderick was a fact he would remember through all the years of his life."[13]

Edward Baker's failure to win election to Congress from California did not kill his political ambitions. Like his friend Abraham Lincoln in faraway Illinois, he still hoped that he could win an important political office and help the Republican Party make its influence felt in the country. In the presidential platforms it adopted in both 1856 and 1860, the Republican Party had clearly stated its intention to prevent slavery from expanding into the western territories.[14] Thus, as members of the party explained, the institution would be put on the road to "ultimate extinction" in the whole country.[15]

In February 1859 Oregon had been admitted to the Union as the thirty-third state. Democrats dominated the new state's political landscape, as they did in California, but Republicans there were hopeful that they could make a breakthrough and invited Baker to come north and make a race for one of Oregon's senatorial seats. Oregon Republicans had started approaching him in 1857 about the possibility of coming north, but with his latest electoral defeat in California he decided to make the move. When Oregonians asked why he was moving north, he answered that it was because Oregon had a salubrious climate and offered his children educational advantages.[16] His family followed him north in 1860. Baker quickly proceeded to demonstrate his oratorical powers and political instincts by speaking to audiences all over the new state. He made trips back to San Francisco and, on August 1, 1860, was able to write Lincoln from the California city to congratulate him on his nomination as the Republican Party's presidential candidate.[17] Baker's efforts in Oregon were successful, and on October 2, 1860, the new state's legislature elected him as one of its two US senators, making him the first Republican ever elected to a distinguished public office on the Pacific coast. On the same date, Baker wrote Lincoln to advise him of his election and to promise his continued support.[18]

The campaign for president in 1860 was hotly contested in California. Lincoln was running as the Republican candidate, but he had three opponents. The most formidable was his 1858 debate adversary, the anti-Lecompton Democratic senator from Illinois, Stephen A. Douglas, but Vice President John Breckinridge of Kentucky—a pro-slavery Democrat—and the Constitutional Union Party candidate John Bell of Tennessee also commanded followings. On October 29, 1860, while he was en route from Oregon to his Senate duty in Washington, DC, Edward Baker stopped in San Francisco where he made an impassioned pro-Republican, pro-Lincoln speech. In it, he stated his views on slavery, which were very close to Broderick's, and assured his listeners that the Republican Party under Lincoln would support them. "The Genius of America," Baker said, "will at last lead her sons to freedom."[19] The California historian Theodore H. Hittell later said that this address was widely considered "the greatest speech ever delivered in California."[20] At about the same time that Baker spoke, former governor John Weller, still a Chivalry Democrat, delivered a speech in which he said: "I do not know whether Lincoln will be elected or not. But I do know that if he is elected and attempts to carry out his doctrine, the south will surely withdraw from the Union; and I should consider them less than men if they did not."[21] When the California votes were cast, Lincoln received more than thirty-eight thousand, Douglas more than thirty-seven thousand, Breckinridge close to thirty-four thousand, and Bell a little more than nine thousand.[22] California's four electoral votes went to Lincoln, helping him gain the 180 electoral votes needed to win the national election.[23]

Baker took his Senate seat in Washington, DC, on December 5, 1860, but took pains during the Christmas break to return to Springfield, Illinois, to greet President-Elect Lincoln. It was an emotional reunion for the two men. While Baker was in Springfield, Lincoln asked him to introduce him when he appeared on the East Front of the Capitol in Washington to take his presidential oath on March 4, 1861. Baker was in the same carriage with Lincoln and James Buchanan when they rode from the White House to the Capitol, where Baker redeemed his promise by intoning, in soaring tones: "Fellow citizens, I introduce to you Abraham Lincoln, the President-Elect of the United States."[24]

Baker took an active part in Senate debates in early 1861. He also made frequent visits to the White House to confer with President Lincoln on important issues, and sometimes just to enjoy the company of Lincoln and his wife, Mary. On one visit, some Republican politicians from California came to see Lincoln to complain about Baker's influence in selecting political appointees in their state.[25] Since Baker was the only Republican senator on the Pacific coast, he had been advising Lincoln about appointments not only in Oregon but also in California. The Californians believed he had no business doing that and presented Lincoln with a paper that included severe criticism of Senator Baker. Lincoln read the letter and angrily thrust it into the fire, later explaining that it "was an unjust attack upon my dearest personal friend," adding that they "did not know what they were talking about when they made him responsible, almost abusively, for what I had done, or proposed to do."[26]

After the Confederate attack on Fort Sumter, Baker volunteered to organize a regiment of California volunteers and prepare them to do battle in behalf of the Union.[27] He was initially commissioned as a colonel, the same rank he carried in the Mexican War, but Lincoln believed he was entitled to be commissioned as a brigadier general and appointed him to that rank. He did not receive congressional confirmation, however.[28] Now colonel—or perhaps general—Baker was in command of a brigade of troops, including regiments from Massachusetts, New York, and Pennsylvania, on a reconnaissance mission on October 21, 1861, at a place called Ball's Bluff, on the Virginia side of the Potomac River some thirty-five miles northwest of Washington. Ever determined, ever aggressive, he went up the bluff and into the fields beyond with his men. Doing so, he came under heavy Confederate gunfire and was killed.[29] Many of his troops were also killed, and many others were badly wounded, including a young Massachusetts militiaman named Oliver Wendell Holmes Jr., who would later become one of the most famous and influential Supreme Court justices in American history.[30] Lincoln was "devastated" when he received the news of Baker's death. That night, he was unable to sleep and paced the floor in "profound sorrow." At the funeral, he "wept uncontrollably."[31] A correspondent for the *Boston Journal* later expressed doubt that "any other of the many tragic events of President Lincoln's life ever stunned him so much as that unheralded message" which advised him of Baker's death on October 21, 1861.[32]

Baker's body was temporarily interred in the Congressional Cemetery in Washington, but then taken back to California, where it was buried on Lone Mountain overlooking San Francisco, near the body of David Broderick.[33] Thus did Archy Lee's heroic defender in the courtroom of George Pen Johnston become the first and only sitting US senator to die in military combat.

Baker's name was remembered in California, in Oregon, and in the nation's capital. A prominent street was named for him in San Francisco, as were forts in California, Nevada, and the District of Columbia. In Oregon, his name was given to Baker County and Baker City. In Washington, DC, a marble statue of Baker clad in a Roman toga was installed in the Capitol in 1876 and moved to the Hall of Columns in 1979.[34] In 2011 the state's legislature and governor decided that his birthday, February 24, would be remembered every year as Edward Dickinson Baker Day in Oregon.[35]

The fate of James H. Hardy, the lawyer who fought so hard to return Archy Lee to slavery in Mississippi, was very different from Baker's. In 1859, Hardy became a judge of California's Sixteenth Judicial District, which embraced Marin County, north of San Francisco, thanks to an appointment of the pro-slavery Governor Weller.[36] He was serving in that office when charges were brought against Supreme Court justice David Terry for his participation in the duel that killed Senator Broderick. Dueling, after all, was illegal in California, and a US senator had lost his life in a shooting contest with a California Supreme Court justice. But Hardy handled Terry's trial with what was called "indecent haste," and the result was that Terry escaped any punishment.[37]

Three years later, however, Hardy was called to task for his handling of the Terry trial, and for many other instances of blatantly pro-slavery and pro-Confederate bias. Democrats still controlled the legislature in 1862, but not all of them were pleased with the war then being waged between the North and South, so a group of pro-Union Democrats and Republicans united against the Chivalry Democrats to bring impeachment charges against Hardy and, after a trial, to successfully remove him from the bench. He thus became the first and only California judge ever removed from his office by impeachment.[38] Soon after this, Hardy moved to Virginia City in the Nevada Territory. He returned to San Francisco after the conclusion of the Civil War, remaining there until his death in 1874 at the tender age of forty-two.[39]

George Pen Johnston lived a comparatively calm and peaceful life after his duel with William Ferguson. He practiced law in San Francisco and served for a time as editor of a newspaper, but he made no efforts to achieve public office. Ferguson's death had left him with regrets. When he died in March 1884 he was only fifty-seven years old. Reporting his death, the newspapers remembered him as a good man. The *Alta* wrote that he was "kind and affable in his disposition, brave as a lion, sympathetic in his nature, and died probably without leaving an enemy on earth."[40] They cannot have forgotten the part he played in Archy Lee's 1858 struggle for freedom.

David Terry went to Nevada after his duel with Broderick, where he practiced mining law, though he returned from time to time to California. In 1863, he left California to join the Confederates, traveling through Mexico to reach the battle grounds.[41] He joined the Texas Rangers and crossed the Mississippi to take part in some furious fighting, including the battle of Chickamauga, where he was wounded, but after the Confederate defeat he went to Mexico and attempted to grow cotton.[42] In 1869, ten years after his duel with Broderick, he returned to California, where he again practiced law.[43] He championed the rights of women but opposed Chinese labor (anti-Chinese sentiments were then almost as strong as anti-black sentiments in California) and expressed bitter opposition to the railroads, which were then taking a dominant position in California commerce. In 1878 and 1879, he served as a delegate to a convention that met in Sacramento to write a new constitution for California. He played an important role in the convention, which opposed Chinese immigration and put limits on monopolies (notably the state's powerful railroads) but included the provision of the original constitution (now obviously unneeded) stating that "neither slavery nor involuntary servitude, unless for the punishment of crime, shall ever be tolerated in this State."[44] Then in 1884, he became the attorney for a woman named Sarah Althea Hill, who was engaged in a bitter legal dispute with William Sharon, one of the West's most powerful financiers, who had served as US senator from Nevada from 1875 to 1881. Hill had been Sharon's mistress and was suing him to enforce a contract she claimed he had made with her. Terry became so deeply involved in Hill's claims against Sharon that he took her as his wife and became involved in a bitter feud with Stephen J. Field, then serving as a justice of the US Supreme Court by appointment of Abraham Lincoln. Field had been one of the associate justices of the California Supreme Court when it decided Archy Lee's case. He had already earned a reputation as one of the most assertive judges on the nation's highest court, where he would continue to serve until his resignation in 1897, thus earning the distinction of being the longest-serving US Supreme Court justice up to that time.[45] But he had made important rulings against Sarah Althea Hill, prompting David Terry to vow personal vengeance against him. In 1889, Field was traveling through California's San Joaquin Valley in the course of his federal circuit-riding duties. He was accompanied by a bodyguard named David Neagle, commissioned to travel with him because of Terry's threats. At a train station restaurant in the town of Lathrop south of Stockton, Terry and his wife encountered Field and Neagle. Terry walked up to the Supreme Court justice and struck him twice in the face.[46] Neagle then drew his gun and shot Terry dead. Both Neagle and Field were taken to court in San Francisco to determine if Terry's death was justified, and they were quickly exonerated. But David Terry won the distinction of being the only Supreme Court justice in California's history who had killed a sitting US senator in a duel and himself been killed in the course of a physical attack on a sitting US Supreme Court justice.

The Democratic Party's domination of California politics began to give way with the outbreak of the Civil War. Many speeches were made in support of the Confederate secession by Democrats who supported slavery. There was also talk of the possibility of forming a separate nation on the West Coast—to be called the "Pacific Republic"—that would be independent of both the United States and the Confederate States.[47] A flag of the proposed nation, adorned with a bear, like the California state flag, was even flown for a short time in Stockton.[48] But the great majority of Californians opposed the idea, and it went nowhere. Californians knew that they had benefited greatly from the state's admission to the Union, and they did not wish to give up their benefits. They were also aware that the Republican Congress in Washington, DC, had declared its intention to subsidize the construction of the long sought-after transcontinental railroad connecting the Middle West with the Pacific coast, a project that would unite California and the Union in fact as well as in law.[49] The cause of pro-Unionism was also promoted by the arrival in California in April 1860 of an eloquent Unitarian minister from Boston named Thomas Starr King. King was an abolitionist who spoke widely throughout the northern part of the state in favor of California's remaining in the Union, affirming the prevailing opinion that California and the United States were indissoluble.[50] Reflecting the views of most Californians, the legislature passed a resolution stating that the people of California were "devoted to the Constitution and Union of the United States" and that they would "not fail in fidelity and fealty to that Constitution and Union, now in the hour of trial and peril." The resolution was approved by both houses of the legislature on May 17, 1861, and signed by the Democratic governor John G. Downey three days later.[51]

A small number of men left California to join the Confederates on the field of battle, but many more volunteered to protect the state and fight in behalf of the Union. More than sixteen thousand Californians volunteered during the war to make up two full regiments of cavalry, eight full regiments of infantry, one battalion of native California cavalry, and one battalion of mountaineers, most of whom were assigned to home guard duty.[52] A "California Battalion" of five hundred men sailed east and joined the 2nd Massachusetts Cavalry, and a "California Column" marched east from southern California through Arizona to New Mexico to protect those territories from Confederate attack.[53]

Even more important than the fighting men from California who joined the Union cause, however, was the gold that was sent by sea from

California via Panama to the Atlantic states. The wealth extracted from California's mines was truly the "treasure" that it was called during the early 1850s, and it was now pouring into the Union coffers and helping Abraham Lincoln and his armies buy the armaments, the transportation vehicles, the food, the medical supplies, and all the other essential items needed to keep his armies in the field. Two or three steamers left San Francisco each month loaded with California "treasure." In 1864 alone, some forty-six million dollars worth of minerals was sent. Lincoln was impressed by the mineral wealth of California and the other western states, which he believed was "practically inexhaustible."[54] He was not the only one, however, for U. S. Grant was also quoted as saying: "I do not know what we would do in this great national emergency were it not for the gold sent from California."[55]

California Republicans, once frozen out of elected office, won some elections, running with Democrats of David Broderick's free soil–leaning persuasion under the joint title of the Union Party. One of the first notable political victors was Leland Stanford, who served as governor of the state in 1862 and 1863. Stanford had been a merchant in Sacramento when Archy Lee's case was argued there. Edwin Bryant Crocker, one of the first lawyers to represent Archy, was the brother of one of Stanford's business partners, Charles Crocker. With Stanford, Collis P. Huntington, and Mark Hopkins, Charles Crocker later became one of the "Big Four" railroad moguls who built the western section of the transcontinental railroad that was completed in 1869, uniting the East and West Coasts of the country with iron rails. Edwin Bryant Crocker himself became the chief legal counsel of the railroad and served as a justice of the California Supreme Court by appointment of Stanford in 1863 and 1864. Frederick F. Low, another Republican, followed Stanford to the governor's chair in 1864, where he served through 1867, thus becoming the first California governor to serve four years. But Low was followed by Henry Haight, a Democrat who served through 1871.

Republican legislators in California were able to pass a bill in 1863 that removed all restrictions on black court testimony in the state.[56] Abraham Lincoln won a much larger majority of California's presidential

votes in 1864 than he had in 1860. In December 1865, California ratified the Thirteenth Amendment to the US Constitution, thus helping to
abolish slavery in every state in the Union. California's US senators were
still chosen from the Democratic Party until 1867, when a Republican
named Cornelius Cole was elected. The Fifteenth Amendment to the US
Constitution, eliminating racial restrictions on voting, became effective
nationally in 1870, though it did so without the help of California, which
did not ratify the amendment until 1962.[57]

No evidence has ever surfaced that Charles Stovall was able to persuade
the governor of Mississippi to issue an extradition request for Archy
Lee. Since Archy had left for British Columbia, such a request would
in any event have been virtually unenforceable. Charles's father Simeon
Stovall continued to live in Carroll County after the outbreak of the
Civil War, maintaining his home plantation there despite the fighting that was raging through much of his state. The Confederate army
sometimes seized local property, mills, or factories there, because they
found it so difficult to maintain their fighting supplies, and without such
seizures they could not continue to fight.[58] Historian Timothy B. Smith
has noted that Carroll County was profoundly affected by the Civil War
fighting. It sent hundreds of men into battle, and some of them never
returned. The county felt the economic effects of the war, including raids
into the area and shortages of food and supplies. According to Smith,
one of the bitterest effects of the war was felt by the people of Carroll
County when, in February 1864, a part of the Third Cavalry of US Colored Troops came into Carroll County, completely surprising the people
and almost paralyzing them with fear.[59]

Simeon Stovall died in May 1870, still in Carroll County. What
happened to Charles Stovall is much more difficult to determine. He may
have joined a Confederate fighting force and attempted to help the government first organized in Montgomery, Alabama, and from June 1861
carried on at Richmond, Virginia. But if he did so the records are unclear.
Many Confederate records were lost or destroyed. He may have moved
to Callahan County, Texas, but little is known of that possibility because

Callahan County did not become fully organized until the 1870s. One researcher has determined that he died after 1862 in Callahan County, Texas, but without offering definite proof.[60]

Mifflin Wistar Gibbs, the black man who had been one of the leaders of San Francisco's A.M.E. Zion Church but followed Archy Lee to Victoria in 1858, had considerable success in British Columbia. He was one of the black community's strongest advocates in the northern land, as well as one of its most successful businessmen. He and his partner, Peter Lester, operated a store that competed with the Hudson's Bay Company. Called Lester & Gibbs, it advertised itself as "dealers in groceries, provisions, boots, shoes, etc.," and solicited business from "miners and the public generally to their very superior stock."[61] He also won an important contract to build a railroad to carry coal across Vancouver Island. As one of the local government leaders wrote, Gibbs was "a superior man and very gentlemanly."[62] But he still hoped to return to the United States, the land of his birth and the land of renewed hopes for a better future. He was finally able to do so in 1870. He went to Oberlin, Ohio, where he studied law, and afterward moved on to Little Rock, Arkansas. There, under the protection of the Reconstruction administration of Republican president U. S. Grant, he was elected as the first black municipal judge in the United States. In 1897, at the age of seventy-four, he earned an additional distinction when Republican president William McKinley named him to be the US consul in Tamatave, Madagascar.[63]

In 1902, Gibbs's autobiography *Shadow and Light* was published in Washington, DC, with an introduction by his friend, the pioneering black educator, Booker T. Washington. In it, Gibbs recalled some of the events that had taken place when he lived in California, and the awful threats that in 1858 had forced him and so many of his fellow blacks to seek shelter in a foreign land, away from their "mother country." He also quoted from famous philosophers who he believed had helped him understand the events he had lived through. One was the French diplomat Talleyrand, who had said: "The lily and thistle may grow together in harmonious proximity, but liberty and slavery delight in the separation."[64] Gibbs died in Little Rock in 1915.[65]

Reverend J. J. Moore, the founder of San Francisco's African Methodist Episcopal Zion Church, also returned to the United States after the Civil War, serving for a time in San Francisco and then departing for the East, where in 1868 he was elected as a bishop of his church and, in 1884, published a *History of the A.M.E Zion Church in America*. Moore was generally regarded as one of the greatest preachers of his time.[66]

Mary Ellen ("Mammy") Pleasant did not migrate to Victoria with Archy, Gibbs, and Moore, although some writers have claimed that she went into the part of Canada that is now known as Ontario to help John Brown prepare for his raid on Harper's Ferry in 1859.[67] If she did that, however (the evidence on the issue is not entirely clear), she returned not long after to San Francisco, where she carried on her business activities and made sustained efforts to help black people avoid discrimination. In 1866 and 1868, she brought a pioneering lawsuit against one of the streetcar companies in the city, seeking damages after the driver of one of the cars refused to stop so she could board.[68] "We don't take colored people in the cars," the driver had shouted out. She won a judgment in the trial court, but it was overturned on appeal when the California Supreme Court ruled that "there was no proof of special damage, nor of any malice, or ill will, or want or violent conduct on the part of the defendant."[69] Despite the loss, the lawsuit established Mary Ellen Pleasant as a courageous civil rights crusader. It also established her legendary status as San Francisco's "Mammy" Pleasant. She continued to feed the legend with writings and recollections through the rest of her long life, which ended in her eighty-ninth year in 1904. As late as 1965, her legend was as robust as ever when, in honor to one of her lifetime requests, the words "She was a friend of John Brown" were placed on her grave.[70]

Archy Lee had reason to be happy in British Columbia—at least at first. In 1858, he was listed in the *Victoria Gazette* among fifty-four men who had applied for British citizenship. Fifty-three of the applicants were blacks, many from San Francisco.[71] When Colonel Baker visited Victoria in 1860, the fugitives from San Francisco who had not forgotten his courageous defense of Archy in the court of George Pen Johnston gave him a "grand reception."[72] In December 1862, however, the *Pacific Appeal*, a black newspaper published in San Francisco, reported that Archy had come back from Victoria and was working as a barber in Washoe, Nevada Territory.[73] A little over a year and a half later, Archy had apparently returned to the North. In an article titled "Notes of a Trip to Victoria," the *Appeal* told its readers that he was "among the notables of Victoria," remembered as the man "upon whose fate once hung the destinies of the people of California." In the same article, he was described as a "a sober, honest, hard-working man, a respectable citizen of Victoria, and a loyal subject of Her Majesty." But the writer of the *Appeal*'s 1864 story added a curious comment, saying: "It affords me much pleasure to be able to contradict the reports which have been circulated prejudicial to the character of Archie [*sic*] Lee; he follows the lucrative occupation of draying, and has accumulated some property, and is much respected by the community."[74] What were the "prejudicial" reports? The reporter didn't say, leaving it to readers to imagine what they might be. The *Appeal*'s article was widely reprinted, even as far away as Boston, where the famous abolitionist William Lloyd Garrison printed it in his newspaper *The Liberator*.[75]

Only a little over two years later, however, Archy's location seemed to have changed again. In the summer of 1866, he was mentioned in San Francisco's newspapers in connection with a robbery alleged to have been committed aboard one of the steamships that regularly made port in San Francisco. As detailed in the press, the circumstances of what happened were so unusual that they may have constituted a swindle rather than a robbery. It seems that a man from Ohio named Samuel Blackford had arrived in San Francisco as a passenger aboard the steamship *Moses Taylor*, which regularly carried freight and passengers between California and San Juan del Sur on the west coast of Nicaragua. Blackford had lived in California for a couple of years in the early 1850s, but he had returned to his original home before deciding in 1866 to come back to the West Coast, perhaps for just a visit—or maybe to work, the evidence is not clear. As soon as he got off the *Moses Taylor*, however, he claimed that while aboard the boat he had been robbed of "$2,300 in greenbacks." He went to the police and, over a period of several weeks, exchanged information with one of the officers and a local attorney who claimed that they knew about the robbery and that a third man was holding the money, refusing to give it up unless he was given a large reward. But the case got more complicated, and soon the police officer and the attorney were arrested and brought into the local Police Court on suspicion of having participated in a conspiracy to take Blackford's money. After listening to many witnesses, the judge discharged them for want of sufficient evidence. In the meantime, there was discussion about a black man sometimes called Charles Williams (and sometimes referred to as Archie [sic] Lee) who was apparently living in San Francisco. Blackford thought Lee may have been the man who was holding his money, but there was a total lack of evidence that he was doing so. And by the time the newspapers reported the dismissal of the case, it appeared that Archy Lee had completely disappeared.[76]

Archy's mother, Maria, made repeated efforts to discover where her son was living and what happened to him. She wrote letters to San Francisco but was unable to learn anything. His family heard rumors that he was with some Indians and that they were treating him for some kind of sickness, but they did not know whether to believe the rumors or dismiss them as efforts by the Stovalls to find him and bring him back to Mississippi. After the war ended, Archy's brothers Pompey and Quitman lived in Jackson, Mississippi.[77]

Nothing more is known of Archy until November 1873, when his name appeared again in newspapers. The *Sacramento Daily Union* told its readers that "a colored man, who was evidently seriously ill," had been found lying under a tree near the old mouth of the American River, at a point where parties had been obtaining sand for grading purposes. Two or three officers went to the place and found the man the *Union* identified as "Archie [sic] Lee—the original Archie, who was the bone of contention in early days when Judge Burnett rendered his famous decision under the fugitive slave law, giving 'the law to the North and the nigger to the South.'" The *Union* said that Archie had until recently been "stout and hearty, but exposure and dissipation have injured him greatly, and the officers found him very ill." The officers told him he should go to the hospital, but he objected, saying he would "keep [out] of the way," he would "go furder up in de woods, and not bodder anybody." After the officers convinced him that "the hospital was not such a very bad place," he relented and went there.[78]

A week later, the *Union* told its readers that a correspondent of the San Francisco *Chronicle* had intimated that the man found near Sacramento was "not the original Archie who was the subject of Judge Burnett's decision." But the *Union* said the *Chronicle* was "in error," for James Lansing, the city marshal who had custody of Archy at the time his case came up before the state Supreme Court, stated that "the man recently sent to the Hospital is the same person, and Archie himself is very positive that he is."[79]

A black newspaper in San Francisco called *The Elevator: A Weekly Journal of Progress, Equality Before the Law* affirmed the *Union*'s reporting with a long article reviewing the facts of Archy Lee's struggle for freedom in 1858, telling readers that he "was the hero of one of the most exciting times of 15 years ago," adding: "His career in this State began here, and here it seems likely to end."[80]

Archy's life did in fact end there, for he died soon after he was hospitalized. But the story of his struggle for freedom—the story that remembered him as "California's Dred Scott"—did not die. It became part of America's history. Archy was gone, but "The Year of Archy Lee" lived on.

# Acknowledgments

WRITING THIS BOOK WAS AN ADVENTURE. AS I HAVE LEARNED WHILE doing previous books, discovering an intriguing but little known story buried in the pages of American history, attempting to learn more about it, examining records and recollections that preserve some of the details of the story, and reading what, if anything, previous writers have written about it, can lead to a string of discoveries, some surprising, others disappointing, and yet others simply too fascinating to put the story aside. I first came on the story of Archy Lee's struggle for freedom in a short paragraph buried in the middle of a long academic history of California. It immediately captured my interest, in part because my background draws me to important legal squabbles of the past and how they were resolved, in part because my many years of reading California history had never explained the importance of Archy Lee's story and the impact it had on the broader history of the United States. As I pursued the story, however, I learned that it touched on many other aspects of American history: economic, social, political, geographic, religious, racial, and intriguingly personal. Most importantly, I learned that it had played an important part in the struggle over slavery that was then building in intensity and anger throughout the United States. As I continued to research Archy Lee's story, I learned that it occurred in the same year in which the epochal Lincoln-Douglas debates took place in Illinois; the same year in which the nation was convulsed by the congressional debates over the Lecompton Constitution and the possible spread of slavery into Kansas and other western territories; the same year in which the first Atlantic cable was successfully laid by a brother of one of the justices who decided Archy Lee's case in the California Supreme Court, making it possible for communications to fly across the ocean more rapidly than ever before; the same year in which Donati's Comet, the most beautiful comet seen in the nineteenth century and the first ever to be photographed, appeared in the California sky, in the Illinois town in which Abraham Lincoln was preparing for one of his debates with Stephen Douglas, above the Atlantic and into Europe, later to be extolled in a celebratory speech given in San Francisco by Edward D. Baker, Archy Lee's principal California lawyer, the determined foe of slavery who did more than any other man to help Archy achieve his freedom; the same year in which Archy Lee joined hundreds of other free blacks from California on a flight to freedom in the British Crown Colony of Victoria, soon to become part of the Confederation of Canada; and the same year in which New York's anti-slavery senator William H. Seward issued his famous warning of the approach of the "irrepressible conflict" and Mississippi's adamantly pro-slavery senator Jefferson Davis, soon to become president of the Confederate States of America, warned his state legislature that the election of an anti-slavery president would lead inevitably to secession and the dissolution of the American Union.

My research quickly discovered a short book about Archy Lee published in a small collector's edition in San Francisco in 1969 and reissued in 2008 by a small press in Berkeley. The book traces the basic facts of Archy Lee's story, but without tying them into the broader events then occurring in the state and the nation. I discovered that Archy Lee's story was mentioned in a growing number of books about the travails of blacks in California before the Civil War but without examining the national reach of the story. I discovered a handful of academic studies of Archy Lee's experience in the California courts, published in scholarly journals stored on the dimly lit shelves of academic libraries. I did not ignore those studies—I have made every effort to set forth the details of the story told in this book, particularly the legal details, with accuracy and scholarship—but I did not attempt to equal their length for fear that general readers would quickly lose interest in such technical discussions. I also learned that the Archy Lee legal victory in San Francisco had been celebrated in 1858 in the western city's African Methodist Episcopal Zion Church, when the congregation sang a joyous hymn adapted from one originally written by Charles Wesley and given the new title of "The Year of Archy Lee." I also learned that the church is still in operation in San Francisco today, although in a different location from the one it occupied in 1858. I learned that the free blacks who came to California in the antebellum years—there were several thousands of them, though they constituted a small minority of the state's total population—were intensely religious and obtained much of their protection and spiritual consolation from the churches they attended. I learned, after all, that "The Year of Archy Lee" was a story worth telling, in all its aspects and details.

My reading told me much about what happened in 1858, but I wanted to know more and hunted for good sources. In the California State Archives in Sacramento I discovered the original, handwritten text of the California Supreme Court's 1858 decision in *Ex parte Archy*, a case often described as "California's Dred Scott case." In the National Archives in San Bruno, California, I discovered the transcripts of the trial held before US Commissioner George Pen Johnston in 1858, the case that ultimately established Archy Lee's legal freedom. I discovered a great file of newspapers published in California in 1858 in the California Digital Newspaper Collection headquartered at the University of California in Riverside, an online site that contains a massive collection of original newspaper accounts of Archy Lee's struggle for freedom and other amazing events that occurred in 1858. When I discovered newspaper files that were not included in the digital collection, I traced down files of the newspapers collected elsewhere. One that was particularly helpful was a microfilm copy of the 1858 editions of the *Daily Evening Bulletin*, an important newspaper published in San Francisco in the early 1850s and for many years thereafter.

I should name some of the individuals who helped me trace down details of the story or offered encouragement for my work. They include Christine Adams of the California Historical Society in San Francisco; Gail L. Allen of the Douglas County Historical Society in Gardnerville, Nevada; Scott Daniels, Scott Rook, and Matthew Cowan of the Oregon Historical Society in Portland, Oregon; Shawyne Garren of the Douglas County Recorder's Office in Minden, Nevada; Renee Glass of the Springfield-Greene County Library in Springfield, Missouri; Michael

P. Maher of the Nevada Historical Society in Reno, Nevada; Charles L. Miller of the National Archives at San Francisco in San Bruno; the reference archivists at the California State Archives in Sacramento; Kelly-Ann Turkington of the Royal BC Museum in Victoria, British Columbia; and Carol Myers of the San Diego History Center in San Diego. My agent, Matthew Carnicelli, my editor at Lyons Press, Eugene Brissie, Ellen Urban, production editor, and Joshua Rosenberg, copyeditor, all helped in substantial ways to produce the book. For all those I have neglected to remember here, I can offer only my apologies.

# Chronology

**1840**
Approximate year of Archy Lee's birth in Pike County, Mississippi.

**1850**
*September 9.* California admitted to Union as free state.
*September 18.* Federal Fugitive Slave Act becomes law.
*October 1.* Federal census in Carroll County, Mississippi, shows that Charles Stovall's father, Simeon Stovall, owns a total of thirty slaves, including twenty-two males and eight females.

**1852**
*April 15.* California legislature passes its own version of the fugitive slave law.
*August 30.* California Supreme Court upholds constitutionality of the California fugitive slave law in the case of *In re Perkins*.

**1855**
*April 15.* California's fugitive slave law is allowed to lapse.
*November 20–22.* First State Convention of Colored Citizens meets in Colored Methodist Church on Seventh Street in Sacramento.

**1856**
*January 19.* District Judge Benjamin Hayes declares that fourteen blacks held in Los Angeles, including a woman later known as "Biddy" Mason, cannot be taken to Texas as slaves because under California law they are "forever free."

*November 4.* Presidential election. In California, James Buchanan receives fifty-two thousand votes, Millard Fillmore thirty-five thousand, and John C. Frémont thirty thousand.

*December 9–12.* Second Annual Convention of the Colored Citizens of the State of California meets in African Methodist Episcopal Church on Seventh Street in Sacramento.

## 1857

*January.* Archy Lee leaves Carroll County, Mississippi, traveling through Memphis, Tennessee, to Cape Girardeau County, Missouri, with Charles Stovall, son of Simeon Stovall.

*January 9.* David Broderick elected US senator from California.

*January 13.* William Gwin elected US senator from California to succeed himself.

*April 16.* Charles Stovall again leaves Carroll County, Mississippi, saying he will travel over the plains to California "for his health."

*About June 20.* Stovall meets Archy at the crossing of the North Platte River, and they join to continue their journey to California. Passing through Carson Valley in land later part of Nevada, he leaves his team of enfeebled cattle behind to cross over the mountains to California.

*About October 2.* Archy Lee and Charles Stovall arrive together in Sacramento, California.

*October 13.* Third convention of Colored People meets in St. Cyprian's African Methodist Episcopal Church on Jackson Street in San Francisco.

*November 16.* San Francisco's *Daily Evening Bulletin* reports that the newly adopted constitution of the State of Oregon forbids blacks from entering the state.

## 1858

*About January 3.* Stovall puts Archy on riverboat to be taken to San Francisco and thence on to Mississippi. Archy escapes to Sacramento's black-owned Hackett House.

*January 4.* California's legislature convenes for its ninth session in Sacramento.

*January 6.* Stovall files affidavit with justice of the peace, who issues warrant for Archy's arrest as fugitive slave. Police officer arrests Archy in Hackett House, where he is hiding.

*January 7.* County Judge Robert Robinson issues writ of habeas corpus sought by Charles Parker, one of the black owners of the Hackett House, requiring the city marshal to produce Archy in his court at 2:00 p.m. and show authority for his detention.

*January 8.* California's Know-Nothing governor J. Neely Johnson leaves office and is succeeded by pro-southern John B. Weller. Judge Robinson holds hearing on petition for writ of habeas corpus. At Charles Parker's side are attorneys Edwin B. Crocker and John H. McKune. Charles Stovall is represented by pro-slavery attorney James H. Hardy. When Judge Robinson asks Archy if he wants to be set free, Archy is silent. Stovall then files petition with US Commissioner George Pen Johnston, who is in Sacramento to attend governor's inauguration, to return Archy to Mississippi as a slave under federal Fugitive Slave Act.

*January 9.* Commissioner Johnston returns to San Francisco to confer with US Circuit Judge Matthew Hall McAllister.

*January 13.* Johnston returns to Sacramento and decides he does not have jurisdiction to order Archy back to Mississippi since Archy Lee did not cross state lines in running away from Stovall but made his strike for freedom within the boundaries of the State of California.

*January 18.* Assemblyman A. G. Stakes introduces severely anti-slavery bill providing that where any slave will be or has been brought by his owner into California, if only travelling through the state or in good faith sojourning therein without the intention of permanently residing, and such slave escapes, he shall not be free but shall be delivered up to his owner.

*January 23.* Since Johnston declined jurisdiction, County Judge Robert Robinson again takes up Archy Lee's case. Archy's attorney is now Joseph W. Winans. Robinson again asks Archy if he wishes to remain in California or return to Mississippi. This time he answers: "I don't understand what you are speaking of, but I want it to come out right. I don't want to go back to Mississippi."

*January 26.* Judge Robinson decides that Archy will go free, but he is immediately rearrested, as Stovall's attorneys have filed a petition that will take Archy's case before the California Supreme Court. Archy is again confined in jail.

*February 2.* Assemblyman A. G. Stakes introduces bill in legislature "to prohibit the immigration of free negroes and other obnoxious persons into this State." In Washington, President Buchanan submits Lecompton Constitution to Congress, recommending the admission of Kansas to the Union as a slave state.

*February 3.* In California, State Senator Samuel Johnson presents a petition from citizens to repeal laws prohibiting Negroes and mulattoes from giving testimony; he says he is opposed to the petition but presents it on behalf of his constituents. In Washington, DC, Illinois's US senator Stephen Douglas condemns the Lecompton Constitution as a violation of "popular sovereignty" and a mockery of justice.

*February 5.* California Supreme Court hears "Archy's case." Chief Justice David S. Terry and Associate Justice Peter H. Burnett are on the bench, but Associate Justice Stephen J. Field is ill and does not attend.

*February 12.* California Supreme Court meets to announce its decision. Opinion written by Burnett says that Archy is a free man, but the Court will nonetheless order that he be returned to Mississippi as a slave. Justice Field later states that he opposes the decision. Archy is returned to jail, while a large crowd follows behind. Archy tries three times to escape, but he is not successful and is returned to prison. Newspapers roundly ridicule the Supreme Court decision.

*February 17.* San Francisco Board of Education orders that blacks not be permitted to attend any school except the one established for them, and directs that those in attendance at any other public school be removed.

*February 18.* Newspaper in City of Stockton south of Sacramento reports that Archy has been taken there and put in jail for "safekeeping."

*February 24.* San Francisco's *Daily Evening Bulletin* reports that Archy's whereabouts are not known, with many speculating that he has been sent back to Mississippi either by sea or by overland travel across the

Great Plains. Black San Franciscan named James Riker signs affidavit for writ of habeas corpus to free Archy from Stovall's confinement.

*March.* Apprehensive about the arrival of federal troops in the Great Salt Lake Valley, about thirty thousand followers of Brigham Young leave to settle farther south.

*March 5.* Crowds gather along San Francisco's busy waterfront, expecting Archy to be secretly put aboard a steamship headed for Panama. Police take boat out into the Bay, board the Panama-bound steamer *Orizaba,* and rescue Archy from Stovall and other men who are attempting to put him aboard. Stovall says the Supreme Court has given Archy to him, and "he'd be G-d d—d" if any other court would take him away from him. But the police are able to rescue him and take him to the county jail to await a hearing the following Monday morning. "The colored population are all out, and Archy is the observed of all observers." San Francisco blacks hold an emergency meeting in the Athenaeum on Washington Street, where they raise money for Archy's defense.

*March 6.* Stovall is arraigned in police court on charge of kidnapping Archy Lee, but charges against him are dismissed because his arrest warrant was sworn to before deputy county clerk instead of a "proper judicial magistrate."

*March 8.* Hearing opens before County Judge T. W. Freelon. Corridors of City Hall on Kearny Street are crowded with spectators, both black and white. Hearing is continued.

*March 17.* With affidavit signed by Charles Stovall, case is brought back before US Commissioner George Pen Johnston. Attorneys for Archy Lee and Stovall agree to dismissal by Judge Freelon. Archy is taken from City Hall on Kearny Street to Merchants' Exchange on Battery Street, with crowd numbering between five and six hundred following, shouting and pushing. Two angry blacks, including a preacher who has come from the gold country, are arrested.

*March 18.* Archy is brought before Commissioner Johnston. Courtroom is filled, but only with whites, as colored people are excluded. Stovall's attorney James H. Hardy asks Johnston to decide case immediately, as Stovall is leaving for Panama and wants to take Archy with him. Archy's lead attorney is Colonel Edward D. Baker.

*March 19.* Attorney Edwin M. Stanton, who will become secretary of war under Abraham Lincoln, arrives in San Francisco to help US district attorney assert federal ownership of New Almaden quicksilver mine south of San Jose. California assemblyman J. B. Warfield of Nevada County introduces bill to prevent immigration to and residence of Negroes and mulattoes in state. Johnston convenes court in courtroom of Judge Hall McAllister, saying he does not want to decide case "on technical points" but on "issues of fact." Hardy argues that since fugitive slaves have no right to testify and no right to counsel under the federal Fugitive Slave Act, Baker has no right to participate in case. Baker says that, before right to counsel can be decided, it must first be decided if Archy is in fact a slave.

*March 20.* Charles Stovall files affidavit "in explanation of the original affidavit filed in the present proceedings," saying that Archy committed a crime against the laws of Mississippi when he stabbed "a white man whose name was Smiley, with a certain knife, with a felonious intention," and "because of said offence said Archy did flee from the said state of Mississippi."

*March 22.* Unfounded rumor circulates that Archy Lee has been taken aboard a revenue cutter for transfer to a mail steamer *Sonora* leaving for Panama. Blacks are patrolling waterfront. In a speech delivered in US Senate, California's Senator Broderick declares his support of free labor and opposition to slavery, saying: "Slavery is old, decrepit, and consumptive; freedom is young, strong, and vigorous."

*March 23.* US Senate votes to admit Kansas under Lecompton Constitution.

*March 25.* Black citizens gather in San Francisco's A.M.E. Zion Church in support of Archy Lee.

*March 29.* Assembly bill preventing Negroes and mulattoes from entering California is defeated through parliamentary maneuvers. Archy Lee's case resumes before Commissioner Johnston. Witnesses testify.

*March 30.* Case continues before Commissioner Johnston in crowded courtroom. Case is continued until the following Tuesday, a week later.

*March 31.* San Francisco's *Daily Alta California* publishes interview with Archy Lee.

*April 1.* In Washington, House of Representatives votes to resubmit Lecompton Constitution to popular vote.

*April 5.* Steamer *John L. Stephens* leaves San Francisco for Panama with Mary Ellen ("Mammy") Pleasant on board.

*April 6.* Commissioner Johnston hears closing arguments made by James H. Hardy for Stovall and by W. H. Tompkins and Edward D. Baker for Archy.

*April 7.* Hardy has gone to Sacramento, presumably to obtain more evidence. In his place G. J. Whelan represents Stovall. Edward D. Baker speaks of the differences between the fugitive slave laws of 1793 and 1850, displaying his eloquence.

*April 14.* US Circuit Courtroom is crowded as Johnston reads decision declaring that Archy Lee is not subject to the Fugitive Slave Act and is thus a free man. A joyous group led by Colonel Baker, James Riker, and Peter Anderson, one of the leaders of California's Colored Convention movement, walk to jailhouse to receive Archy. In the evening, a large gathering of blacks in the African Methodist Episcopal Zion Church talk of danger they feel living in California and consider possibility of emigrating to some more hospitable land or territory, possibly to Vancouver Island in the British colonies or the State of Sonora in Mexico. But no decisions are made.

*April 15.* Even larger congregation gathers in A.M.E. Zion Church and sings the hymn to "The Year of Archy Lee." Archy may be housed in boardinghouse run by "Mammy" Pleasant.

*April 20.* Archy Lee and large group of San Francisco blacks leave San Francisco on steamer *Columbia* for Victoria.

*April 23.* Assembly bill to prevent Negroes and mulattoes from entering California dies as it is recommitted to committee in State Senate.

*April 26.* California's state legislature adjourns. Samuel Brooks, former San Joaquin County treasurer and recent nominee of Governor Weller to the office of state controller, meets George Pen Johnston at San Francisco's Apollo Hall, calls him a "Black Republican" and says he "robbed Stovall of his Nigger."

*April 30.* US Supreme Court issues decision in *Fossat* case relating to ownership of New Almaden quicksilver mine.

*May 6.* Archy Lee and other blacks are in Victoria.

*June 2.* Brilliant comet is seen streaking across the sky. After the Great Comet of 1811, it is the most brilliant comet to appear in the nineteenth century. Baker observes it in San Francisco, where the *Daily Evening Bulletin* tells readers that the comet has come to prompt mankind to repent of its many transgressions before the approach of death.

*June 7.* *Sacramento Daily Union* says that Archy Lee and the other people who left San Francisco for the northern country "are delighted with the equality and fraternity accorded them."

*June 16.* Abraham Lincoln delivers his "House Divided" speech to Republican state convention in Illinois, saying "A house divided against itself cannot stand. I believe the government cannot endure permanently half slave and half free. I do not expect the Union to be dissolved; I do not expect the house to fall; but I do expect it will cease to be divided. It will become all one thing, or all the other."

*July 24.* Lincoln challenges Stephen Douglas to series of joint debates.

*August 2.* Lecompton Constitution is rejected in Kansas by vote of 11,812 against to 1,926 in favor.

*August 5.* Laying of the telegraph cable joining Valentia, Ireland, and Trinity Bay, Newfoundland, is completed by Cyrus West Field, Stephen Field's brother.

*August 16.* Queen Victoria sends message to President Buchanan over Atlantic Telegraph cable.

*August 19.* George Pen Johnston clashes with attorney named William L. Ferguson in San Francisco's Bank Exchange Saloon.

*August 21.* Johnston and Ferguson meet in duel on Angel Island, where Ferguson is shot.

*August 21.* Lincoln and Douglas meet in first debate in Ottawa.

*August 27.* Lincoln and Douglas meet in second debate in Freeport.

*September 14.* On eve of his third debate with Douglas, Lincoln sits on porch of his hotel in Jonesboro, Illinois, for an hour or more to observe Donati's Comet.

*September 15.* Lincoln and Douglas meet in third debate in Jonesboro.

*September 16.* Edward D. Baker delivers eulogy for deceased William L. Ferguson in State Senate in Sacramento.

*September 18.* Lincoln and Douglas meet in fourth debate in Charleston.

*September 27.* Baker delivers official oration in San Francisco to commemorate laying of Atlantic cable. He also refers to Donati's Comet. The oration is said to be his "most poetic."

*October 7.* Lincoln and Douglas meet in fifth debate in Galesburg, Illinois.

*October 13.* Lincoln and Douglas meet in sixth debate in Quincy.

*October 14.* Lincoln and Douglas meet in seventh and final debate in Alton.

*October 25.* New York senator William H. Seward, speaking at Rochester, New York, delivers a speech in which he calls the sectional controversy "an irrepressible conflict between opposing and enduring forces, and it means that the United States must and will, sooner or later, become either a slaveholding nation or entirely a free-labor nation."

*October 29.* US Circuit Judge Matthew Hall McAllister and US District Judge Ogden Hoffman Jr. issue highly publicized injunction shutting down operation of New Almaden quicksilver mine pending final determination of its ownership.

*November 16.* US senator Jefferson Davis addresses Mississippi's legislature, defending slavery and stating that if opponents of slavery should ever seek to amend the Constitution to abolish slavery he would urge Mississippi to resist, even if it became necessary to go through "all the storms and clouds of war."

## 1859

*September 13.* California chief justice David S. Terry shoots Senator David Broderick in a duel.

*September 16.* Broderick dies of wound suffered in duel with Terry.

*September 20.* Edward D. Baker delivers long and impassioned eulogy of Broderick before the largest crowd ever assembled in California up to that date. He reveals that Broderick's last words were: "I died because I was opposed to a corrupt administration and the extension of slavery."

## 1860

*October 2.* Edward D. Baker is elected US senator from Oregon. He is the first Republican to win an important political position on the Pacific coast.

*October 26.* On his way to Washington, DC, Baker stops in San Francisco, where he delivers a stirring speech before a large crowd in the American Theater. It is called his "Apostrophe to Freedom" Speech.

*November 6.* Lincoln is elected president.

*December 24.* Baker is reunited with Lincoln in Springfield, Illinois. Lincoln asks him to introduce him at his inauguration in Washington.

## 1861

*March 4.* Edward Baker rides with President-Elect Lincoln, outgoing President Buchanan, and Senator James Pearce of Maryland from White House to Capitol for Lincoln's inauguration. On portico of Capitol, Baker introduces Lincoln to crowd.

*August 21.* Having volunteered to lead a regiment of Union army troops, Edward Baker is killed at Ball's Bluff on the Virginia side of the Potomac River. Lincoln is devastated by his death.

## 1862

*December 20. Pacific Appeal,* a weekly black newspaper in San Francisco, reports that Archy Lee has returned from British Columbia and is working as barber in Washoe, Nevada.

## 1863

*November 13.* Joined by a group of supporters, California's Senator John Conness presents a cane once owned by David Broderick to Abraham Lincoln, who heaps praise on Broderick.

## 1866

*June.* Samuel Blackford arrives in San Francisco on steamship *Moses Taylor* and claims that he has been robbed of "$2,300 in greenbacks." He thinks that Archy Lee may have his money. A police investigation reveals no evidence linking Archy to the theft, although there are reports that he is in San Francisco.

*July 19. Alta* reports that Archy Lee has "skedaddled."

## 1873

*November 14.* Black newspapers in San Francisco and Sacramento report that Archy Lee was found seriously ill on a bank of the American River just outside Sacramento, buried in sand up to his head, probably because of a fever, and refusing any help. He had been camping there for several months. He is sent to County Hospital, where he dies.

# NOTES

Full details for each reference in the notes may be found in the bibliography.

## INTRODUCTION

1. Charles Wesley, *Hymns for New-Year's Day*, Hymn 3.
2. "Second Meeting of the Colored People," *Daily Evening Bulletin*, April 16, 1858, 3; see *The African Methodist Episcopal Hymn and Tune Book Adapted for the Doctrines and Usages of the Church*, 5th ed., 74–75.
3. California Constitution of 1849, Art. I, Sec. 18. The Constitution was adopted in 1849 but approved by Congress and the president in 1850.
4. "Obituary," *The Elevator*, June 27, 1874, 2.
5. Howay, "The Negro Immigration into Vancouver Island in 1858," 102.
6. McClain, "Pioneers on the Bench: The California Supreme Court, 1849–1879," 51.
7. Ethington, *The Public City: The Political Construction of Urban Life in San Francisco, 1850–1900*, 186.
8. McGinty, *John Brown's Trial*, details the judicial proceedings that followed Brown's Harper's Ferry raid. The name of the town was Harper's Ferry, Virginia, in 1859; it is Harpers Ferry, West Virginia, today.
9. During the 1850s, a series of trials were brought under the Fugitive Slave Act of 1850 testing the ability of slave owners to recapture slaves who had fled to the North. Lubet, *Fugitive Justice: Runaways, Rescuers, and Slavery on Trial*, tells the stories of three of the most important of these trials. Vandervelde, *Redemption Songs: Suing for Freedom before Dred Scott*, x, xi, 3, describes a determined and dramatically resourceful research effort in St. Louis that turned up the records of about three hundred judicial proceedings commenced between 1814 and 1860 in which blacks, some free and some slave, tried to obtain court orders establishing their freedom under state laws. The same book tells the dramatic stories of a dozen of those efforts.

## A SLAVE FROM PIKE COUNTY

1. Ownby and Wilson, *Mississippi Encyclopedia*, 997.
2. John Hebron Moore, *Agriculture in Ante-Bellum Mississippi*, 57.
3. Although kind or benevolent masters were sometimes reluctant to whip their slaves, whipping was very common in Mississippi and other slave states for the simple reason that slaves made profits for their masters when they worked hard and rapidly but not

when they did not. Slaves were often whipped for picking "trashy" cotton (cotton with leaves, rocks, or dirt mixed in) or for not picking enough. When they were whipped, they were often given fifty to one hundred lashes, and runaway slaves were often scarred by whip marks. See Libby, *Slavery and Frontier Mississippi, 1720–1835*, 43, 54, 80, 81–82. Charles S. Sydnor, a Mississippi historian with more sympathy for slaveholders than for slaves, stated that whipping was used "to force or persuade slaves to labor" because "the ordinary incentives to labor which operate on free men were lacking in slavery." He added that "the usual mode of punishing negroes [*sic*] was with the whip" and that this was so severely applied that permanent marks were sometimes left on their bodies. Sydnor, *Slavery in Mississippi*, 86–87.

4. A "major function of Anglo-American law for three centuries [was] the creation and maintenance of a system in which human beings were regularly sold, bred, and distributed like beasts." Noonan, *Persons and Masks of the Law: Cardozo, Holmes, Jefferson and Wythe as Makers of the Masks*, 10.

5. Petition of C.A. Stovall for Habeas Corpus to Supreme Court of California, subscribed and sworn to on January 26, 1858, certified copy in Case Files of the US Commissioner, RG 21, National Archives and Records Administration, San Bruno, California.

6. The letter was sent to Carter G. Woodson, editor of the *Journal of Negro History*, in response to the article entitled "Slavery in California" by Delilah L. Beasley, published in that journal in January 1918 (vol. 3, no. 1:33–44). The letter was published in the same journal under the heading of "Notes" in October 1918 (vol. 3, no. 3: 333), and again in Delilah Beasley's *The Negro Trail Blazers of California; a Compilation of Records from the California Archives in the Bancroft Library at the University of California in Berkeley, and from the Diaries, Old Papers and Conversations of Old Pioneers in the State of California*, 83.

7. See Lapp, *Blacks in Gold Rush California*, 25.

8. Donald E. Bishop, *Descendants of Bartholomew Stovall (1665–1721) (First Five American Generations)*, 1–244, 245.

9. A visit to an online genealogical site on October 16, 2017, revealed 399,376 entries under the name Stovall. See https://www.ancestry.com/search/?name=_Stovall&name_x=1_1. References to individuals associated with the family of Simeon Stovall are, however, rare. See Wiltshire, *Mississippi Index of Wills 1800–1900*, 192–93 (eight Stovalls); Wiltshire, *Mississippi Pioneers, with Abstracts of Wills 1834–1875 & Divorces, 1857–1875*, 311 (eight Stovalls); Boyd, *Family Maps of Carroll County, Mississippi*, 50, 216 (one reference to Simeon Stovall).

10. 1850 Federal Census Slave Schedules, Southern Division of Carroll County, State of Mississippi, October 1, 1850.

11. 1860 Federal Census Slave Schedules, Fifth Police District of Carroll County, State of Mississippi, October 6, 1860.

12. Witnesses who testified in California in 1858 uniformly declared that Archy was worth "about $1,500 'at home.'" See, e.g., "The Sacramento Fugitive Slave Case," *San Francisco Bulletin*, January 25, 1858, 2; "Case of Archy—The Fugitive Slave," *Sacramento Daily Union*, January 25, 1858, 2; "The Sacramento Fugitive Slave Case," *New York Times*, March 1, 1858, 3. Moore, *Agriculture in Ante-Bellum Mississippi*, 180, states

that the average price of able-bodied field hands in the New Orleans market rose from seven hundred dollars in 1845 to eleven hundred dollars in 1850 and eighteen hundred dollars in 1860. Howay, "The Negro Immigration into Vancouver Island in 1858," 103, gives the value of Archy Lee in Mississippi as fifteen hundred dollars.

13. 1850 Federal Census, Mississippi, Carroll County.

14. 1860 Federal Census, Mississippi, Carroll County.

15. See Sydnor, *Slavery in Mississippi*, 191–92.

16. See Howay, "The Negro Immigration into Vancouver Island in 1858," 102–3 (referring to the Stovall property in Mississippi).

17. Testimony of D. R. Doyle, January 23, 1858, in *Sacramento Daily Union*, "Case of Archy—The Fugitive Slave," January 25, 1858, 2.

18. *The Twenty-Seventh Annual Catalogue of the Officers and Students of Centre College, at Danville, Kentucky, for the Year Ending June 26th, 1851*. Danville, KY. Published by the Students. Printed at the Lexington Observer & Reporter Office, 1851. Catalogue of Students, 14.

19. Testimony of Ira Cross in *C.A. Stovall vs. Archy (a slave)* taken before US Commissioner George Pen Johnston in San Francisco in March 1858, Case Files of the US Commissioner.

20. Under the slave code of Mississippi, slaves could not be taught to read or write. This command was rarely violated, and only under particular circumstances. See discussion in *Sydnor, Slavery in Mississippi*, 53–54.

21. By the end of the 1830s, the production of cotton in Mississippi already exceeded that of all other states. Beckert, *Empire of Cotton: A Global History*, 104. A total of 1,705,650 acres were added to the state's production in the 1850s, enabling it to continue to be the leading cotton-producing state in the South up to the Civil War. John Hebron Moore, *The Emergence of the Cotton Kingdom in the Old Southwest: Mississippi, 1770–1860*, 285, 286.

22. See John Hebron Moore, *Agriculture in Ante-Bellum Mississippi*, 13–36, 97; McPherson, *Battle Cry of Freedom*, 6–7, 100–102; Stampp, *The Peculiar Institution: Slavery in the Ante-Bellum South*, 408–9; Beckert, *Empire of Cotton: A Global History*, 242–43.

23. In a speech in the US Senate on March 4, 1858, Senator James Henry Hammond of South Carolina said the North "dare not make war on cotton. No power on earth dares to make war upon it. Cotton is king." Hammond, *Selections from the Letters and Speeches of the Hon. James H. Hammond, of South Carolina* (New York: John F. Trow & Co., 1866), 317–22, from *Congressional Globe*, 35th Congress 1st session, 961–92. See also Charles Francis Adams Jr., "The Reign of King Cotton," *Atlantic Monthly* (April 1861), 451–65; Beckert, *Empire of Cotton*, 41, 81, 85, 88, 91, etc.

24. "Archy's Story," *Daily Alta California*, March 31, 1858, 2; "Archy's Story," *Sacramento Union*, April 2, 1858, 3.

25. Without offering any evidence, Secrest, *Dark and Tangled Threads of Crime: San Francisco's Famous Police Detective, Isaiah W. Lees*, 71, erroneously states that Archy "eventually returned to live out his life in Mississippi."

26. "Archy's Story," *Daily Alta California*, March 31, 1858, 2; "Archy's Story," *Sacramento Union*, April 2, 1858, 3.

27. "The Archy Case Continued," *Daily Alta California*, March 30, 1858, 1.
28. Shirley Ann Wilson Moore, *Sweet Freedom's Plains: African Americans on the Overland Trails, 1841–1869*, 3.
29. Mattes, *Platte River Road Narratives*, 2–5.
30. For extensive discussion about blacks traveling over the plains, see Shirley Ann Wilson Moore, *Sweet Freedom's Plains*, especially chs. 3, 4, and 5.
31. Ibid., 3.
32. Ibid., 9, 111–12.
33. Lapp, *Blacks in Gold Rush California*, 25.
34. "The Archy Case Again Continued," *Daily Alta California*, March 31, 1858, 1.
35. Wallis, *The Best Land Under Heaven: The Donner Party in the Age of Manifest Destiny*, 35.
36. Affidavits of Charles A. Stovall and William D. Stovall in *C.A. Stovall vs. Archy (a slave)*, given before US Commissioner George Pen Johnston, San Francisco, March 1858, Case Files of the US Commissioner; "The Archy Case Continued," *Daily Alta California*, March 30, 1858, 1.
37. See Lapp, *Blacks in Gold Rush California*, 29; Shirley Ann Wilson Moore, *Sweet Freedom's Plains: African Americans on the Overland Trails, 1841–1869*, 145–47.
38. Sydnor, *Slavery in Mississippi*, 249–50.
39. Stampp, *The Peculiar Institution: Slavery in the Ante-Bellum South*, 378–79.
40. "Letter from San Francisco," *Sacramento Daily Union*, March 22, 1858, 4.
41. According to historian George R. Stewart, what later became known as the California Trail was originally called the Oregon Trail because the trails to those two regions followed the same routes before branching off far to the northwest. See George R. Stewart, *The California Trail: An Epic with Many Heroes*, 8.
42. "Brief for Respondent" by E. D. Baker, of counsel, and Crosby & Tompkins, attorneys for Respondent, in *C.A. Stovall vs. Archy (a slave)*, before US Commissioner George Pen Johnston, San Francisco, Case Files of the US Commissioner.
43. Paher, *Nevada Ghost Towns and Mining Camps*, 55–56.
44. Testimony of J. Milburn, March 29, 1858, given in *C.A. Stovall vs. Archy (a slave)* before US Commissioner George Pen Johnston, San Francisco, Case Files of the US Commissioner.
45. *In re Archy*, 9 Cal. 147, 161 (1858).

## THE BLACK HEART OF THE GOLD COUNTRY

1. News of the gold discovery reached San Francisco in March 1848 and California's old Mexican capital of Monterey in June, but it was not communicated to the broader world until President James K. Polk confirmed it in his annual address on December 5. *Congressional Globe*, 30th Congress, 2nd Session, December 5, 1848, 4; Morris, *Encyclopedia of American History*, 6th ed., 247.
2. Hart, *A Companion to California*, new ed., 190.
3. The precise numbers of the estimates are $245,301 in 1848, $10,151,360 in 1849, $41,273,106 in 1850, $75,938,232 in 1851, $81,294,700 in 1852, $67,613,487 in 1853, and $55,485,395 in 1855. Ibid., 189–90.

4. The word *genocide* has been used to describe violence directed against ethnic and racial groups in many parts of the world. It has also been used to describe the dramatic decline of the population of the California Indians in the nineteenth century. This use has aroused doubts as to whether it is appropriate. See David E. Stannard, *American Holocaust: The Conquest of the New World* (New York: Oxford University Press, 1992); Dominick J. Schaller and Jürgen Zimmerer, eds., *The Origins of Genocide: Raphael Lemkin as a Historian of Mass Violence* (New York: Routledge, 2009); Brendan C. Lindsay, *Murder State: California's Native American Genocide, 1846–1873* (Lincoln: University of Nebraska Press, 2012); Benjamin Madley, *An American Genocide: The United States and the California Indian Catastrophe, 1846–1873* (New Haven, CT: Yale University Press, 2016). The word was coined in 1944 by a Polish lawyer to describe the slaughter of millions of Jews during World War II, and it was legally defined in 1948 when the United Nations General Assembly adopted the Convention on the Prevention and Punishment of the Crime of Genocide. Whether the fate that befell the California Indians in the nineteenth century was comparable to that of the Jews in the twentieth-century Holocaust is a question that has been debated. Historian Alan Taylor has described the use of the word in this context as "rhetorically double-edged," writing that it sheds "more heat than light" and "ultimately obscures the decentralized and populist nature" of the killing of the California Indians. See Alan Taylor, "'An American Genocide' by Benjamin Madley," *New York Times Book Review,* May 27, 2016. Historian Richard White acknowledges that the impact of the word "has been diminished through overuse," but he has accepted Madley's use of it to describe the truly terrible treatment of the California Indians. See Richard White, "Naming America's Own Genocide," *The Nation,* August 17, 2016.

5. "Comparative Table of Population," in *The Seventh Census of the United States: 1850: An appendix. J.D.B. DeBow, Superintendent of the United States Census.* Washington: Robert Armstrong, Printer, 1853; *Population of the United States in 1860; Compiled from the Original Returns of the Eighth Census under the Direction of the Secretary of the Interior, by Joseph C.G. Kennedy, Superintendent of Census.* Washington: Government Printing Office, 1864.

6. See Mason, *The Census of 1790: A Demographic History of Colonial California,* 45, stating that the founders of the pueblo of Los Angeles "were generally known to have been of Indian and African ancestry."

7. Salomon, *Pío Pico: The Last Governor of Mexican California,* 12.

8. Ibid., 3–9, 13.

9. Lapp, *Blacks in Gold Rush California,* 33.

10. Ibid., 18, 39.

11. Ibid., 267–69.

12. Shirley Ann Wilson Moore, *Sweet Freedom's Plains: African Americans on the Overland Trails, 1841–1869,* 157.

13. Chan, "A People of Exceptional Character," 67; Lapp, *Blacks in Gold Rush California,* 50.

14. D.S. Cutter & Co., *Sacramento City Directory for the Year A.D. 1860,* Sacramento: H.S. Crocker & Co., 1859, xxix (giving populations for 1859).

15. Lapp, *Blacks in Gold Rush California*, 57.

16. Ibid., 65.

17. Ibid., 70–74.

18. Ibid., 42.

19. Chan, "A People of Exceptional Character," 67.

20. Lapp, *Blacks in Gold Rush California*, 21.

21. Ibid., xi.

22. *New Bedford Mercury*, August 22, 1849, as quoted in Lapp, *Blacks in Gold Rush California*, 13.

23. Gudde, *California Place Names*, 258.

24. Loosley, *Foreign Born Population of California, 1848–1920*, 33, as quoted in Chan, "A People of Exceptional Character," 49.

25. Completed in 1856, the small Sacramento Valley Railroad extended inland only twenty-three miles to the foothill town of Folsom. The Central Pacific Railroad, which eventually climbed over the Sierra Nevada and went on to meet the Union Pacific Railroad at Promontory Summit, Utah, in 1869, was formed in October 1861, but it did not begin construction until late 1862 and early 1863. Orsi, *Sunset Limited: The Southern Pacific Railroad and the Development of the American West, 1850–1930*, 5–10, 17.

26. "California Legislature—Fifth Session," *Sacramento Daily Union*, February 27, 1854, 3 (bill fixing permanent location of the state capital signed by the governor on February 25, 1854).

27. Lapp, *Blacks in Gold Rush California*, 22, 78.

28. Affidavit of Samuel J. Noble, in *C.A. Stovall vs. Archy (a slave)*, given before US Commissioner George Pen Johnston, San Francisco, March 1858, Case Files of the US Commissioner.

29. *In re Archy*, 9 Cal. 147, 161 (1858).

30. "The Archy Case Continued," *Daily Alta California*, March 29, 1858, 1.

31. Bancroft, *History of California*, 7:313.

32. See Richards, *The California Gold Rush and the Coming of the Civil War*, 39 (Gwin owned several plantations in Mississippi, plus three that he rented out, and almost 200 slaves); Matthews, *The Golden State in the Civil War: Thomas Starr King, the Republican Party, and the Birth of Modern California*, 34–35 (Gwin never severed his ties to Mississippi, including the ownership of 200 slaves).

33. See Brands, *The Age of Gold*, 279; Quinn, *The Rivals*, 68–69; Richards, *The California Gold Rush and the Coming of the Civil War*, 71–73, 79–82. Gerald Stanley, "Senator William Gwin: Moderate or Racist?," 243–55, argues persuasively that Gwin was a racist and that he favored slavery throughout his political career.

34. California Constitution of 1849, Art. I, Sec. 18; Shirley Ann Wilson Moore, "'We Feel the Want of Protection': The Politics of Law and Race in California, 1848–1878," 103.

35. Starr, *California: A History*, 96.

36. Fehrenbacher, *The Slaveholding Republic*, 83–87, 269–72; Ibid., 96, 97.

37. US Const., Art. IV, Sec. 2, cl. 3.

38. Fugitive Slave Act of February 12, 1793, Ch. 7, Sec. 3, 1 Stat. 302, 304.

39. Fugitive Slave Act of September 18, 1850, Ch. 60, Sec. 6, 9 Stat. 462, 463.

40. See Stacey L. Smith, *Freedom's Frontier: California and the Struggle over Unfree Labor, Emancipation, and Reconstruction*, 8.

41. Richards, *The California Gold Rush and the Coming of the Civil War*, 37–40; David Alan Johnson, *Founding the Far West: California, Oregon, and Nevada, 1840–1890*, 245–50.

42. David A. Williams, *David C. Broderick: A Political Portrait*, 52; Richards, *The California Gold Rush and the Coming of the Civil War*, 180–82.

43. Gienapp, *The Origins of the Republican Party, 1852–1856*, 305–46.

44. "Sewardism," *Daily Alta California*, March 10, 1855, 2.

45. Shafter, *Life, Diary, and Letters of Oscar Lovell Shafter*, 186.

46. David A. Williams, *David C. Broderick: A Political Portrait*, 28–29.

47. Although it has often been written that Broderick was active in the Tammany Society in New York, his biographer David Williams has written that he was never a member and that he openly incurred its hostility from time to time. Many of his friends and associates were members. Williams, *David C. Broderick: A Political Portrait*, 15.

48. On April 14, 1850, David C. Broderick, Frederick D. Kohler, George W. Green, and William McKibbin founded San Francisco's Empire Engine Co. No. 1. Broderick was the first foreman. See http://guardiansofthecity.org/sffd/companies/volunteer/empire_broderick_engine_co_no1.html (accessed November 20, 2016). See also David A. Williams, *David C. Broderick: A Political Portrait*, 54–55; Quinn, *The Rivals*, 41–42, 56, 57, 58.

49. 1 Cal. Stat (1850), Ch. 38, An Act to regulate elections, Art. II, Sec. 10. The particular wording of this law limited the right to vote to "every white male citizen of the United States, and every white male citizen of Mexico, who shall have elected to become a citizen of the United States, under the treaty of peace exchanged and ratified at Queretaro, on the 30th day of May, 1848 of the age of twenty-one years, who shall have been a resident of the State six months next preceding the election, and the county or district in which he claims his vote thirty days."

50. Cal. Constitution of 1849, Art II, Sec. 1.

51. 1 Cal. Stat. (1850), Ch. 99, An Act concerning Crimes and Punishments, Third Division, Sec. 14.

52. Lapp, *Blacks in Gold Rush California*, 192.

53. 3 Cal. Stat. (1852), Ch. 33, An Act Respecting Fugitives from Labor, and Slaves Brought to This State Prior to Her Admission into the Union; see Finkelman, "The Law of Slavery and Freedom in California 1848–1860," 452; Stacey L. Smith, *Freedom's Frontier*, 9; Lapp, *Blacks in Gold Rush California*, 139–40.

54. *In re Perkins*, 2 Cal. 424, 438, 439 (1852); "The Fugitive Slave Case," *Daily Alta California*, August 31, 1852, 2. See discussion in Finkelman, "The Law of Slavery and Freedom in California 1848–1860," 454–57; Albin, "The Ordeal of Three Slaves in Gold Rush California," 215–27. This case was commenced as a petition for a writ of habeas corpus. The California Constitution of 1849 specifically empowered the Supreme Court to issue writs of habeas corpus "at the instance of any person held in actual custody." Cal. Const. of 1849, Art. VI, Sec. 4. The legislature enacted a statute

containing specific provisions governing habeas corpus on April 20, 1850. 1 Cal. Stat. (1852), Ch. 122, An Act concerning the Writ of Habeas Corpus. Hugh C. Murray was born in St. Louis, Missouri, in 1821, and raised in nearby Alta, Illinois. He died in Sacramento in September 1857, just as Archy Lee and Charles Stovall were approaching the city. Shuck, *Bench and Bar in California*, 435–36; McClain, "Pioneers on the Bench: The California Supreme Court, 1849–1879," 9–10, 20.

55. *Mason v. Smith* (The Bridget "Biddy" Mason Case), 1856, State of California County of Los Angeles, Before the Hon. Benjamin Hayes, Judge of the District Court of the First Judicial District State of California, County of Los Angeles. University of California, Los Angeles, Department of Special Collections, Charles E. Young Research Library, in Golden States Insurance Company Records. Benjamin Ignatius Hayes was born in Baltimore. In 1850, he became the first American-trained lawyer to practice in Los Angeles. See also "California Freedom Papers," *Journal of Negro History* 3, no. 1 (January 1918): 50–54; Leonard Pitt and Dale Pitt, *Los Angeles A to Z: An Encyclopedia of the City and County*, 192.

56. Hayden, "Biddy Mason's Los Angeles, 1858–1891," 86–99; Pitt and Pitt, *Los Angeles A to Z*, 149–50, 317.

57. David A. Williams, *David C. Broderick: A Political Portrait*, 35–37.

58. Quintard Taylor, *In Search of the Racial Frontier: African Americans in the American West, 1528–1990*, 90–91.

59. See *Proceedings of the First State Convention of the Colored Citizens of the State of California. Held at Sacramento Nov. 20th, 21st, and 22d, in the Colored Methodist Chuch [sic]*. Sacramento: Democratic State Journal Print, 1855.

60. "Colored People's Convention," *Sacramento Daily Union*, October 20, 1857, 3.

61. "The Colored Men's Convention," *Sacramento Daily Union*, October 21, 1857, 2.

62. Ibid.

63. Lapp, *Blacks in Gold Rush California*, 159–60.

64. See John Wesley, *Thoughts upon Slavery*.

65. In the history of the A.M.E. Zion Church that he published in 1884, John Jamison Moore stated that as the Methodist Episcopal Church "grew popular and influential, the prejudice of caste began to engender negro [sic] proscription, and as the number of colored members increased, the race-friction and proscription increased, which finally overcame the tolerance of the colored members of the M. E. Society." John Jamison Moore, D. D., *History of the A.M.E. Zion Church in America*, 15.

66. Leviticus 25:8-55 (English Standard Version). "You shall count seven weeks of years, seven times seven years, so that the time of the seven weeks of years shall give you forty-nine years. Then you shall sound the loud trumpet on the tenth day of the seventh month. On the Day of Atonement you shall sound the trumpet throughout all your land. And you shall consecrate the fiftieth year, and proclaim liberty throughout the land to all its inhabitants. It shall be a jubilee for you, when each of you shall return to his property and each of you shall return to his clan. That fiftieth year shall be a jubilee for you; in it you shall neither sow nor reap what grows of itself nor gather the grapes from the undressed vines. For it is a jubilee. It shall be holy to you. You may eat the produce of the field."

67. Quintard Taylor, *In Search of the Racial Frontier*, 87. Lapp, *Blacks in Gold Rush California*, 159, says that "while Reverend Barney Fletcher was called 'Reverend' at that time, he was apparently not fully ordained until later."
68. Langley, *San Francisco Directory for the Year 1858*, 374.
69. Lapp, *Blacks in Gold Rush California*, 160; Quintard Taylor, *In Search of the Racial Frontier*, 88; History of First A.M.E. Zion Church, San Francisco, online at http://www.firstamezionsf.org/.
70. Quintard Taylor, *In Search of the Racial Frontier*, 88.
71. "The Colored Men's Convention," *Sacramento Daily Union*, October 21, 1857, 2.
72. Gibbs, *Shadow and Light: An Autobiography*, 44–45; Lapp, *Blacks in Gold Rush California*, 16, 39, 97–98; Quintard Taylor, *In Search of the Racial Frontier*, 91. See also Parker and Abajian, *A Walking Tour of the Black Presence in San Francisco during the Nineteenth Century*, 9–10; "Mirror of the Times," *The Elevator*, May 28, 1869, 2: "Lester and Gibbs, (now of Victoria) dealers in Boots and Shoes, 184 Clay St."
73. Historian Lynn M. Hudson has written that "prostitution was central to the mining economies of California, Nevada, and other western states, and some of Pleasant's patrons probably expected sexual services along with room and board. However, the legend of Pleasant as black madam obscures the entrepreneurial aspect of her career.... Rather than either a madam or entrepreneur, she was probably both." See Hudson, *The Making of "Mammy Pleasant": A Black Entrepreneur in Nineteenth-Century San Francisco*, 60.

## "I WANT IT TO COME OUT RIGHT"

1. "Crowds Gather in Sacramento," *Daily Evening Bulletin*, January 5, 1858, 2.
2. "Inaugural Address of Governor Weller," *Daily Evening Bulletin*, January 9, 1858, 1.
3. "Inauguration Ceremonies—Inaugural Address—Brilliant Scene—Imposing Military Parade—Evening Festivities," *Daily Alta California*, January 10, 1858, 2.
4. "City Intelligence. Fugitive Slave—Habeas Corpus," *Sacramento Daily Union*, January 8, 1858, 3.
5. Downey, "The Force of Nature & The Power of Man: Historic Walking Tours of Old Sacramento's Underground and Hollow Sidewalks," 102; "Auction Sales," *Sacramento Daily Union*, May 18, 1858, 2; "Real Estate," *Sacramento Daily Union*, May 19, 1858, 3; Quintard Taylor, *In Search of the Racial Frontier: African Americans in the American West, 1528–1990*, 85; Burg, *Sacramento's K Street: Where Our City Was Born*, 27.
6. "City Intelligence. Fugitive Slave—Habeas Corpus," *Sacramento Daily Union*, January 8, 1858, 3.
7. See J. Edward Johnson, "E. B. Crocker," 338–42; Guinn, *History of the State of California and Biographical Record of the Sacramento Valley, California*, 364.
8. Macon B. Allen (sometimes written as Marcus Bolling Allen) is believed to have become the first duly-licensed black attorney in the United States in 1844 or 1845. See https://www.biography.com/people/macon-bolling-allen-21342461, accessed on November 5, 2017.
9. See Lapp, *Archy Lee: A California Fugitive Slave Case*, 4.
10. 1 Cal. Stat. (1852), Ch. 122, Sec. 1, An Act concerning the Writ of Habeas Corpus.
11. "Slave Case in Sacramento," *Daily Alta California*, January 10, 1858, 2.

12. "City Intelligence. Fugitive Slave—Habeas Corpus," *Sacramento Daily Union*, January 8, 1858, 3.

13. "Case of Archy, The Fugitive Slave. Opinion of Judge Robinson," *Sacramento Daily Union*, January 27, 1858, 3.

14. "The Sacramento 'Slave case,'" *Daily Evening Bulletin*, January 11, 1858, 2.

15. Ownby and Wilson, *Mississippi Encyclopedia*, 627. The population of Issaquena County was 93 percent slaves.

16. "George Pen Johnston. His Death Last Night. After a Painful and Lingering Illness," *Daily Alta California*, March 5, 1884, 8.

17. Petition and Affidavit of C. A. Stovall, filed January 8, 1858, before Geo. Pen Johnston, US Commissioner, and Warrant from Geo. Pen Johnston to marshals dated January 8, 1858; in Case Files of the US Commissioner, RG 21, National Archives and Records Administration, San Bruno, California.

18. Frank M. Stewart, "Impeachment of Judge James H. Hardy, 1862," 63.

19. Warrant from Geo. Pen Johnston to marshals dated January 8, 1858; in Case Files of the US Commissioner.

20. Lapp, *Archy Lee: A California Fugitive Slave Case*, 8.

21. Brief for Claimant Stovall (summarizing arguments of Winans and including concessions), filed January 10, 1858, before Geo. Pen Johnston; in Case Files of the US Commissioner.

22. Ibid. See *Dred Scott v. Sandford* (1857), 19 How. (60 U.S.) 393.

23. "Letter from Sacramento. The 'Archy' Slave Case—Anticipated Conflict of the State and Federal Courts," *Daily Evening Bulletin*, January 13, 1858, 2.

24. Ibid.

25. Gordan, *Authorized by No Law: The San Francisco Committee of Vigilance of 1856 and the United States Circuit Court for the Districts of California*, 5–6; 10 Stat. 631, Ch. 143, an act to establish a Circuit Court of the United States in and for the State of California, March 2, 1855.

26. See Ward McAllister, *Society As I Have Found It*.

27. Swisher, *History of the Supreme Court of the United States: Volume V, The Taney Period 1836–64*, 776.

28. "The Slave Case of 'Archy,'" *Daily Evening Bulletin*, January 13, 1858, 3.

29. "Case of Archy—The Fugitive Slave," *Sacramento Daily Union*, January 25, 1858, 2.

30. "Case of Archy, The Fugitive Slave. Opinion of Judge Robinson," *Sacramento Daily Union*, January 27, 1858, 3.

31. "The Sacramento Fugitive Slave Case," *Daily Evening Bulletin*, January 25, 1858, 2; Lapp, *Archy Lee: A California Fugitive Slave Case*, 8–9.

32. "Letter from Sacramento. The 'Archy' Slave Case—Anticipated Conflict of the State and Federal Courts," *Daily Evening Bulletin*, January 13, 1858, 2.

33. "The Sacramento Fugitive Slave Case," *Daily Evening Bulletin*, January 25, 1858, 2.

34. "Case of Archy—The Fugitive Slave," *Sacramento Daily Union*, January 25, 1858, 2.

35. Edward H. Baker should not be confused with Edward D. Baker, who later became one of Archy's most active attorneys in San Francisco.

36. "Case of Archy—The Fugitive Slave," *Sacramento Daily Union*, January 25, 1858, 2.

37. Ibid.
38. Ibid.
39. Ibid.
40. Ibid.
41. Affidavit of Samuel J. Noble, in *C.A. Stovall vs. Archy (a slave)*, given before US Commissioner George Pen Johnston, San Francisco, March 1858, Case Files of the US Commissioner.
42. "Case of Archy, The Fugitive Slave. Opinion of Judge Robinson," *Sacramento Daily Union*, January 27, 1858, 3.
43. See Finkelman, "Comity," 192–93. US Const., Art. IV, Sec. 2, cl. 1, called the Comity clause, provides that "the citizens of each state shall be entitled to all privileges and immunities of citizens in the several states."
44. "Case of Archy, The Fugitive Slave. Opinion of Judge Robinson," *Sacramento Daily Union*, January 27, 1858, 3.
45. *In re Perkins*, 2 Cal. 424 (1852). See discussion in Ch. 2.
46. "Case of Archy, The Fugitive Slave. Opinion of Judge Robinson," *Sacramento Daily Union*, January 27, 1858, 3.
47. Ibid. Robinson's opinion as reported in this article is considerably longer and more technical than the brief summary given here. Those interested in the full opinion may consult the *Union* article. Because the opinion was quickly overruled by the California Supreme Court's own decision in the case of *In re Archy*, 9 Cal. 147 (1858) (see discussion in Ch. 4), and because it is much beyond the scope and purpose of this narrative history, only this brief summary is given here.
48. "The Sacramento Fugitive Slave Case," *Daily Evening Bulletin*, January 25, 1858, 2; Lapp, *Archy Lee: A California Fugitive Slave Case*, 8–9.

## "THE ARCHY CASE"

1. "The Archy Slave Case," *Sacramento Daily Union*, February 10, 1858, 2.
2. Ibid.
3. "The Archy Slave Case," *Daily Alta California*, February 12, 1858, 1.
4. "Court Records," *Sacramento Daily Union*, October 12, 1857, 2 (two-year lease is concluded for Supreme Court and State Library on second story of Jansen's new brick building on the southwest corner of Fourth and J streets in Sacramento); Burg, *Sacramento's K Street: Where Our City Was Born*, 27.
5. California Constitution of 1849, Art. VI, Sec. 4 (power of Supreme Court justices to issue writs of habeas corpus); 1 Cal. Stat. (1852), Ch. 122, Sec. 3, an Act concerning the Writ of Habeas Corpus (writs may be granted by the Supreme Court, or any judge thereof).
6. Buchanan, *David S. Terry of California: Dueling Judge*, 7, 15, 93.
7. Ibid., 17; McClain, "Pioneers on the Bench: The California Supreme Court, 1849–1879," 20.
8. Buchanan, *David S. Terry of California*, 11–12, 39; Rahm, "Chief Justice David S. Terry and the Language of Federalism," 119, 120–21.

9. Buchanan, *David S. Terry of California*, 36–70, 76, 92; Gordan, *Authorized by No Law: The San Francisco Committee of Vigilance of 1856 and the United States Circuit Court for the Districts of California*, 31–43.

10. McClain, "Pioneers on the Bench: The California Supreme Court, 1849–1879," 20.

11. See Nokes, *The Troubled Life of Peter Burnett, Oregon Pioneer and First Governor of California*, 65–70. Nokes describes the law that Burnett was able to have passed in Oregon, called "Peter Burnett's lash law," that subjected free blacks in Oregon to whipping if they did not leave the state within a specified period. The law was later repealed, although it was convincing evidence of the anti-black sentiments in Oregon and of Burnett's own anti-black racism.

12. Bancroft, *History of California*, 6:312.

13. Ibid.; Bancroft, *History of Oregon*, 1:438–39.

14. David A. Williams, *David C. Broderick: A Political Portrait*, 34.

15. *Journal of the Senate of the State of California at Their First Session* (1850), 347–48; David A. Williams, *David C. Broderick: A Political Portrait*, 34–35; Lapp, *Blacks in Gold Rush California*, 130.

16. "News of the Morning," *Sacramento Daily Union*, January 14, 1857, 2.

17. Kens, *Justice Stephen Field*, 13–74; McGinty, "Before the Judge," 20–23, 83.

18. Field, *Personal Reminiscences of Early Days in California with Other Sketches*, 59; see Kens, *Justice Stephen Field*, 35.

19. Field, Stephen J. *Personal Reminiscences of Early Days in California with Other Sketches*, 60.

20. Argument of James H. Hardy, of counsel for Petitioner, Stovall, in *In re Archy*, 9 Cal. 147, 147–56 (1858).

21. Argument of Winans, of counsel for Archy, in *In re Archy*, 9 Cal. Reports 147, 156–61.

22. "Case of Archy, the Fugitive Slave," *Sacramento Daily Union*, February 6, 1858, 3.

23. *In re Archy*, 9 Cal. 147, 171 (1858); "Case of Archy, the Fugitive Slave," *Sacramento Daily Union*, February 12, 1858, 2.

24. "Case of Archy, the Fugitive Slave," *Sacramento Daily Union*, February 12, 1858, 2.

25. In the Matter of Archy on Habeas Corpus," February 11, 1858. Cal. Supreme Court Opinions, Vol. D, 248–54. California State Archives, Sacramento, CA; *In re Archy*, 9 Cal. 147 (1858).

26. *In re Archy*, 9 Cal. 147, 162 (1858); quoting from statement of Justice Benjamin Mills in *Rankin v. Lydia*, 9 Ky. 467, 470 (1820). The Northwest Ordinance, which was passed by the Congress of the Confederation on July 13, 1787, while the Constitutional Convention was in session, laid down legal rules for the establishment of government north of the Ohio River. Among its most important provisions was one prohibiting involuntary servitude, except in punishment for crime. For discussion, see Finkelman, "Slavery and the Northwest Ordinance: A Study in Ambiguity," 343–79.

27. *Dred Scott v. Sandford*, 19 How. (60 U.S.) 393, 407 (1857).

28. *Somerset v. Stewart* (1772), 98 Eng. Rep. 499–510. See Wise, *Though the Heavens May Fall: The Landmark Trial That Led to the End of Human Slavery*, 182. This case has been subject to some misunderstanding. It did not abolish slavery in England. It

merely determined that the slave James Somerset could not be forced against his will to be transported to slavery in Jamaica. See Wiecek, "*Somerset*: Lord Mansfield and the Legitimacy of Slavery in the Anglo-American World," 86–146. Finkelman, *An Imperfect Union: Slavery, Federalism, and Comity*, 16, says that *Somerset* was "the most important judicial precedent on slavery at the Foundation."

29. Walker, *Reports of Cases Adjudged in The Supreme Court of Mississippi*, 36; see Finkelman, *Supreme Injustice: Slavery and the Nation's Highest Court*, 2, 24, 57, 231–31. The opinion in this case was apparently announced by Joshua G. Clarke, a Maryland-born attorney who lived in Pennsylvania before he came to Mississippi in 1804. He served as a justice of the Mississippi Supreme Court from 1818 to 1821 and died in 1828. He owned some slaves in Mississippi and was widely respected for his legal ability, but it is doubtful if the views he expressed in this case were widely accepted by other southern judges. See Andrew T. Fede, "Judging Against the Grain? Reading Mississippi Supreme Court Judge Joshua G. Clarke's Views on Slavery Law in Context," *FCH Annals: Journal of the Florida Conference of Historians* 20 (May 2013): 11–29.

30. *In re Archy*, 9 Cal. 147, 157 (1858).

31. *In re Archy*, 9 Cal. 147, 161–71 (1858).

32. *In re Archy*, 9 Cal. 147, 171 (1858); see McClain, "Pioneers on the Bench: The California Supreme Court, 1849–1879," 22.

33. "Impeach the Supreme Mugginses," *Daily Evening Bulletin*, February 19, 1858, 2. ("We have been informed that Judge Field's health prevented him from taking any part in the ridiculous decision recently rendered by the Supreme Court in the 'Archy' case.") (A "muggins" is a foolish and gullible person.) Grodin, "The California Supreme Court and State Constitutional Rights: The Early Years," 144, says that that Field "was on leave from the court, and out of the state at the time Archy's case was decided." Upham, "The Meaning of the 'Privileges and Immunities of Citizens' on the Eve of the Civil War," 1142, states that Field was "conspicuously absent and remained deafeningly silent about this controversial decision throughout his entire life," thus suggesting that he deliberately avoided participating in it because of its high profile and controversial overtones. I have found no evidence for either of these points.

34. "The Archy Case," *Sacramento Daily Union*, February 18, 1858, 3, quoting from the *Butte Record*; "The Supreme Mugginess on the Bench," *Daily Evening Bulletin*, February 13, 1858, 2.

35. "The Archy Case," *Sacramento Daily Union*, February 12, 1858, 2.

36. "The Archy Case," *Daily Alta California*, February 12, 1858, 1.

37. "Our Sacramento Correspondence," *Daily Alta California*, February 13, 1858, 1.

38. "The Supreme Mugginess on the Bench," *Daily Evening Bulletin*, February 13, 1858, 2.

39. "That Decision," *Sacramento Daily Union*, February 16, 1858, 2, quoting from *Marysville Express*.

40. Ibid., quoting from the *San Joaquin Republican*.

41. "The Archy Case," *Sacramento Daily Union*, February 18, 1858, 3, quoting from the *San Francisco Argus*.

42. Burnett's recollections of his early life were published in 1880 without any mention of the Archy Case. He recalled then that he was born and reared in the slave section of the United States, implying that this had shaped his views about slavery, and did not even hint that his views about the institution had changed. He did state, however, that he supported the Union during the Civil War and voted for Abraham Lincoln when he ran for a second term as president in 1864. See Burnett, *Recollections and Opinions of an Old Pioneer*, 405–6.

43. Hoffheimer, "Race and Terror in Joseph Baldwin's *The Flush Times of Alabama and Mississippi*," 729 (referring to the "extreme form of his racism").

44. Shuck, *Bench and Bar in California*, 277; McClain, "Pioneers on the Bench: The California Supreme Court, 1849–1879," 22 (changing Baldwin's "nigger" to "Negro"); Eaves, *A History of California Labor Legislation: With an Introductory Sketch of the San Francisco Labor Movement*, 101.

## A STRUGGLE ON THE WATER

1. "The Slave 'Archy'," *Red Bluff Beacon*, February 17, 1858, 2, quoting from *Sacramento Daily Union* and *State Journal*; "Summary of the Fortnight's News," *Daily Alta California*, February 20, 1858, 1.

2. "Archy," *Daily Alta California*, February 21, 1858, 2.

3. "The Boy Archy," *Sacramento Daily Union*, February 26, 1858, 2, quoting from *San Joaquin Republican*.

4. "The Denouement of the Archy Case—Great Excitement on Steamer Day," *Daily Alta California*, March 6, 1858, 2; "The Affidavit in the Archy Case," *Sacramento Daily Union*, March 8, 1858, 2, quoting affidavit of James Riker dated March 4, 1858.

5. "Where Is 'Archy'?" *Daily Evening Bulletin*, February 24, 1858, 3.

6. Ibid.

7. Ibid.

8. "The Denouement of the Archy Case—Great Excitement on Steamer Day," *Daily Alta California*, March 6, 1858, 2. According to a report in the *Bulletin*, Archy said he was taken away from Stockton on Monday, March 1. "Arrest of 'Archy' and His Master," *Daily Evening Bulletin*, March 5, 1858, 2.

9. "Arrest of 'Archy' and His Master," *Daily Evening Bulletin*, March 5, 1858, 2.

10. "The Sacramento Fugitive Slave Case," *New York Times*, March 1, 1858, 3.

11. "Pacific Mail S.S. Co.'s Line to Panama," *Sacramento Daily Union*, March 4, 1858, 1.

12. "Nicaragua Steamship Co.'s Line," *Sacramento Daily Union*, March 4, 1858, 1.

13. "Summary of the Fortnight's News," *Daily Alta California*, March 5, 1858, 1.

14. Lapp, *Blacks in Gold Rush California*, 99, 100; Langley, *San Francisco Directory for the Year 1858*, 236, 381.

15. Shuck, *Bench and Bar in California*, 49.

16. "The Affidavit in the Archy Case," *Sacramento Daily Union*, March 8, 1858, 2.

17. "The Denouement of the Archy Case—Great Excitement on Steamer Day," *Daily Alta California*, March 6, 1858, 2. For a book about Isaiah W. Lees and his long career as a San Francisco police detective, see Secrest, *Dark and Tangled Threads of Crime: San*

*Francisco's Famous Police Detective, Isaiah W. Lees* (Sanger, CA: Quill Driver Books/Word Dancer Press, 2004).

18. "The Denouement of the Archy Case—Great Excitement on Steamer Day," *Daily Alta California*, March 6, 1858, 2.

19. Ibid.

20. Ibid.

21. Ibid.

22. "News of the Morning," *Sacramento Daily Union*, March 6, 1858, 2.

23. The Denouement of the Archy Case—Great Excitement on Steamer Day," *Daily Alta California*, March 6, 1858, 2.

24. "Arrest of 'Archy' and his Master," *San Francisco Bulletin*, March 5, 1858, 2.

25. "The Denouement of the Archy Case—Great Excitement on Steamer Day," *Daily Alta California*, March 6, 1858, 2.

26. Ibid.

27. Ibid.

28. Ibid.

29. "Arrest of 'Archy' and His Master," *Daily Evening Bulletin*, March 5, 1858, 2.

30. "The Denouement of the Archy Case—Great Excitement on Steamer Day," *Daily Alta California*, March 6, 1858, 2.

31. Ibid.

32. Ibid.

33. For a brief discussion of Reverend Moore's background, see Ch. 2.

34. "The Colored People on the 'Archy' Case," *Daily Evening Bulletin*, March 6, 1858, 3.

35. Ibid.

36. Ibid.

37. "Funds for Archy," *Sacramento Daily Union*, March 25, 1858, 3.

## THE OPPOSING FORCES

1. Fugitive Slave Act of September 18, 1850, Ch. 60, Sec. 6, 9 Stat. 462, 463.

2. Fugitive Slave Act of September 18, 1850, Ch. 60, Sec. 7, 9 Stat. 462, 463.

3. Affidavit of C. A. Stovall dated March 17, 1858, filed March 17, 1858, before George Pen Johnston, in *Charles A. Stovall vs. Archy (a slave)*, Case Files of the US Commissioner, RG 21, National Archives and Records Administration, San Bruno, California.

4. Warrant of Arrest given March 17, 1858, by George Pen Johnston, in *Charles A. Stovall vs. Archy (a slave)*, Case Files of the US Commissioner.

5. "Letter from San Francisco," *Sacramento Daily Union*, March 8, 1858, 3.

6. Burlingame, *Abraham Lincoln: A Life*, 1:214; Blair and Tarshis, *Colonel Edward D. Baker*, 56.

7. Blair and Tarshis, *Colonel Edward D. Baker*, 58–61.

8. Ibid., 56.

9. David A. Williams, *David C. Broderick: A Political Portrait*, 122.

10. Senkewicz, *Vigilantes in Gold Rush San Francisco*, 84–85; Starr, *California: A History*, 87, 106; McGloin, *San Francisco: The Story of a City*, 58.

11. Blair and Tarshis, *Colonel Edward D. Baker*, 69. The Cora trial opened on January 8, 1856. Baker addressed the jury on January 14. After forty-one hours of deliberation, the jury was discharged on January 17, 1856. They stood six for manslaughter, four for murder in the first degree, and two for acquittal. Shuck, *Eloquence of the Far West. No. 1. Masterpieces of E.D. Baker*, 289–90. While a hung verdict is not the ultimate "success" for a defense attorney in a murder trial, it is much more favorable than a conviction, giving the accused person yet another opportunity to prove that he (or she) is not guilty. The exact circumstances of the encounter between Richardson and Cora have been recounted in various ways. This is not surprising in view of the fact that Cora's trial continued for nine days and that the testimony of witnesses in such a trial typically differs, particularly when the murder charge is met with a claim of self-defense.
12. McGinty, "Hung Be the Heavens with Black," 34–35.
13. David A. Williams, *David C. Broderick: A Political Portrait*, 128; McGinty, "Hung Be the Heavens with Black," 39.
14. David A. Williams, *David C. Broderick,*: A Political Portrait 131.
15. See discussion in Ch. 4.
16. Buchanan, *David S. Terry of California: Dueling Judge*, 20–70.
17. "The Case of 'Archy Lee' on Habeas Corpus," *Daily Evening Bulletin*, March 17, 1858, 3.
18. "Archy under the Fugitive Slave Law," *Daily Evening Bulletin*, March 18, 1858, 3.
19. "Letter from San Francisco," *Sacramento Daily Union*, March 22, 1858, 4.
20. Ibid.
21. Ibid.
22. "The Case of Archy To-day," *Daily Evening Bulletin*, March 18, 1858, 3.
23. "The Archy Case," *Daily Evening Bulletin*, March 20, 1858, 3.
24. Ibid.
25. Ibid.
26. Lubet, *Fugitive Justice: Runaways, Rescuers, and Slavery on Trial*, 159–60.
27. Amestoy, *Slavish Shore: The Odyssey of Richard Henry Dana Jr.*, 174–95.
28. Lubet, *Fugitive Justice: Runaways, Rescuers, and Slavery on Trial*, 226–27; Amestoy, *Slavish Shore: The Odyssey of Richard Henry Dana Jr.*, 201.
29. "The Archy Case," *Daily Evening Bulletin*, March 20, 1858, 3.

## "JEHOVAH HAS TRIUMPHED"

1. "The Archy Case in Another Shape," *Sacramento Daily Union*, March 20, 1858, 3.
2. "The Last Scene in the Archy Case," *Daily Alta California*, March 24, 1858, 2.
3. "C.A. Stovall Left by the Sonora and Archy Remained," *Sacramento Daily Union*, March 24, 1858, 2.
4. "News of the Morning," *Sacramento Daily Union*, March 23, 1858, 21.
5. "Card to the Public by a Committee of Colored People," *Daily Evening Bulletin*, March 27, 1858, 3.
6. "The Archy Case—Trial of Willis Corse—Case of Adams & Co.—Arrival," *Sacramento Daily Union*, March 30, 1858, 2.
7. "The Archy Case Continued," *Daily Alta California*, March 30, 1858, 1.

8. Affidavit of C. A. Stovall, signed March 20, 1858, filed March 29, 1858, before Geo. Pen Johnston, US Commissioner, in Case Files of the US Commissioner, RG 21, National Archives and Records Administration, San Bruno, California.

9. Affidavit of William D. Stovall signed March 26, 1858, filed March 29, 1858, before Geo. Pen Johnston, US Commissioner, in Case Files of the US Commissioner.

10. "The Archy Case Continued," *Daily Alta California*, March 30, 1858, 1.

11. Ibid.

12. "The Archy Case Again Continued," *Daily Alta California*, March 31, 1858, 1.

13. "Archy's Story," *Daily Alta California*, March 31, 1858, 2.

14. "Court Proceedings. Wednesday, April 7th, 1858. Before US Commissioner Geo. Pen. Johnston. The Archy Case," *Daily Alta California*, April 8, 1858, 1.

15. Baker's oratory and legal skills were often and enthusiastically praised. One of the most interesting men who did this was Henry S. Foote, a lawyer and politician who had served Mississippi as both US senator and governor before coming to California in 1854, where he practiced law and was active in politics for four years. After hearing Baker speak and watching him try cases, Foote wrote that he was "universally recognized as altogether the most eloquent speaker at the California bar, and, on familiar acquaintance with him, I discovered that he was very far from being merely a brilliant and forceful rhetorician, for I repeatedly heard him, both then and afterward, when engaged in the argument of legal causes of the greatest complexity and difficulty, and never did I find him at all unequal to the occasion." Foote, *War of the Rebellion; or, Scylla and Charybdis, Consisting of Observations upon the Causes, Course, and Consequences of the Late Civil War in the United States*, 213.

16. *Somerset v. Stewart* (1772), 98 Eng. Rep. 499–510.

17. Brief for Respondent, E.D. Baker of Counsel, Crosby and Tompkins, attorneys for Respondent, Before Geo. Pen Johnston, US Commissioner, in *C.A. Stovall vs. Archy (claimed as a slave)*, Case Files of the US Commissioner.

18. "Court Proceedings. Wednesday, April 7th, 1858. Before US Commissioner Geo. Pen. Johnston. The Archy Case," *Daily Alta California*, April 8, 1858, 1.

19. Brief of James H. Hardy "Before Hon. George Penn [*sic*] Johnston U.S. Commissioner for the Districts of California," in *Charles A. Stovall vs. Archy (A Slave)*, Case Files of the US Commissioner.

20. "Archy Discharged—Further from Puget Sound and the Gold Mines," *Sacramento Daily Union*, April 15, 1858, 2. In the title to his short but well-researched book, *Archy Lee: A California Fugitive Slave Case,* Rudolph M. Lapp adopted the argument of Hardy and Stovall that Archy Lee was a "fugitive slave." But the facts clearly demonstrated that Archy Lee had not fled from slavery into California, where the state constitution clearly provided that there were no slaves, and George Pen Johnston's decision clearly confirmed those facts. It may make some sense to argue that the legal struggle over Archy Lee's status was a "fugitive slave case," but the facts and Commissioner Johnston's decision both clearly establish that he was not a "fugitive slave," although he had been a slave in Mississippi.

21. "Release of Archy Lee, and the End of It," *Daily Alta California*, April 15, 1858, 2. A short summary of the courtroom proceedings that began in Sacramento and ended with the order declaring Archy Lee a free man in San Francisco is set forth in Eunsun

Celeste Han, "All Roads Lead to San Francisco: Black Californian Networks of Community and the Struggle for Equality, 1849–1877," 110–23.

22. "Release of Archy Lee, and the End of It," *Daily Alta California*, April 15, 1858, 2.

23. "The Colored People Talk of Emigrating," *Daily Evening Bulletin*, April 15, 1858, 3.

24. "Second Meeting of the Colored People," *Daily Evening Bulletin*, April 16, 1858, 3. See Eaves, *A History of California Labor Legislation: With an Introductory Sketch of the San Francisco Labor Movement*, 103.

25. "Second Meeting of the Colored People," *Daily Evening Bulletin*, April 16, 1858, 3.

26. Freeman is identified as T. P. Freeman in the *Bulletin*. See "Second Meeting of the Colored People," *Daily Evening Bulletin*, April 16, 1858, 3. He is listed in the San Francisco City Directory as Thomas P. Freeman, a colored shoemaker at 83 Jackson Street. See Langley, *San Francisco Directory for the Year 1858*, 128.

27. See Thomas Moore, *The Works of Thomas Moore, Esq.*, 6 vols. New York: G. Smith, 1825, IV: 269.

## "SEND THEM TO THE DEVIL"

1. "The Legislature of 1858," *Sacramento Daily Union*, January 4, 1858, 2.

2. California Constitution of 1849, Art. I, Sec. 18.

3. "Inaugural Address of Governor Weller," *Evening Bulletin*, January 9, 1858, 1.

4. The name of the Virginia-born lawyer and California state assemblyman A. G. Stakes of San Joaquin County has frequently (and erroneously) been printed as "A. G. Stokes." Entries in the California State Roster, city archives, census records, tax assessment lists, and contemporary newspaper accounts all confirm that his last name was Stakes.

5. "California Legislature. Ninth Session," *Sacramento Daily Union*, January 13, 1858, 1.

6. "California Legislature. Ninth Session," *Sacramento Daily Union*, January 19, 1858, 1.

7. Ibid.

8. "Now and Then," *Sacramento Daily Union*, January 19, 1858, 2.

9. "Legislative Summary," *Sacramento Daily Union*, February 3, 1858, 2.

10. "Legislative Summary," *Sacramento Daily Union*, March 20, 1858, 2.

11. "California Legislature. Ninth Session," *Sacramento Daily Union*, February 4, 1858, 1.

12. In 1863, Republican legislators were able to pass a bill that removed all restrictions on black testimony. The law was signed by Governor Leland Stanford. See "Laws of This Session," *Daily Alta California*, March 22, 1863, 1 ("Among the important general bills approved are those permitting Negroes to testify against whites in civil and criminal court"). See also Chandler, "Friends in Time of Need: Republicans and Black Civil Rights in California during the Civil War Era," 349.

13. "California Legislature. Ninth Session," *Sacramento Daily Union*, March 30, 1858, 1.

14. Ibid.

15. Ibid.

16. "Court Proceedings. Wednesday, April 7th, 1858. Before U.S. Commissioner Geo. Pen. Johnston. The Archy Case," *Daily Alta California*, April 8, 1858, 1.

17. "Speech of J.B. Moore Delivered in the Assembly of this State on Wednesday Evening, April 7th, 1858," *Sacramento Daily Union*, April 9, 1858, 1; "A Model Speech," *Daily Alta California*, April 10, 1858, 1.

18. *Journal of the Ninth Session of the Assembly of the State of California*, 525.

19. *Journal of the Ninth Session of the Senate of the State of California*, 553.

20. *Journal of the Ninth Session of the Senate of the State of California*, 661.

21. Article quoting from *Puget's Sound Democrat* copied in *The National Era*, July 22, 1858. See also Eunsun Celeste Han, "All Roads Lead to San Francisco: Black Californian Networks of Community and the Struggle for Equality, 1849–1877," 169–67.

## "ALL ONE THING, OR ALL THE OTHER"

1. "Senate Special Session," *Congressional Globe*, March 4, 1857, 371.

2. David A. Williams, *David C. Broderick: A Political Portrait*, 150–8, quoting from Sacramento *Weekly Times*, January 10, 1857, and December 10, 1856.

3. Bancroft, *History of California*, 6:710–43, quoting from San Francisco *Post*, March 8, 1879.

4. *Dred Scott v. Sandford*, 19 How. (60 U.S.) 393, 407 (1857).

5. *Dred Scott v. Sandford*, 19 How. (60 U.S.) 452 (1857).

6. See McGinty, *Lincoln and the Court*, 38–64, for more extensive discussion.

7. 10 Stat. 277, Ch. 59, An Act to Organize the Territories of Nebraska and Kansas, May 30, 1854.

8. David A. Williams, *David C. Broderick: A Political Portrait*, 174; McPherson, *Battle Cry of Freedom*, 166.

9. "Thirty-Fifth Congress, First Session," *Congressional Globe*, December 23, 1857, 163–64.

10. "Thirty-Fifth Congress, First Session," *Congressional Globe*, December 23, 1857, 163–92; *Speech of Hon. D. C. Broderick, of California, Against the Admission of Kansas, Under the Lecompton Constitution: Delivered in the Senate of the United States, March 22, 1858*, 10. See Bancroft, *History of California*, 6:719–55.

11. "Thirty-Fifth Congress, First Session," *Congressional Globe*, March 4, 1858, 962.

12. "Thirty-Fifth Congress, First Session," *Appendix to the Congressional Globe*, March 22, 1858, 193.

13. Ibid.

14. Ibid; *Speech of Hon. D. C. Broderick, of California, Against the Admission of Kansas, Under the Lecompton Constitution: Delivered in the Senate of the United States, March 22, 1858*, 16.

15. Kennedy, *The Contest for California in 1861: How Colonel E.D. Baker Saved the Pacific States to the Union*, 40, 41–42.

16. McPherson, *Battle Cry of Freedom*, 168–69.

17. 12 Stat. 126, Ch. 20, An Act for the admission of Kansas into the Union, January 29, 1861.

18. Basler, *The Collected Works of Abraham Lincoln*, 2:461 (emphasis in original, but division into paragraphs ignored). The biblical phrase is from Matthew 12:25 and Mark 3:25.

19. Ibid., 2:399.

20. Ibid., 2:400–409.

21. Ibid., 2:522.

22. Burlingame, *Abraham Lincoln: A Life*, 1:484.

23. Basler, *The Collected Works of Abraham Lincoln*, 3:177.

24. Ibid., 3:322. One transcript of this statement quotes Douglas as using the word *nigger* rather than *Negro*. Both Douglas and Lincoln were frequently (although not consistently) quoted as having used that word. Although it is clear that Douglas used it to denigrate African Americans, it is not as clear that Lincoln did so.

25. Ibid, 3:145–46.

26. Ibid, 3:276; Eric Foner, *The Fiery Trial: Abraham Lincoln and American Slavery*, 65; see also Eric Foner, *Free Soil, Free Labor, Free Men: The Ideology of the Republican Party Before the Civil War*, ix, 116, 225.

27. Basler, *The Collected Works of Abraham Lincoln*, 3:226.

28. Ibid., 3:249.

29. Ibid., 3:254.

30. Ibid., 3:112.

31. Ibid., 3:231.

32. Ibid., 3:255.

33. Ibid., 3:339.

34. Leroy, *Mr. Lincoln's Book*, 73–77, 145, 149.

35. Stahr, *Seward: Lincoln's Indispensable Man*, 174–75.

36. Rowland, *Jefferson Davis, Constitutionalist: His Letters, Papers, and Speeches*, 23: 356–57.

37. "S.H. Brooks Insults Geo. Pen Johnston at a Ball," *Sacramento Daily Union*, May 1, 1858, 2.

38. California Constitution of 1849, Art. XI, Sec. 2.

39. 6 Cal. Stat. (1855), Ch. 127, an Act amendatory of and supplemental to an Act entitled "An Act concerning Crimes and Punishments," passed April 16, 1850.

40. "In Support of a Principle," *Daily Alta California*, August 23, 1858, 2.

41. "Sharp Shooting," *Sacramento Daily Union*, June 14, 1858, 2; "Card of George Pen Johnston," *Sacramento Daily Union*, June 16, 1858, 3; "News of the Morning," *Sacramento Daily Union*, June 19, 1858, 2.

42. Blair and Tarshis, *Colonel Edward D. Baker*, 83; Stowell, et al., eds., *The Legal Papers of Abraham Lincoln: Legal Documents and Cases*, 4:348.

43. "The Duel Between George Pen Johnston and W. I. Ferguson—Its Origin and the Progress of the Difficulty—The Gwin Family," *Sacramento Daily Union*, August 23, 1858, 2; "Summary of the Fortnight's News," *Daily Alta California*, September 21, 1.

44. "In Support of a Principle," *Daily Alta California*, August 23, 1858, 2.

45. "News of the Morning," *Sacramento Daily Union*, August 23, 1858, 2.

46. "Arrest of George Penn [*sic*] Johnston," *Daily Alta California*, October 15, 1858, 1; "Geo [*sic*] Pen Johnston Acquitted," *Sacramento Daily Union*, November 11, 1858, 2.

47. "Case of Geo [*sic*] Pen Johnston," *Sacramento Daily Union*, December 8, 1858, 2; "Summary of the Fortnight's News," *Daily Alta California*, December 20, 1858, 1.

## NORTH TO FREEDOM

1. Beasley, *The Negro Trail Blazers of California; a Compilation of Records from the California Archives in the Bancroft Library at the University of California in Berkeley, and from the Diaries, Old Papers and Conversations of Old Pioneers in the State of California*, 83.

2. Holdredge, *Mammy Pleasant*, 49–54. Lapp, *Blacks in Gold Rush California*, 152, says "Archy, according to one chronicler of this period, made his home at the boardinghouse of Mary Ellen 'Mammy' Pleasants [*sic*]." Hudson, *The Making of "Mammy Pleasant": A Black Entrepreneur in Nineteenth-Century San Francisco*, 38, says that "Mary Ellen Pleasant hid Archy Lee in her home, concerned about the frenzied atmosphere after the case and the risks it might pose." Lapp's book is a pioneering and generally reliable text. Hudson's book is a scholarly reexamination of Mary Ellen Pleasant's long life, the real events that took place in it, and the mysteries that swirled around her in life and in death. It is documented with many and very detailed notes. Holdredge's book has no notes and no index. One student of San Francisco in Pleasant's time has criticized it and another book also written by Holdredge as containing "so many errors that it is difficult to regard them as anything more than some kind of historical novel." Secrest, *Dark and Tangled Threads of Crime: San Francisco's Famous Police Detective, Isaiah W. Lees*, xv. Hudson does not attempt to second-guess either Delilah Beasley's assertions about Archy Lee or Helen Holdredge's assertions about John Brown but merely sets them forth for readers to examine.

3. John Brown took precautions to prevent advanced word about his planned Harper's Ferry raid from leaking out. It is difficult to believe that at a distance of more than two thousand miles Mammy Pleasant would have known anything about it before it happened. Hudson says that Mary Pleasant and her husband went north into Chatham, in what is now Ontario, Canada, in 1858, where they were able to personally help Brown prepare for Harper's Ferry. At p. 40, Hudson writes: "Among the legends that Mary Ellen Pleasant has inspired, none are more heroic than her role in John Brown's raid." At p. 42, however, Hudson admits that "most historians hedge on the question of Pleasant's involvement in the raid."

4. Beezley and Meyer, *The Oxford History of Mexico*, 327 (slavery abolished).

5. "Meeting of Colored People," *Sacramento Daily Union*, April 16, 1858, Sec. 4, 2.

6. Bancroft, *History of California*, 6:593–600; Dunlap, *California People*, 212; Richards, *The California Gold Rush and the Coming of the Civil War*, 138–42; Stampp, *America in 1857: A Nation on the Brink*, 189–90; Stacey L. Smith, *Freedom's Frontier: California and the Struggle over Unfree Labor, Emancipation, and Reconstruction*, 69.

7. Bancroft, *History of California*, 6:312; Bancroft, *History of Oregon*, 1:438–39.

8. Lapp, *Blacks in Gold Rush California*, 241.

9. "Equality for Colored Men," *Daily Alta California*, July 23, 1856, 1; "Summary of the Fortnight's News," *Daily Alta California*, August 5, 1858, 1; Kilian, *Go Do Some Great Thing: The Black Pioneers of British Columbia*, 18.

10. The Act was passed on August 28, 1833, to take effect on August 1, 1834. Winks, *The Blacks in Canada: A History*, 111.

11. Winks, *The Blacks in Canada: A History*, 275.

12. According to historian Charlotte S. M. Girard, it has long been believed that James Douglas was not only a Creole (one born in the West Indian Colonies) but a mulatto (partly black or colored). She studied original sources in an effort to precisely determine his heritage and identified his mother and his probable grandmother. Girard, "Sir James Douglas' [*sic*] Mother and Grandmother," 26. After consulting with Girard and others, Douglas's biographer John Adams concluded that Douglas's

mother was "a free coloured West Indian." Adams, *Old Square-Toes: The Life of James and Amelia Douglas*, 3. The term "coloured" then generally referred to anyone of mixed black and white ancestry.

13. Winks, *The Blacks in Canada: A History*, 273–75; Edwards, "The War of Complexional Distinction: Blacks in Gold Rush California & British Columbia," 38–39; Kilian, *Go Do Some Great Thing: The Black Pioneers of British Columbia*, 24; *Dictionary of Canadian Biography*, http://www.biographi.ca/en/bio/douglas_james_10E.html, accessed October 9, 2017.

14. Winks, *The Blacks in Canada: A History*, 273.

15. Kilian, *Go Do Some Great Thing: The Black Pioneers of British Columbia*, 27.

16. "Off for the Fraser River Mines," *Daily Alta California*, April 17, 1858, 2.

17. "Shipping Intelligence," *Daily Alta California*, April 21, 1858, 2.

18. The number of blacks who were aboard the *Commodore* has been variously reported. In "The Rush for Frazer [*sic*] River," the *Daily Alta California*, April 21, 1858, 2, it is stated that there were "about one hundred and fifty negroes, among whom the celebrated 'Archy' figured conspicuously."

19. "Emigration for Vancouver's Island," *Sacramento Daily Union*, April 21, 1858, 2.

20. "A Colored Correspondent," *Sacramento Daily Union*, April 23, 1858, 2. In a puzzling set of news reports, a newspaper several hundred miles north of San Francisco reported that Archy did not leave for Victoria on the *Commodore*, but instead went north into the California mines. The *Red Bluff Beacon* told its readers: "That individual, Archy, about whom more talk has been made for the last few months than any other in California, Mrs. Cora Anna Weekes not excepted, came up on the Pike on Saturday morning, and was actually here, in Red Bluff, a few hours. We desired to have an interview with the 'Great Mississippian,' but failed to get an opportunity.... He has gone into the Northern mines." "Matters at Red Bluff," *Sacramento Daily Union*, April 21, 1858, 1, quoting from the *Red Bluff Beacon*. In San Francisco, the *Daily Alta California* told its readers that it was "confidently asserted that 'Archy' did not leave in the *Commodore* last week for Puget Sound, but is in the northern mines in this State, delving in Mother Earth for the shining metal which is eventually to make him a 'colored gentleman' of affluent circumstances." "About Archy," *Daily Alta California*, May 1, 1858, 2. The obviously anti-Archy, anti-black sarcasm in these reports suggests that they were fictitious or, if not that, that they were based on a confusion of identities. Archy was not in Red Bluff.

21. "Later [*sic*] from the North," *Daily Alta California*, May 6, 1858, 1.

22. Winks, *The Blacks in Canada: A History*, 273.

23. "Letter from Victoria," *Daily Alta California*, May 6, 1858, 1.

24. Ibid., 1.

25. "Later [*sic*] from the North," *Daily Alta California*, May 6, 1858, 1.

26. "The Northern Diggings," Sacramento Daily Union, May 8, 1858, 1.

27. "Another Account," *Sacramento Daily Union*, May 22, 1858, 2.

28. "Meeting of Colored Citizens," *Sacramento Daily Union*, May 8, 1858, 2.

29. [No title], *Daily Alta California*, May 12, 1858, 2; "Colored Emigration," *Daily Alta California*, May 12, 1858, 2.

30. "The African Hegira," *Sacramento Daily Union*, May 14, 1858, 1, quoting from the *Daily Evening Bulletin* of May 12, 1858.

31. "Letter from Victoria," *Daily Alta California*, May 31, 1858, 1; "Colored People in Victoria," *Sacramento Daily Union*, June 2, 1858, 2.

32. "From Victoria," *Sacramento Daily Union*, June 7, 1858, 4.

33. Winks, *Blacks in Canada: A History*, 273.

34. *Victoria Gazette*, August 28, 1858, as quoted in Edwards, "The War of Complexional Distinction: Blacks in Gold Rush California & British Columbia," 40.

35. Edwards, "The War of Complexional Distinction: Blacks in Gold Rush California & British Columbia," 40–41.

36. Cornwallis, *The New El Dorado; or, British Columbia*, 283–84.

37. Gibbs, *Shadow and Light: An Autobiography*, 50.

38. Ibid., 63.

39. Ibid., 64.

40. Ibid., 64–65.

41. "Notes of a Trip to Victoria," *Pacific Appeal*, February 6, 1864, 2.

## "WE FEEL THE IMPULSE"

1. *Transcript of the Proceedings, in Case No. 366, Andres Castillero, Claimant, vs. The United States Defendant, for the Place Named New Almaden*, 5, 6.

2. See McGinty, *Lincoln's Greatest Case: The River, the Bridge, and the Making of America*, 79–81. Stanton lost the McCormick case in the trial court but prevailed on appeal to the Supreme Court. Burlingame, *Abraham Lincoln: A Life*, 1:339–41, details Stanton's insults to Lincoln in Cincinnati. Stahr, *Stanton: Lincoln's War Secretary*, 76–78, admits that Stanton was probably rude to Lincoln in Cincinnati but expresses skepticism about some of the recollections of their encounter there.

3. See Basler, *The Collected Works of Abraham Lincoln*, 5:312–13 (order making Henry W. Halleck general-in-chief). Marszalek, *Commander of All Lincoln's Armies: A Life of General Henry W. Halleck*, 134, says that Secretary of War Stanton opposed Halleck's selection as general-in-chief, considering him a "man totally destitute of principle" and "probably the greatest scoundrel and most barefaced villain in America."

4. *United States v. Charles Fossat*, 61 US 413 (1958); "The Forsat [*sic*] Case Confirmed," *Sacramento Daily Union*, June 21, 1858, 3.

5. "The New Almaden Case and Judge Ogden Hoffman Jr., in Washington," *Daily Alta California*, April 9, 1858, 1; "The New Almaden Mine Case," *New York Times*, October 7, 1859, 4.

6. "An Injunction Granted in the New Almaden Case," *Daily Alta California*, October 30, 1858, 2.

7. "The New Almaden Land Case," *Daily Alta California*, September 25, 1858, 2.

8. "An Injunction Granted in the New Almaden Case," *Daily Alta California*, October 30, 1858, 2; Cutler McAllister, ed., *United States of America v. Parrott, et al., Reports of Cases Argued and Determined in the Circuit Court of the United States for the Districts of California*. Vol. 1 (New York: John S. Voorhies, 1859), 271–350. The interests of the

claimants under Castillero were represented by Henry Halleck's partner, Archibald C. Peachy. For further discussion of Stanton's work in obtaining the injunction, see Stahr, *Stanton: Lincoln's War Secretary*, 87–88.

9. Bancroft, *History of California*, 6:556–67.

10. Basler, *The Collected Works of Abraham Lincoln*, 6:205–6. Leonard Swett, an attorney Lincoln knew well from his law practice in Illinois, was the agent authorized to go to California and take custody of New Almaden from the marshal.

11. Bancroft, *History of California*, 6:560–61.

12. For a history of the New Almaden mine, see Johnston, *Mercury and the Making of California Mining, Landscape, and Race*. For an extensive discussion of litigation in the Supreme Court relating to New Almaden, see Swisher, *History of the Supreme Court of the United States: Volume V, The Taney Period 1836–64*, 786–802. For a short review of New Almaden's history and litigation, see Cahan, Hinckle, and Ocken, *The Court That Tamed the West: From the Gold Rush to the Tech Boom*, 74–77.

13. "Rejection of the Limantour Claim," *Daily Alta California*, November 20, 1858, 2; see discussion in Fritz, *Federal Justice: The California Court of Ogden Hoffman, 1851–1891*, 155–56, 165–73; Stahr, *Stanton: Lincoln's War Secretary*, 82–89, 569–31.

14. Fritz, *Federal Justice in California: The Court of Ogden Hoffman, 1851–1891*, 170.

15. "Cyrus West Field," *Sacramento Daily Union*, September 18, 1858, 3 (copied from the *Springfield American*); Gordon, *A Thread Across the Ocean: The Heroic Story of the Transatlantic Cable*, 24.

16. Judson, *Cyrus W. Field: His Life and Work*, 97–98.

17. The reported distance was 1,698 nautical miles and 1,950 statute miles. Judson, *Cyrus W. Field: His Life and Work*, 97.

18. Howe, "American Victorianism as a Culture," 507.

19. Nevins and Thomas, *The Diary of George Templeton Strong*, II: 408–9.

20. "Meeting of the Committee on the Celebration of the Atlantic Telegraph Cable," *Daily Alta California*, September 19, 1858, 2.

21. "The Cable Jubilee," *Daily Alta California*, September 29, 1858, 1; "The Celebration—Continued," *Daily Alta California*, September 30, 1959, 1.

22. "The Cable Jubilee," *Daily Alta California*, September 29, 1858, 1; Shuck, *The California Scrap-Book: A Repository of Useful Information and Select Reading*, 17–26.

23. Bond, *An Account of Donati's Comet of 1858*, 5.

24. "Letter from Placerville," *Sacramento Daily Union*, September 20, 1858, 2.

25. Untitled, *California Farmer and Journal of Useful Sciences*, September 17, 1858, 52.

26. See Pasachoff, Olson, and Hazen, "The Earliest Comet Photographs: Usherwood, Bond, and Donati 1858," 27 (May 1996): 129–45, explaining that Donati's Comet was the first to be photographed but that it is not entirely clear whether the photograph was made on September 27 or September 28, 1858, or whether it was taken by George Bond of Harvard or William Usherwood, an English artist and photographer.

27. Sergeant, *The Greatest Comets in History: Broom Stars and Celestial Scimitars*, 133.

28. Horace White in added chapter to Herndon and Weik, *Herndon's Lincoln*, 405.

29. In an online site, George Bishop, highly praised author of *The Night of the Comet: A Novel*, wrote: "A person of a novelistic bent might imagine that Donati's Comet helped

NOTES

inspire these words from Lincoln, and thus, in a roundabout way, a comet helped to bring about the end of slavery in the United States." See http://georgebishopjr.com/tag/donatis-comet/, accessed October 4, 2017.

30. The Cable Jubilee," *Daily Alta California*, September 29, 1858, 1; Shuck, *California Scrap-Book: A Repository of Useful Information and Select Reading*, 17–26.

31. Gordon, *A Thread Across the Ocean: The Heroic Story of the Transatlantic Cable*, 139, 145.

32. Ibid., 200–201, 203–8.

## THE YEAR LIVES ON

1. David A. Williams, *David C. Broderick: A Political Portrait*, 219.
2. Ibid., 209.
3. Ibid., 230.
4. Ibid., 214.
5. Buchanan, *David S. Terry of California: Dueling Judge*, 98.
6. David A. Williams, *David C. Broderick: A Political Portrait*, 239.
7. Ibid., 197; Lynch, *The Life of David C. Broderick, a Senator of the Fifties*, 248, 251–52; Kennedy, *The Contest for California in 1861: How Colonel E.D. Baker Saved the Pacific States to the Union*, 56, 60.
8. David A. Williams, *David C. Broderick: A Political Portrait*, 240.
9. Buchanan, *David S. Terry of California*, 111–12, 124–25.
10. See Gudde, *California Place Names: The Origin and Etymology of Current Geographical Names*, 89.
11. "Proceedings of the National Republican Convention," *Sacramento Daily Union*, June 11, 1860, 2; "National Republican Convention," *Sacramento Daily Union*, June 13, 1860, 1; Untitled article, *Brooklyn Evening Star*, May 16, 1860, 2; Shutes, *Lincoln and California*, 34.
12. Shutes, *Lincoln and California*, 28.
13. "Reply to John Conness upon Presentation of a Cane," *Cincinnati Gazette*, November 17, 1863, in Basler, *The Collected Works of Abraham Lincoln*, 7:13n1; David A. Williams, *David C. Broderick: A Political Portrait*, 252–53; Shutes, *Lincoln and California*, 38–39.
14. Republican Party Platforms: "Republican Party Platform of 1856," June 18, 1856. Online by Gerhard Peters and John T. Woolley, *The American Presidency Project*. http://www.presidency.ucsb.edu/ws/?pid=29619; "Republican Party Platform of 1860," May 17, 1860. Online by Gerhard Peters and John T. Woolley, *The American Presidency Project*. http://www.presidency.ucsb.edu/ws/?pid=2962.
15. See Basler, *The Collected Works of Abraham Lincoln*, 2:461 ("A House Divided": Speech at Springfield, Illinois, June 16, 1858); Oakes, *Freedom National: The Destruction of Slavery in the United States, 1861–1865*, 22, 31, 32, 52, 67, 277; Eric Foner, *The Fiery Trial: Abraham Lincoln and American Slavery*, 65, 101, 128–29; Eric Foner, *Free Soil, Free Labor, Free Men: The Ideology of the Republican Party Before the Civil War*, ix, 116, 223, 225.
16. Blair and Tarshis, *Colonel Edward D. Baker*, 93.

17. Edward D. Baker to Abraham Lincoln from San Francisco, August 1, 1860, Abraham Lincoln Papers, Library of Congress; Blair and Tarshis, *Colonel Edward D. Baker*, 101.

18. Edward D. Baker to Abraham Lincoln, October 2, 1860, Abraham Lincoln Papers, Library of Congress; Blair and Tarshis, *Colonel Edward D. Baker*, 105–7.

19. "Republican Meeting in San Francisco," *Sacramento Daily Union*, October 29, 1860, 1.

20. Hittell, *History of California*, IV: 272.

21. Winfield J. Davis, *History of Political Conventions in California, 1849–1892*, 127.

22. "Official Vote of the State of California," *California Farmer*, December 7, 1860, 116. It is impossible to state exact popular vote totals for the candidates, as under the electoral system then in place in California votes were cast for named electors who were pledged to support named candidates, and the votes for the different electors varied, although only slightly.

23. Morris, *Encyclopedia of American History*, 6th ed., 270.

24. Blair and Tarshis, *Colonel Edward D. Baker*, 122.

25. See written Protest signed by California Republicans, March 28, 1861, Abraham Lincoln Papers, Library of Congress.

26. Brooks, *Abraham Lincoln: The Nation's Leader in the Great Struggle through Which Was Maintained the Existence of the United States*, 416; Burlingame, *Abraham Lincoln: A Life*, 2:82.

27. On March 8, 1861, Secretary of War Simon Cameron granted Baker authority to raise a military command to be known as the California Regiment. See Blair and Tarshis, *Colonel Edward D. Baker*, 126. On April 21, Baker met in New York with a group of men to organize the regiment. See Morgan, *A Little Short of Boats: The Battles of Ball's Bluff & Edwards Ferry, October 21–22, 1861*, 10.

28. Blair and Tarshis, *Colonel Edward D. Baker*, 137–38. In response to complaints that the office of a US senator and a commission as general were incompatible, Baker had initially declined the appointment.

29. The circumstances of Baker's death, including conflicting accounts left by eye-witnesses and other participants in the battle, are examined in great detail in Morgan, *A Little Short of Boats: The Battles of Ball's Bluff & Edwards Ferry, October 21–22, 1861*, 223–31; another informative account of the battle is in Farwell, *Ball's Bluff: A Small Battle and Its Long Shadow*.

30. Grant, *Oliver Wendell Holmes Jr.: Civil War Soldier, Supreme Court Justice*, 39, 46–54, 59, 62, 169, 176–78. For the circumstances under which Holmes was wounded, see Morgan, *A Little Short of Boats: The Battles of Ball's Bluff & Edwards Ferry, October 21–22, 1861*, 150–52; Farwell, *Ball's Bluff: A Small Battle and Its Long Shadow*, 95–96.

31. Burlingame, *Abraham Lincoln: A Life*, 2:200.

32. Charles Carlton Coffin in Rice, ed., *Reminiscences of Abraham Lincoln by Distin-guished Men of His Time*, 174.

33. Blair and Tarshis, *Colonel Edward D. Baker*, 158–69. The bodies of Baker and his wife were transferred in 1940 to the military cemetery in the Presidio of San Francisco, where they were marked only by a simple headstone.

34. See https://www.aoc.gov/art/other-statues/edward-dickinson-baker, accessed 1/1/2018.

35. See https://www.oregonlaws.org/ors/187.245, accessed 12/31/2017.
36. Frank M. Stewart, "Impeachment of Judge James H. Hardy, 1862," 61.
37. Ibid., 62.
38. Ibid., 61.
39. Ibid., 69.
40. "George Pen Johnston," *Daily Alta California*, March 5, 1884, 4; Hittell, *History of California,* IV:248–49.
41. Buchanan, *David S. Terry of California*, 130–32.
42. Ibid., 132–39.
43. Ibid., 162–69.
44. Ibid., 3, 170–90. See Constitution of the State of California. Adopted in Convention, at Sacramento, March Third, Eighteen Hundred and Seventy-Nine; Ratified by a vote of the People on Wednesday, March Seventh, Eighteen Hundred and Seventy-Nine, Sec. 18.
45. Only Justice William O. Douglas (1898–1980), whose term began in 1939 and ended in 1975, served longer.
46. Testimony as to Terry's attack on Field varied, with one witness claiming that Terry merely brushed Field with an open hand, as if to insult him. The testimony of Field and Neagle was that Terry had struck Field with two violent blows. See Kens, *Justice Stephen Field: Shaping Liberty from the Gold Rush to the Gilded Age*, 281.
47. Starr, *Americans and the California Dream, 1850–1915*, 103–4; Shutes, *Lincoln and California*, 45, 51–52, 146.
48. "Pacific Republic Flag in Stockton," *Sacramento Daily Union*, January 17, 1861, 2; "The Flag of the Pacific Republic Hoisted at Stockton," *Daily Alta California*, January 19, 1861, 2.
49. Orsi, *Sunset Limited: The Southern Pacific Railroad and the Development of the American West, 1850–1930*, 7–9; Shutes, *Lincoln and California*, 144–62.
50. Matthews, *The Golden State in the Civil War: Thomas Starr King, the Republican Party, and the Birth of Modern California*, 63, says that although "no other single Californian was so important to the war effort as King, he did not carry on the fight alone." She points out that King's efforts complemented the efforts of the Republican Party to keep California in the Union. In the words of the California historian Kevin Starr: "The legend grew up that King saved California for the Union. It was only a legend, but like all such things it contained an element of symbolic truth." See Starr, *Americans and the California Dream, 1850–1915*, 103.
51. Senate Concurrent Resolution No. 18, *Statutes of California Passed at the Twelfth Session of the Legislature, 1861* (Sacramento: Charles T. Botts, State Printer, 1861), 686; "Union Resolution," *Sacramento Daily Union*, May 22, 1861, 2.
52. Matthews, *The Golden State in the Civil War: Thomas Starr King, the Republican Party, and the Birth of Modern California*, 115; Shutes, *Lincoln and California*, 81–82; Faust, ed., *Historical Times Illustrated Encyclopedia of the Civil War*, 105.
53. Faust, ed., *Historical Times Illustrated Encyclopedia of the Civil War*, 105–6, 113; Matthews, *The Golden State in the Civil War: Thomas Starr King, the Republican Party, and the Birth of Modern California*, 114–23.

54. Reck, *A. Lincoln: His Last 24 Hours*, 20.
55. Spaulding, "The Attitude of California to the Civil War," 125; Richards, *The California Gold Rush and the Coming of the Civil War*, 230.
56. "Laws of This Session," *Daily Alta California*, March 22, 1863, 1 ("Among the important general bills approved are those permitting Negroes to testify against whites in civil and criminal court").
57. US Const., amend. XV, Sec. 1: "The right of citizens of the United States to vote shall not be denied or abridged by the United States or by any state on account of race, color, or previous condition of servitude." California's legislature rejected the amendment on January 28, 1870, and did not ratify it until April 3, 1962. Avila, Lee, and Ao, "Voting Rights in California: 1982–2006," 136–17.
58. Riesie Gillespie Gee, *History of Middleton, Carroll County, Mississippi*, tells of such seizures in Carroll County.
59. Timothy B. Smith, *Mississippi in the Civil War: The Home Front*, 1.
60. Many sources of genealogical research for the Stovall family (but some that are conflicting and uncertain) are available online at Ancestry.com.
61. Kilian, *Go Do Some Great Thing: The Black Pioneers of British Columbia*, 37.
62. Winks, *The Blacks in Canada: A History*, 276.
63. Ibid.; Work, ed., *Negro Year Book: An Annual Encyclopedia of the Negro 1937–1938*, 313. *See also* Parker and Abajian, *A Walking Tour of the Black Presence in San Francisco during the Nineteenth Century*, 10–11.
64. Gibbs, *Shadow and Light: An Autobiography*, 67.
65. Winks, *The Blacks in Canada: A History*, 276; Work, ed., *Negro Year Book: An Annual Encyclopedia of the Negro 1937–1938*, 313. *See also* Parker and Abajian, *A Walking Tour of the Black Presence in San Francisco during the Nineteenth Century*, 10–11.
66. Murphy, Melton, and Ward, eds., *Encyclopedia of African American Religions*, 186; John Jamison Moore, D.D., *History of the A.M.E. Zion Church in America*. Hood, *One Hundred Years of the African Methodist Episcopal Zion Church; or, The Centennial of African Methodism*, 177, wrote: "He was regarded as the greatest black preacher on the Pacific coast, and some spoke of him as the greatest *preacher*, regardless of color."
67. Hudson, *The Making of "Mammy Pleasant": A Black Entrepreneur in Nineteenth-Century San Francisco*, 38–41. See discussion in Ch. 9.
68. Beasley, *The Negro Trail Blazers of California; a Compilation of Records from the California Archives in the Bancroft Library at the University of California in Berkeley, and from the Diaries, Old Papers and Conversations of Old Pioneers in the State of California*, 65.
69. *Pleasants v. North Beach and Mission Railroad Company*, 34 Cal. 586 (1868).
70. Hudson, *The Making of "Mammy Pleasant*," 43. The words were placed there in a ceremony conducted by the San Francisco Negro Historical and Cultural Society. The grave is in Tulocay Cemetery in Napa, California.
71. Kilian, *Go Do Some Great Thing: The Black Pioneers of British Columbia*, 38–39; Lapp, *Blacks in Gold Rush California*, 249.
72. Lapp, *Blacks in Gold Rush California*, 251.
73. "Archy," *Pacific Appeal*, December 20, 1862, 2.
74. "Notes of a Trip to Victoria," *Pacific Appeal*, February 6, 1864, 2.

75. "The Colored Inhabitants of Vancouver Island," *The Liberator* [Boston], April 15, 1864, 1; "Victoria, V.I., Described by a Colored Man—Condition of the Colored Race There," *The Daily Appeal* [Marysville, California], February 17, 1864, 4; see also Philip S. Foner, "The Colored Inhabitants of Vancouver Island," 33.
76. See "The 'Moses Taylor' Robbery Case," *Daily Alta California*, June 23, 1866, 1; "The Alleged Conspiracy Case," *Daily Alta California*, June 27, 1866, 1; "Skedaddled," *Daily Alta California*, July 19, 1866, 1; "Suit to Recover Money," *Sacramento Daily Union*, July 20, 1866, 3: "The negro waiter Archie Lee, who was supposed by the prosecutor in the Ansbro-Bachelder conspiracy case to have stolen the money from Samuel Blackford on the *Moses Taylor*, left the steamer at San Juan del Sur, and it is impossible to find him. Judge Rix to-day discharged both Ansbro and Bachelder."
77. Letter to Carter G. Woodson, editor of the *Journal of Negro History*, from Mrs. R. A. Hunt, Archy Lee's niece, in "Notes" in *Journal of Negro History* 3, no. 3 (October 1918), 333, and Beasley, *The Negro Trail Blazers of California*, 83.
78. "Sent to the Hospital," *Sacramento Daily Union*, November 7, 1873, 3.
79. "Archie Lee," *Sacramento Daily Union*, November 14, 1873, 4.
80. "A Bit of History, after 15 Years," *The Elevator: A Weekly Journal of Progress. Equality Before the Law*, November 15, 1873, 2; "Archy, the Slave," *Pacific Appeal*, January 3, 1874, 1; "A Bit of History," *Los Angeles Herald*, November 21, 1873, 2. Parker and Abajian, *A Walking Tour of the Black Presence in San Francisco during the Nineteenth Century*, 8, states that the *Elevator* was started in 1865 by Philip A. Bell (1807–1889), who had been a well-known abolitionist and journalist in the East.

# BIBLIOGRAPHY

## ARCHIVES AND GOVERNMENT RECORDS

Abraham Lincoln Papers, Library of Congress.

African-American Slavery: California Fugitive Slave Case: *Stovall v. Archy* Legal Papers. BACM Research. www.PaperlessArchives.com.

*C. A. Stovall v. Archy Lee*. Case file (13-2480). National Archives at San Francisco, San Bruno, CA.

*California Constitution of 1849*.

Congressional Globe, 1833–1873.

Constitution of the State of California. Adopted in Convention, at Sacramento, March Third, Eighteen Hundred and Seventy-Nine; Ratified by a vote of the People on Wednesday, March Seventh, Eighteen Hundred and Seventy-Nine.

*Dred Scott v. Sandford* (1857), 19 How. (60 U.S.) 393.

Fugitive Slave Act of September 18, 1850, Ch. 60, Sec. 6, 9 Stat. 462, 463.

*In re Archy*, 9 Cal. 147 (1858).

*In re Perkins*, 2 Cal. 424 (1852).

"In the Matter of Archy on Habeas Corpus." February 11, 1858. Cal. Supreme Court Opinions, Vol. D, 248–54. California State Archives, Sacramento, CA.

*Journal of the Ninth Session of the Assembly of the State of California*. Sacramento: John O'Meara, State Printer, 1858.

*Journal of the Ninth Session of the Senate of the State of California*. Sacramento: John O'Meara, State Printer, 1858.

*Journal of the Senate of the State of California at Their First Session*. San José: J. Winchester, State Printer, 1850.

*Mason v. Smith* (The Bridget "Biddy" Mason Case), 1856, State of California County of Los Angeles, Before the Hon. Benjamin Hayes, Judge of the District Court of the First Judicial District State of California, County of Los Angeles.

*Pleasants [sic] v. North Beach and Mission Railroad Company*, 34 Cal. 586 (1868).

*Somerset v. Stewart* (1772), 98 Eng. Rep. 499–510.

*Speech of Hon. D. C. Broderick, of California, Against the Admission of Kansas, Under the Lecompton Constitution: Delivered in the Senate of the United States, March 22, 1858*. Washington: Printed by Lemuel Towers, 1858.

*Transcript of the Proceedings, in Case No. 366, Andres Castillero, Claimant, vs. The United States, Defendant, for the Place Named New Almaden*. San Francisco: Whitton, Towne & Co., Printers, 1858.

*United States Constitution.*
*United States v. Charles Fossat,* 61 US 413 (1958).
Walker, Robert J. *Reports of Cases, Adjudged in The Supreme Court of Mississippi.* Natchez, MS: Printed at the Courier and Journal Office, 1834.

## NEWSPAPERS
*Brooklyn Evening Star*
*Daily Alta California*
*Daily Evening Bulletin*
*The Elevator: A Weekly Journal of Progress. Equality Before the Law*
*Los Angeles Herald*
*New York Times*
*Pacific Appeal*
*Red Bluff Beacon*
*Sacramento Daily Union*
*San Francisco Bulletin*

## THESES AND DISSERTATIONS
Braden, Gayle Anderson. "The Public Career of Edward Dickinson Baker." PhD diss., Vanderbilt University, 1960.
Downey, Heather Lavezzo. "The Force of Nature & The Power of Man: Historic Walking Tours of Old Sacramento's Underground and Hollow Sidewalks." Master's thesis, California State University, Sacramento, 2010.
Fisher, James A. "A History of the Political and Social Development of the Black Community in California, 1850–1950." PhD diss., State University of New York, Stony Brook, 1971.
Han, Eunsun Celeste. "All Roads Lead to San Francisco: Black Californian Networks of Community and the Struggle for Equality, 1849–1877." PhD diss., Brown University, 2015.
Mantilla, Jeanette Davis. "'Hush, Hush, Miss Charlotte': A Quarter-Century of Civil Rights Activism by the Black Community of San Francisco, 1850–1875." PhD diss., Ohio State University, 2000.
Pilton, James William. "Negro Settlement in British Columbia 1858–1871." MA thesis, University of British Columbia, 1951.

## BOOKS AND ARTICLES
Adams, John. *Old Square-Toes: The Life of James and Amelia Douglas.* Victoria, BC: TouchWood Editions, 2011.
African Methodist Episcopal Hymn and Tune Book Adapted for the Doctrines and Usages of the Church, The. 5th ed. Philadelphia: African Methodist Episcopal Book Concern, 1912.
Albin, Ray. "The Ordeal of Three Slaves in Gold Rush California." *California History* 67, no. 4 (December 1988): 215–27.

Amestoy, Jeffrey L. *Slavish Shore: The Odyssey of Richard Henry Dana Jr.* Cambridge, MA: Harvard University Press, 2015.

Avila, Joaquin G., Eugene Lee, and Terry M. Ao. "Voting Rights in California: 1982–2006." *Review of Law and Social Justice* 17, No. 1 (2007): 131–94.

Bagley, Will. *Scoundrel's Tale: The Samuel Brannan Papers.* Spokane, WA: Arthur H. Clark Company, 1999.

Bancroft, Hubert Howe. *History of California.* 7 vols. San Francisco: The History Company, 1886–1888.

———. *History of Oregon.* Vol. 1, 1834–1848. San Francisco: The History Company, 1886.

Basler, Roy P., ed. *The Collected Works of Abraham Lincoln.* 8 vols. New Brunswick, NJ: Rutgers University Press, 1953.

Beasley, Delilah L. *The Negro Trail Blazers of California; a Compilation of Records from the California Archives in the Bancroft Library at the University of California in Berkeley, and from the Diaries, Old Papers and Conversations of Old Pioneers in the State of California.* Los Angeles: Times Mirror Printing and Binding House, 1919. Reprint: San Francisco: R and E Associates, 1968.

———. "Slavery in California." *Journal of Negro History* 3, no. 2 (January 1918): 33–44.

Beckert, Sven. *Empire of Cotton: A Global History.* New York: Vintage Books, 2015.

Beezley, William H., and Michael C. Meyer. *The Oxford History of Mexico.* New York: Oxford University Press, 2010.

Bell, Howard H. "Negroes in California, 1849–1859." *Phylon* 28, no. 2 (1862): 151–60.

Berwanger, Eugene H. "The Black Law Question in Ante-Bellum California." *Journal of the West* 6, no. 2 (1967): 205–20.

———. *The Frontier against Slavery: Western Anti-Negro Prejudice and the Slavery Extension Controversy.* Urbana: University of Illinois Press, 1967.

Bishop, Donald E. *Descendants of Bartholomew Stovall (1665–1721) (First Five American Generations).* Decorah, IA: Stovall Family Association, 1999.

Bishop, George. *The Night of the Comet: A Novel.* New York: Ballantine Books, 2013.

Blair, Harry C., and Rebecca Tarshis. *Colonel Edward D. Baker: Lincoln's Constant Ally.* Portland: Oregon Historical Society, 1960.

Bond, George Phillips. *An Account of Donati's Comet of 1858.* Cambridge, UK: John Bartlett, 1858.

Boyd, Gregory A. *Family Maps of Carroll County, Mississippi.* Norman, OK: Arphax Publishing Co., 2009.

Brands, H. W. *The Age of Gold: The California Gold Rush and the New American Dream.* New York: Doubleday, 2002.

Brooks, Noah. *Abraham Lincoln: The Nation's Leader in the Great Struggle through Which Was Maintained the Existence of the United States.* Washington, DC: *National Tribune*, 1888.

Broussard, Albert S. *Expectations of Equality: A History of Black Westerners.* Wheeling, IL: Harlan Davidson; Cody WY: Buffalo Bill Historical Center, 2012.

Buchanan, A. Russell. *David S. Terry of California: Dueling Judge.* San Marino, CA: Huntington Library, 1956.

Burg, William. *Sacramento's K Street: Where Our City Was Born*. Charleston, SC: History Press, 2012.

Burlingame, Michael. *Abraham Lincoln: A Life*. 2 vols. Baltimore: Johns Hopkins University Press, 2008.

Burnett, Peter H. *Recollections and Opinions of an Old Pioneer*. New York: D. Appleton and Co., 1880.

Burrill, Donald R. *Servants of the Law: Judicial Politics on the California Frontier, 1849–1889: An Interpretive Exploration of the Field-Terry Controversy*. Lanham, MD: University Press of America, 2011.

Cahan, Richard, Pia Hinckle, and Jessica Royer Ocken. *The Court That Tamed the West: From the Gold Rush to the Tech Boom*. Berkeley, CA: Heyday, 2013.

"California Freedom Papers," *Journal of Negro History* 3, no. 1 (January 1918): 50–54.

Catteral, Helen Tunnicliff, and James J. Hayden, eds. *Judicial Cases Concerning American Slavery and the Negro*. Vol. 5, *Cases from the Courts of States North of the Ohio and West of the Mississippi Rivers, Canada and Jamaica*. Washington, DC: Carnegie Institution of Washington, 1937.

Chadwick, Bruce. *1858: Abraham Lincoln, Jefferson Davis, Robert E. Lee, Ulysses S. Grant, and the War They Failed to See*. Naperville, IL: Sourcebooks, 2008.

Chan, Sucheng. "A People of Exceptional Character: Ethnic Diversity, Nativism, and Racism in the California Gold Rush." In Starr, Kevin, and Richard J. Orsi, *Rooted in Barbarous Soil: People, Culture, and Community in Gold Rush California*. Berkeley and Los Angeles: University of California Press for the California Historical Society, 2000, 44–85.

Chandler, Robert J. "Friends in Time of Need: Republicans and Black Civil Rights in California during the Civil War Era." *Arizona and the West* 24, no. 4 (Winter 1982): 319–40.

Cheek, William, and Aimee Lee Cheek. *John Mercer Langston and the Fight for Black Freedom, 1829–65*. Urbana and Chicago: University of Illinois Press, 1989.

Cornwallis, Kinahan. *The New El Dorado; or, British Columbia*. London: Thomas Cautley Newby, 1858.

Daniels, Douglas Henry. *Pioneer Urbanites: A Social and Cultural History of Black San Francisco*. Berkeley and Los Angeles: University of California Press, 1990.

Davis, Sam P. "How a Colored Woman Aided John Brown." *Comfort* [Augusta, Maine], November 1903, 3.

Davis, Winfield J. *History of Political Conventions in California, 1849–1892*. Sacramento: California State Library, 1893.

De Graaf, Lawrence B., Kevin Mulroy, and Quintard Taylor, eds. *Seeking El Dorado: African Americans in California*. Seattle: University of Washington Press with the Autry Museum of Western Heritage, 2001.

DeVoto, Bernard. *Across the Wide Missouri*. Boston: Houghton Mifflin, 1947.

Dunlap, Carol. *California People*. Salt Lake City, UT: Gibbs M. Smith, Peregrine Smith Books, 1982.

Eaves, Lucile. *A History of California Labor Legislation: With an Introductory Sketch of the San Francisco Labor Movement*. Berkeley, CA: The University Press, 1910.

Edwards, Malcolm. "The War of Complexional Distinction: Blacks in Gold Rush California & British Columbia." *California Historical Quarterly* 56, no. 1 (Spring 1977): 34–45.

Ethington, Philip J. *The Public City: The Political Construction of Urban Life in San Francisco, 1850–1900*. Berkeley and Los Angeles: University of California Press, 2001.

Fardon, George Robinson. *San Francisco Album: Photographs of the Most Beautiful Views and Public Buildings*. With contributions by Rodger C. Birt, Marvin R. Nathan, Peter E. Palmquist, and Joan M. Schwartz. San Francisco: Chronicle Books, 1999.

Farwell, Byron. *Ball's Bluff: A Small Battle and Its Long Shadow*. McLean, VA: EPM Publications, 1990.

Faust, Patricia L., et al., eds. *Historical Times Illustrated Encyclopedia of the Civil War*. New York: Harper & Row, 1986.

Fawcett, Edgar. *Some Reminiscences of Old Victoria*. Toronto: William Briggs, 1912.

Fede, Andrew T. "Judging Against the Grain? Reading Mississippi Supreme Court Judge Joshua G. Clarke's Views on Slavery Law in Context." *FCH Annals: Journal of the Florida Conference of Historians* 20 (May 2013): 11–29.

Fehrenbacher, Don E. *The Slaveholding Republic: An Account of the United States Government's Relations to Slavery*. Completed and edited by Ward M. McAfee. New York: Oxford University Press, 2001.

Field, Stephen J. *Personal Reminiscences of Early Days in California with Other Sketches. By Stephen J. Field. Printed for a few friends*. Not published. Copyright, 1893 by Stephen J. Field.

Finkelman, Paul. *An Imperfect Union: Slavery, Federalism, and Comity*. Chapel Hill: University of North Carolina Press, 1981.

———. "Comity," in *The Oxford Companion to the Supreme Court of the United States*. 2nd ed., Kermit L. Haw, James W. Ely Jr., and Joel B. Grossman, eds. New York: Oxford University Press, 2005, 192–93.

———. *Dred Scott v. Sandford: A Brief History with Documents*. Boston and New York: Bedford/St. Martins, 1997.

———. "The Law of Slavery and Freedom in California 1848–1860." *California Western Law Review* 17, no. 3 (1980–1981): 437–64.

———. "Slavery and the Northwest Ordinance: A Study in Ambiguity." *Journal of the Early Republic* 6 (1986): 343–70.

———. *Supreme Injustice: Slavery and the Nation's Highest Court*. Cambridge, MA: Harvard University Press, 2018.

Fisher, James A. "The Struggle for Negro Testimony in California, 1851–1863." *Southern California Quarterly* 51, no. 4 (1969): 313–24.

Flamming, Douglas. *African Americans in the West*. Santa Barbara, CA: ABC-CLIO, 2009.

Foner, Eric. *The Fiery Trial: Abraham Lincoln and American Slavery*. New York: W.W. Norton & Co., 2010.

———. *Free Soil, Free Labor, Free Men: The Ideology of the Republican Party Before the Civil War*. New York: Oxford University Press, 1995.

———. *Gateway to Freedom: The Hidden History of the Underground Railroad.* New York: W.W. Norton & Co., 2015.

Foner, Philip S. "The Colored Inhabitants of Vancouver Island." *B.C. Studies: The British Columbian Quarterly* 9 (Winter 1970): 23–33.

Foote, H. S. *War of the Rebellion; or, Scylla and Charybdis, Consisting of Observations upon the Causes, Course, and Consequences of the Late Civil War in the United States.* New York: Harper & Brothers, 1866.

Franklin, William E. "The Archy Case: The California Supreme Court Refuses to Free a Slave." *Pacific Historical Review* 32, no. 2 (1963): 137–54.

Friis, Leo J. "The Archy Case." *California Herald* 2, no. 2 (October 1954): 4, 14.

Fritz, Christian G. *Federal Justice in California: The Court of Ogden Hoffman, 1851–1891.* Lincoln: University of Nebraska Press, 1991.

*Fugitive Slave Law and Its Victims, The.* New York: American-Anti-Slavery Society, 1861.

Gee, Riesie Gillespie. *History of Middleton, Carroll County, Mississippi.* Winona, MS: Lowry Print Co., 1961.

Germenis, Matthew. "Runaway Slave Advertisements in Mississippi: Violence and Dominion." *Journal of Mississippi History* 75, no. 2 (Summer 2013): 97–105.

Gibbs, Mifflin Wistar. *Shadow and Light: An Autobiography.* Introduction by Booker T. Washington. Washington, DC: N. P., 1902.

Gienapp, William E. *The Origins of the Republican Party, 1852–1856.* New York and Oxford: Oxford University Press, 1987.

Girard, Charlotte S. M. "Sir James Douglas' [*sic*] Mother and Grandmother." *BC Studies* 44 (Winter 1979–80), 26–31.

Goode, Kenneth G. *California's Black Pioneers: A Brief Historical Survey.* Santa Barbara, CA: McNally and Loftin, 1974.

Gordan, John D., III. *Authorized by No Law: The San Francisco Committee of Vigilance of 1856 and the United States Circuit Court for the Districts of California.* Pasadena, CA: Ninth Judicial Circuit Historical Society and San Francisco: United States District Court for the Northern District of California Historical Society, 1987.

Gordon, John Steele. *A Thread Across the Ocean: The Heroic Story of the Transatlantic Cable.* New York: Perennial, an Imprint of HarperCollins Publishers, 2003.

Grant, Susan-Mary. *Oliver Wendell Holmes Jr.: Civil War Soldier, Supreme Court Justice.* New York: Routledge, 2016.

Greeley, Horace, ed. *Proceedings of the First Three Republican National Conventions of 1856, 1860 and 1864.* Minneapolis, MN: Charles W. Johnson, 1893.

Grodin, Joseph R. "The California Supreme Court and State Constitutional Rights: The Early Years." *Hastings Constitutional Law Quarterly* 31, no. 2 (2004): 141–62.

Gudde, Erwin G. *California Place Names: The Origin and Etymology of Current Geographical Names,* 4th ed., rev. and enlarged by William Bright. Berkeley and Los Angeles: University of California Press, 1998.

Guinn, J. M. *History of the State of California and Biographical Record of the Sacramento Valley, California: An Historical Story of the State's Marvelous Growth from Its*

*Earliest Settlements to the Present Time: Also Containing Biographies of Well-Known Citizens of the Past and Present.* Chicago: Chapman, 1906.

Hammond, James Henry. *Selections from the Letters and Speeches of the Hon. James H. Hammond, of South Carolina.* New York: John F. Trow & Co., 1866.

Hart, James D. *A Companion to California.* New ed., revised and expanded. Berkeley and Los Angeles: University of California Press, 1987.

Hayden, Delores. "Biddy Mason's Los Angeles, 1858–1891." *California History* 68, no. 3 (1989): 86–99.

Hayden, James J. "The Story of Archy." *Journal of the District of Columbia Bar Association* 3, no. 2 (March 1936): 42–43.

Herndon, William H., and Jesse W. Weik. *Herndon's Lincoln.* Edited by Douglas L. Wilson and Rodney O. Davis. Urbana and Chicago: Knox College Lincoln Studies Center and the University of Illinois Press in association with the Abraham Lincoln Bicentennial Commission, 2006.

Hittell, Theodore Henry. *The General Laws of the State of California, from 1850 to 1864 inclusive.* 2nd ed. 2 vols. San Francisco: H. H. Bancroft and Co., 1870.

———. *History of California.* 4 vols. San Francisco: N.J. Stone & Co., 1897.

Hoffheimer, Michael H. "Race and Terror in Joseph Baldwin's *The Flush Times of Alabama and Mississippi.*" *Seton Hall Law Review* 29 (2009): 725–78.

Holdredge, Helen. *Mammy Pleasant.* New York: G. P. Putnam's Sons, 1953.

Hood, J. S. *One Hundred Years of the African Methodist Episcopal Zion Church; or, The Centennial of African Methodism.* New York: A.M.E. Zion Book Concern, 1895.

Howay, Frederic W. *The Early History of the Fraser River Mines.* Victoria, BC: Charles F. Banfield, 1926.

———. "The Negro Immigration into Vancouver Island in 1858." *British Columbia Historical Quarterly* 3, no. 2 (1939): 101–14.

Howe, Daniel Walker. "American Victorianism as a Culture." *American Quarterly* 27, no. 5 (1975): 507–32.

Hudson, Lynn M. *The Making of "Mammy Pleasant": A Black Entrepreneur in Nineteenth-Century San Francisco.* Urbana and Chicago: University of Illinois Press, 2003.

Johnson, David Alan. *Founding the Far West: California, Oregon, and Nevada, 1840–1890.* Berkeley and Los Angeles: University of California Press, 1992.

Johnson, J. Edward. "E. B. Crocker," *Journal of the State Bar of California* 24, no. 5 (1949), 338–42.

Johnson, Reinhard O. *The Liberty Party, 1840–1848: Antislavery Third-Party Politics in the United States.* Baton Rouge: Louisiana State University Press, 2009.

Johnston, Andrew Scott. *Mercury and the Making of California Mining, Landscape, and Race.* Boulder: University Press of Colorado, 2013.

Judson, Isabella Field. *Cyrus W. Field: His Life and Work.* New York: Harper & Brothers, 1896.

Katz, William Loren. *The Black West.* Garden City, NY: Doubleday, 1971.

Kennedy, Elijah R. *The Contest for California in 1861: How Colonel E.D. Baker Saved the Pacific States to the Union.* Boston: Houghton Mifflin, 1912.

Kens, Paul. *Justice Stephen Field: Shaping Liberty from the Gold Rush to the Gilded Age.* Lawrence: University Press of Kansas, 1997.

Kilian, Crawford. *Go Do Some Great Thing: The Black Pioneers of British Columbia.* Burnaby, BC: Commodore Books, 2008.

Lamb, W. Kaye. "British Columbia Official Records: The Crown Colony Period." *Pacific Northwest Quarterly* 29, no. 1 (January 1938), 17–25.

Langley, Henry G. *San Francisco Directory for the Year 1858.* San Francisco: S.D. Valentine & Co., 1858.

Lapp, Rudolph M. *Archy Lee: A California Fugitive Slave Case.* San Francisco: Book Club of California, 1969. Reprint: Berkeley, CA: Heyday Books, 2008.

———. *Blacks in Gold Rush California.* New Haven, CT: Yale University Press, 1977.

———. "The Negro in Gold Rush California." *Journal of Negro History* 49 (1964): 81–98.

———. "Negro Rights Activities in Gold Rush California." *California Historical Society Quarterly* 45 (March 1966): 3–20.

Leroy, David H. *Mr. Lincoln's Book: Publishing the Lincoln-Douglas Debates.* New Castle, DE: Oak Knoll Press; Chicago: Abraham Lincoln Book Shop, 2009.

*Lewis & Dryden's Maritime History of the Pacific Northwest.* Edited by E. W. Wright. Portland OR: Lewis & Dryden Printing Co., 1895.

Libby, David J. *Slavery and Frontier Mississippi, 1720–1835.* Jackson: University Press of Mississippi, 2004.

Lindsay, Brendan C. *Murder State: California's Native American Genocide, 1846–1873.* Lincoln: University of Nebraska Press, 2012.

Loosley, Allyn C. *Foreign Born Population of California, 1848–1920.* San Francisco: R and E Research Associates, 1971.

Lubet, Steven. *Fugitive Justice: Runaways, Rescuers, and Slavery on Trial.* Cambridge, MA: Belknap Press of Harvard University Press, 2010.

Lynch, Jeremiah. *The Life of David C. Broderick, a Senator of the Fifties.* New York: Baker & Taylor Co., 1911.

Macfie, Matthew. *Vancouver Island and British Columbia: Their History, Resources, and Prospects.* London: Longman, 1865.

Madley, Benjamin. *An American Genocide: The United States and the California Indian Catastrophe, 1846–1873.* New Haven, CT: Yale University Press, 2016.

Marszalek, John F. *Commander of All Lincoln's Armies: A Life of General Henry W. Halleck.* Cambridge, MA: The Belknap Press of Harvard University Press, 2004.

Mason, William Marvin. *The Census of 1790: A Demographic History of Colonial California.* Menlo Park, CA: Ballena Press, 1998.

Mattes, Merrill J. *Platte River Road Narratives: A Descriptive Bibliography of Travel Over the Great Central Overland Route to Oregon, California, Utah, Colorado, Montana, and Other Western States and Territories, 1812–1866.* Urbana: University of Illinois Press, 1988.

Matthews, Glenna. *The Golden State in the Civil War: Thomas Starr King, the Republican Party, and the Birth of Modern California.* New York: Cambridge University Press, 2012.

May, Samuel. *The Fugitive Slave Law and Its Victims*. New York: American Anti-Slavery Society, 1861.

Mayne, R. C. *Four Years in British Columbia and Vancouver Island: An Account of Their Forests, Rivers, Coasts, Gold Fields and Resources for Colonisation*. London: John Murray, 1862.

McAllister, Cutler, ed. *United States of America v. Parrott, et al., Reports of Cases Argued and Determined in the Circuit Court of the United States for the Districts of California*. Vol. 1. New York: John S. Voorhies, 1859.

McAllister, Ward. *Society As I Have Found It*. New York: Cassell Publishing, 1896.

McClain, Charles J. "Pioneers on the Bench: The California Supreme Court, 1849–1879." In *Constitutional Governance and Judicial Power: The History of the California Supreme Court*. Berkeley: Berkeley Public Policy Press, Institute of Governmental Studies, University of California, Berkeley, 2016.

McCurdy, Charles W. "Prelude to Civil War: A Snapshot of the California Supreme Court at Work in 1858." *California Supreme Court Historical Society Yearbook* 1 (1994): 33–54.

McGinty, Brian. "Before the Judge." *Westways* 71, no. 5 (May 1979), 20–23, 83.

———. "The Green and the Gold: The Irish in Early California." *The American West* 15, no. 2 (March/April 1978), 18–21, 65–69.

———. "Hung Be the Heavens with Black." *American History Illustrated* 17, no. 10 (February 1983), 31–39. 39.

———. *John Brown's Trial*. Cambridge, MA. Harvard University Press, 2009.

———. *Lincoln and the Court*. Cambridge, MA: Harvard University Press, 2008.

———. *Lincoln's Greatest Case: The River, the Bridge, and the Making of America*. New York: Liveright Publishing Corporation, 2015.

———. "Stephen J. Field: California's Superjudge." *Old West* 20, no. 2 (Winter 1983), 36–40, 60.

McGloin, John B., S. J. *San Francisco: The Story of a City*. San Rafael, CA: Presidio Press, 1978.

McPherson, James M. *Battle Cry of Freedom: The Civil War Era*. New York: Oxford University Press, 1988.

Montesano, Philip M. "San Francisco Black Churches in the Early 1860's: Political Pressure Group." *California Historical Quarterly* 52 (1973), 145–52.

Moore, John Hebron. *Agriculture in Ante-Bellum Mississippi*. With a new introduction by Douglas Helms. Columbia, SC: University of South Carolina Press, 2010.

———. *The Emergence of the Cotton Kingdom in the Old Southwest: Mississippi, 1770–1860*. Baton Rouge and London: Louisiana State University Press, 1988.

Moore, John Jamison, D. D. *History of the A.M.E. Zion Church in America*. York, PA: Teachers' Journal Office, 1884.

Moore, Shirley Ann Wilson. "'I Want It to Come Out Right,'" foreword to Rudolph M. Lapp, *Archy Lee: A California Fugitive Slave Case*. Berkeley, CA: Heyday Books, 2008.

———. *Sweet Freedom's Plains: African Americans on the Overland Trails, 1841–1869*. Norman: University of Oklahoma Press, 2016.

———. "'We Feel the Want of Protection': The Politics of Law and Race in California, 1848–1878," in John F. Burns and Richard J. Orsi, eds., *Taming the Elephant: Politics, Government, and Law in Pioneer California.* Berkeley: University of California Press, and San Francisco: California Historical Society, 2003, 96–125.

Moore, Thomas. *The Works of Thomas Moore, Esq.* 6 vols. New York: G. Smith, 1825.

Morgan, James A., III. *A Little Short of Boats: The Battles of Ball's Bluff & Edwards Ferry, October 21–22, 1861.* New York and California: Savas Beattie, 2011.

Morris, Richard B. *Encyclopedia of American History.* 6th ed., Jeffrey B. Morris, Assoc. Ed. New York: Harper & Row, 1982.

Murphy, Larry G., J. Gordon Melton, and Gary L. Ward, eds. *Encyclopedia of African American Religions.* New York: Routledge, Taylor and Francis Group, 2011.

*National Cyclopedia of American Biography.* Vol. 13. New York: James T. White, 1906.

Nevins, Allan, and Milton Halley Thomas, eds. *The Diary of George Templeton Strong.* Vol. 2. New York: Macmillan Company, 1953.

Nokes, R. Gregory. *The Troubled Life of Peter Burnett, Oregon Pioneer and First Governor of California.* Corvallis: Oregon State University Press, 2018.

Noonan, John T. Jr. *Persons and Masks of the Law: Cardozo, Holmes, Jefferson, and Wythe as Makers of the Masks.* Berkeley and Los Angeles: University of California Press, 2002.

Oakes, James. *Freedom National: The Destruction of Slavery in the United States, 1861–1865.* New York: W.W. Norton and Co., 2013.

Orsi, Richard J. *Sunset Limited: The Southern Pacific Railroad and the Development of the American West, 1850–1930.* Berkeley and Los Angeles: University of California Press, 2005.

Ownby, Ted, and Charles Reagan Wilson, eds. *Mississippi Encyclopedia.* Jackson: University Press of Mississippi, 2017.

Paher, Stanley W. *Nevada Ghost Towns and Mining Camps.* Las Vegas: Nevada Publications, 1970.

Parker, Elizabeth L., and James Abajian. *A Walking Tour of the Black Presence in San Francisco during the Nineteenth Century.* San Francisco: San Francisco African American Historical and Cultural Society, 1974.

Pasachoff, Jay M., Roberta J. M. Olson, and Martha L. Hazen. "The Earliest Comet Photographs: Usherwood, Bond, and Donati 1858." *Journal for the History of Astronomy* 27 (May 1996): 129–45.

Pitt, Leonard, and Dale Pitt. *Los Angeles A to Z: An Encyclopedia of the City and County.* Berkeley and Los Angeles: University of California Press, 1997.

Pleasant, Mary Ellen. "Memoirs and Autobiography." *The Pandex of the Press* 1, no. 1 (January 1901): 1–6.

*Proceedings of the First State Convention of the Colored Citizens of the State of California Held at Sacramento Nov. 20th, 21st, and 22d, in the Colored Methodist Chuch [sic].* Sacramento: Democratic State Journal Print, 1855.

*Proceedings of the Second Annual Convention of the Colored Citizens of the State of California, Held in the City of Sacramento, Dec. 9th, 10th, 11th, and 12th, 1856.* San Francisco: J. H. Udell and W. Randall, printers, 1856.

Quinn, Arthur. *The Rivals: William Gwin, David Broderick, and the Birth of California*. New York: Crown Publishers, 1994.

Rahm, Richard H. "Chief Justice David S. Terry and the Language of Federalism." *California Legal History* 9 (2014): 119–62.

Reck, W. Emerson. *A. Lincoln: His Last 24 Hours*. Columbia: University of South Carolina Press, 1994.

Rice, Allen Thorndike, ed. *Reminiscences of Abraham Lincoln by Distinguished Men of His Time*. New York: Published for the North American Review, 1888.

Richards, Leonard L. *The California Gold Rush and the Coming of the Civil War*. New York: Vintage Books, a Division of Random House, 2008.

Rowland, Dunbar, ed. *Jefferson Davis, Constitutionalist: His Letters, Papers, and Speeches*. Vol. 3. Jackson: Mississippi Department of Archives and History, 1923.

Salomon, Carlos Manuel. *Pío Pico: The Last Governor of Mexican California*. Norman: University of Oklahoma Press, 2010.

Savage, W. Sherman. *Blacks in the West*. Westport, CT: Greenwood Press, 1976.

———. "The Negro in the Westward Movement." *Journal of Negro History* 25 (1940): 533–34.

Schaller, Dominick J., and Jürgen Zimmerer, eds. *The Origins of Genocide: Raphael Lemkin as a Historian of Mass Violence*. New York: Routledge, 2009.

Scheiber, Harry N., ed. *Constitutional Governance and Judicial Power: The History of the California Supreme Court*. Berkeley, CA: Berkeley Public Policy Press, Institute of Governmental Studies, University of California, Berkeley, 2016.

Secrest, William B. *Dark and Tangled Threads of Crime: San Francisco's Famous Police Detective, Isaiah W. Lees*. Sanger, CA: Quill Driver Books/Word Dancer Press, 2004.

Senkewicz, Robert M., S. J. *Vigilantes in Gold Rush San Francisco*. Stanford, CA: Stanford University Press, 1985.

Sergeant, David. *The Greatest Comets in History: Broom Stars and Celestial Scimitars*. New York: Springer, 2009.

Shafter, Oscar Lovell. *Life, Diary, and Letters of Oscar Lovell Shafter*. San Francisco: Blair-Murdock Company, 1915.

Shuck, Oscar T. *Bench and Bar in California*. San Francisco: Occident Printing House, 1889.

———. *The California Scrap-Book: A Repository of Useful Information and Select Reading*. San Francisco: H. H. Bancroft and Co., 1869.

———. *Eloquence of the Far West. No. 1. Masterpieces of E.D. Baker*. San Francisco: Published by the Editor, 1899.

Shutes, Milton H. *Lincoln and California*. Stanford University, CA: Stanford University Press, 1943.

Smith, Stacey L. *Freedom's Frontier: California and the Struggle over Unfree Labor, Emancipation, and Reconstruction*. Chapel Hill: University of North Carolina Press, 2013.

———. "Remaking Slavery in a Free State: Masters and Slaves in Gold Rush California." *Pacific Historical Review* 80, no. 1 (February 2011): 28–63.

Smith, Timothy B. *Mississippi in the Civil War: The Home Front.* Jackson: University Press of Mississippi, 2010.

Spaulding, Imogen. "The Attitude of California to the Civil War." *Publications of the Historical Society of Southern California* 9, nos. 1 and 2 (1912-1913): 104–31.

Spiegel, Irwin O. "Mammy Pleasant Rides Again." *Los Angeles Bar Bulletin* (September 1963): 407–8.

Stahr, Walter. *Seward: Lincoln's Indispensable Man.* New York: Simon and Schuster, 2012.

———. *Stanton: Lincoln's War Secretary.* New York: Simon and Schuster, 2017.

Stampp, Kenneth M. *America in 1857: A Nation on the Brink.* New York: Oxford University Press, 1990.

———. *The Peculiar Institution: Slavery in the Ante-Bellum South.* New York: Alfred A. Knopf, 1956.

Stanley, Gerald. "Senator William Gwin: Moderate or Racist?" *California Historical Quarterly* 50, no. 3 (September 1971): 243–55.

Stanley, Jerry. *Hurry Freedom: African Americans in Gold Rush California.* New York: Crown Publishers, 2000.

Stannard, David E. *American Holocaust: The Conquest of the New World.* New York: Oxford University Press, 1992.

Starr, Kevin. *Americans and the California Dream, 1850–1915.* New York: Oxford University Press, 1973.

———. *California: A History.* New York: Modern Library, 2005.

Stewart, Frank M. "Impeachment of Judge James H. Hardy, 1862." *Southern California Law Review* 28, no. 1 (1954): 61–69.

Stewart, George R. *The California Trail: An Epic with Many Heroes.* New York and London: McGraw-Hill, 1962.

———. *Ordeal by Hunger: The Story of the Donner Party.* Boston: Houghton Mifflin, 1960.

Stowell, Daniel, et al., eds., *The Papers of Abraham Lincoln: Legal Documents and Cases.* 4 vols. Charlottesville: University of Virginia Press, 2008.

Swisher, Carl B. *History of the Supreme Court of the United States: Volume V, The Taney Period 1836–64.* New York: Macmillan Publishing, 1974.

———. *Stephen J. Field: Craftsman of the Law.* Washington, DC: Brookings Institution, 1930.

Sydnor, Charles S. *Slavery in Mississippi.* With a new introduction by John David Smith. Columbia: University of South Carolina Press, 2013.

Taylor, Alan. "'An American Genocide' by Benjamin Madley." *New York Times Book Review,* May 27, 2016.

Taylor, Martha C. *From Labor to Reward: Black Church Beginnings in San Francisco, Oakland, Berkeley, and Richmond, 1849–1972.* Eugene, OR: Resource Publications, 2016.

Taylor, Quintard. *In Search of the Racial Frontier: African Americans in the American West, 1528–1990.* New York: W. W. Norton, 1998.

Taylor, Quintard, and Shirley Ann Wilson Moore, eds. *African American Women Confront the West, 1600–2000*. Norman: University of Oklahoma Press, 2003.

Taylor, William. *California Life Illustrated*. New York: Carlton and Porter, 1858.

Thurman, Sue Bailey. *Pioneers of Negro Origin in California*. San Francisco: Acme Publishing, 1952.

Tinkham, George H. *California Men and Events: Time 1769–1890*. Stockton, CA: Record Publishing Co., 1915.

Twenty-Seventh Annual Catalogue of the Officers and Students of Centre College, at Danville, Kentucky, for the Year Ending June 26th, 1851, The. Danville, KY. Published by the Students. Printed at the *Lexington Observer & Reporter* Office, 1851.

Upham, David R. "The Meaning of the 'Privileges and Immunities of Citizens' on the Eve of the Civil War." *Notre Dame Law Review* 91 (2016): 1117–66.

Vandervelde, Lea. *Redemption Songs: Suing for Freedom before Dred Scott*. New York: Oxford University Press, 2014.

Wallis, Michael. *The Best Land Under Heaven: The Donner Party in the Age of Manifest Destiny*. New York: Liveright Publishing Corporation, 2017.

Weiß, E. *Bilderatlas der Sternenwelt*, 1888. Esslingen (Germany): J.F. Schreiber, 1888.

Wesley, Charles. *Hymns for New-Year's Day*. London: R. Hawes, n.d. [1750].

Wesley, John. *Thoughts upon Slavery*. London: Re-printed in Philadelphia, with notes, and sold by Joseph Crukshank, 1784.

Wiecek, William M. "*Somerset*: Lord Mansfield and the Legitimacy of Slavery in the Anglo-American World." *University of Chicago Law Review* 42 (1974): 86–146.

Williams, David A. *David C. Broderick: A Political Portrait*. San Marino, CA: Huntington Library, 1969.

Williams, James. *Fugitive Slave in the Gold Rush: Life and Adventures of James Williams*. With Introduction to the Bison Books Edition by Malcolm J. Rohrbough. Lincoln: University of Nebraska Press, 2005.

Wiltshire, Betty Couch. *Carroll County, Mississippi Pioneers, with Abstracts of Wills 1834–1875 & Divorces, 1857–1875*. Bowie, MD: Heritage Books, 1990.

———. *Mississippi Index of Wills 1800–1900*. Westminster, MD: Heritage Books, 2007.

Winks, Robin W. *The Blacks in Canada: A History*. 2nd ed. Montreal and Kingston: McGill Queen's University Press, 1997.

Wise, Steven W. *Though the Heavens May Fall: The Landmark Trial That Led to the End of Human Slavery*. Cambridge, MA: Da Capo Press, 2005.

Work, Monroe N., ed. *Negro Year Book: An Annual Encyclopedia of the Negro 1937–1938*. Tuskegee Institute, AL: Negro Year Book Publishing Co., 1937.

# INDEX